Test Driven Development in Ruby

A Practical Introduction to TDD Using Problem and Solution Domain Analysis

■ ■ ■

Bala Paranj

Apress®

Test Driven Development in Ruby: A Practical Introduction to TDD Using Problem and Solution Domain Analysis

Bala Paranj
Atlanta, Georgia, USA

ISBN-13 (pbk): 978-1-4842-2637-7   ISBN-13 (electronic): 978-1-4842-2638-4
DOI 10.1007/978-1-4842-2638-4

Library of Congress Control Number: 2017934648

Managing Director: Welmoed Spahr
Editorial Director: Todd Green
Acquisitions Editor: Steve Anglin
Development Editor: Matthew Moodie
Technical Reviewer: Ronald Petty
Coordinating Editor: Mark Powers
Copy Editor: April Rondeau
Compositor: SPi Global
Indexer: SPi Global
Artist: SPi Global
Cover image designed by Freepik.

Distributed to the book trade worldwide by Springer Science+Business Media New York, 233 Spring Street, 6th Floor, New York, NY 10013. Phone 1-800-SPRINGER, fax (201) 348-4505, e-mail orders-ny@springer-sbm.com, or visit www.springeronline.com. Apress Media, LLC is a California LLC and the sole member (owner) is Springer Science + Business Media Finance Inc (SSBM Finance Inc). SSBM Finance Inc is a **Delaware** corporation.

For information on translations, please e-mail rights@apress.com, or visit http://www.apress.com/rights-permissions.

Apress titles may be purchased in bulk for academic, corporate, or promotional use. eBook versions and licenses are also available for most titles. For more information, reference our Print and eBook Bulk Sales web page at www.apress.com/bulk-sales.

Any source code or other supplementary material referenced by the author in this book is available to readers on GitHub via the book's product page, located at www.apress.com/9781484226377. For more detailed information, please visit http://www.apress.com/source-code.

Printed on acid-free paper

This book is dedicated to the memory of my father.

Contents at a Glance

Contents

About the Author

Bala Paranj has a master's degree in electrical engineering from Wichita State University. He has been working in the software industry since 1996. He started his career as a technical support engineer and later became a web developer. He most commonly uses Perl, Java, and Ruby. He has consulted for companies in the United States, Australia, and Jamaica in finance, telecommunications, and other domains.

He is the founder of the developer training company rubyplus.com. He publishes podcasts and screencasts in Ruby. He has been organizing Ruby, Rails and TDD related events since 2007. He also has developed several open-source gems that were extracted from his side projects.

He lives in Los Altos Hills, California, with his girlfriend and his dog, Chico. He enjoys hiking, tennis, and tango. You can buy the TDD in Ruby course at https://rubyplus.com/sales/new?id=11

You can contact the author with any questions about his book at feedback@rubyplus.com.

About the Technical Reviewer

Ronald Petty, M.B.A., M.S. is the founder of Minimum Distance LLC, a management consulting firm based in San Francisco. He spends his time helping technology-based startups do the right thing. He is also an instructor at UC Berkeley Extension.

Foreword

I have known Bala for more than a decade. In all this time, he has consistently been a leader in the Ruby community in the San Francisco Bay Area. Bala has mentored many Ruby and Rails developers, including me. He is very approachable and has a very appealing style of conversation.

Case in point, last week I was waiting for him at the Starbucks near Google's HQ in Mountain View to get his opinions on a project I am working on. While I waited, I met a fellow coffee enthusiast who, upon finding out that I work for Intuit (the TurboTax company), asked me for some career advice. Ten minutes later, Bala walked in. After a quick introduction to what we were talking about, Bala took the lead on the mentoring. No more than a minute had passed before the protégé said, "Can I please record this?" Yes, Bala is that impressive!

Bala thinks differently. He is a genius. In fact, when the above conversation was done, the protégé asked us for our contact information. Whereas I proceeded to enter my name, number, and email into his phone, Bala said, "Just go to my website and click on download vCard. Boom."

Bala's excellence in communicating rather abstract concepts clearly and concisely is very clear in the way the lessons and examples are laid out in this book. He builds up the examples one step at a time so that it is crystal clear what he intends you to learn. He uses various techniques to make sure the concepts stick in your mind.

My two key takeaways from this book are as follows:

1. Understanding the problem is the most important part of solving the problem.

2. Test Driven Development does not magically result in a good design. There is more to design than just reducing duplication in code.

This is an excellent book, and I highly recommend that you read it if you plan to create great software.

—John Varghese
Devops Evangelist at Intuit

Acknowledgments

My first thanks go to Steve Anglin, who approached me with the idea of writing a Ruby book. As a first-time author, I was both petrified and excited at the same time. He was very understanding about my situation and provided me the freedom to choose the topic and timing of the book.

I would like to thank Rhonda Jezek for pairing with me on most of the examples in this book, and Daniel Pritchard for believing in me and encouraging me to write the book. I also would like to thank the members of my Silicon Valley Ruby meetup, who provided valuable feedback about the early material in this book at the bootcamps and tutorials. Thanks to Emily Bache for providing me with very candid technical feedback, and Randy Coulman for his inspiring presentations and technical review of one of the chapters. I would also like to thank Mayank Suri for challenging me and pushing me out of my comfort zone in order to accomplish bigger goals in my career.

This book builds on top of the work of others like Kent Beck, Robert Martin, Eric Evans, Gerard Meszaros, Michael Feathers, and others mentioned in the book. I cannot thank Ryan Davis enough for building a simple and elegant testing framework with a gentle learning curve for beginners.

This book would not have been a reality without Steve Anglin, Mark Powers, and Matthew Moodie. I am deeply indebted to the Apress team for recognizing my talent and providing me with a channel for my voice. Last but not least, thanks to Ronald Petty for patiently reviewing my book and pointing out the mistakes.

This book is the result of my search for solutions to overcome the difficulties I faced when I started to learn TDD. It also distills the design knowledge I have acquired over my career. I sincerely hope that this book shows empathy for beginners and makes it easier for them to learn TDD.

Introduction

Experience is simply the name we give our mistakes.

—Oscar Wilde

This book is the result of my struggle to learn Test Driven Development. I started documenting the difficulties that I faced and what I did to overcome them. I started sharing my tips with the members of my Silicon Valley Ruby meetup and on my blog. You will learn both from my mistakes and from other developers in this book.

Mistakes are the portals of discovery.

—James Joyce

More importantly, if you document your mistakes and start analyzing them, you too will discover new tips that you can share with others. Mastering TDD is a journey. I hope you enjoy the journey as much as I have enjoyed writing this book. Good luck.

CHAPTER 1

The Basics

This chapter will discuss coding kata, basic terminology, overcoming difficulty in TDD, and how to improve your TDD skills over time. We will look at the distinction between *intent* and *implementation* and its role in coming up with elegant solutions. We will briefly discuss the basics of Test Driven Development (TDD) and how problem-solving skills fit into TDD. We will also cover designing test cases, assertion, Canonical Test Structure, and how to avoid common mistakes.

Terminology

This section will introduce you to the basic terminology required to grasp the material in this book. We will look at basic terms such as *kata*, *coding kata*, *domain*, *problem domain*, and *solution domain*.

Kata

Kata is a Japanese word meaning *form*. In martial arts, it describes a choreographed pattern of movements used to train yourself to the level of muscle memory. The focus is on making small improvements during practice. Figure 1-1 shows a choreographed pattern of movements in martial arts.

Figure 1-1. *A choreographed pattern of movements*

© Bala Paranj 2017
B. Paranj, *Test Driven Development in Ruby*, DOI 10.1007/978-1-4842-2638-4_1

Coding Kata

A *coding kata* is a short exercise that is thirty minutes to an hour long. It can be coded in many different ways. It is likely that coding katas have many solutions. The focus is on learning when you work through them. The goal is to practice in order to improve your skills, not to achieve perfection.

Domain

What comes to mind when you hear terms such as *equity, debt, gross margin,* and *net income*? How about *contour, contrast, opacity,* and *form*? Here's another example: *parallel, ordinate, arc,* and *angle.* A *domain* is defined as a specific sphere of activity or knowledge. The first example corresponds to finance. The second example corresponds to visual communication, and the third corresponds to geometry. Figure 1-2 shows three different domains–finance, visual communication, and math–consisting of abstractions found in those domains.

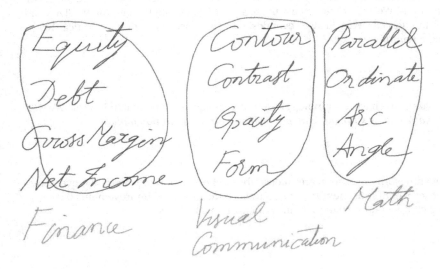

Figure 1-2. *Examples of domains*

Problem Domain

The *problem domain* refers to real-world things and concepts related to a problem.

Solution Domain

The *solution domain* refers to real-world things and concepts related to a solution.

Domain Expert

A *domain expert* is someone with special knowledge or skill in a particular domain. For instance, an accountant is an expert in the accounting domain. The development of accounting software requires knowledge in two different domains, namely accounting and software.

Domain Knowledge

Domain knowledge is expertise in a particular problem domain. It is a critical ingredient in coming up with abstractions that create elegant solutions.

Defining the Problem Domain and the Solution Domain

When you read a problem statement in a textual form, you will find concepts in the problem statement. You can list the concepts you find and group them to come up with the problem domain name. Figure 1-3 illustrates the process of coming up with the problem domain name from a given problem statement.

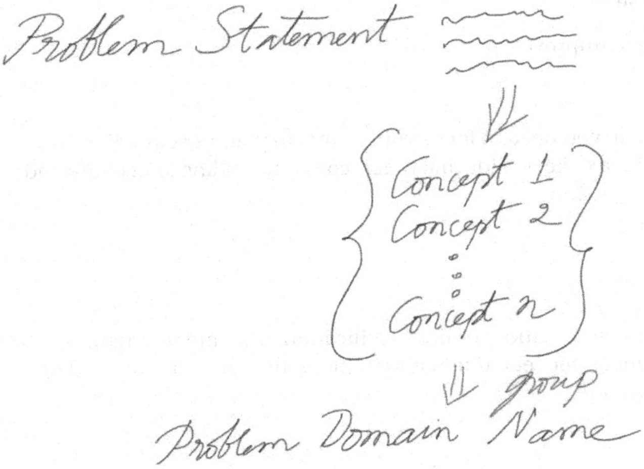

Figure 1-3. *Process of finding the domain name*

Let's now see an example of problem domain and solution domain. Let's say you have leaking sink problem in your kitchen. You search on the Internet for the term **leaking sink**. The phrase **leaking sink** is found in the problem domain. Once you read about the solution to this problem, you learn about things like: clevis screw, stopper rod, clevis, retaining nut and so on. These terms belong to the solution domain. You watch a video and find out that you need to buy a retaining nut to fix the leak. You now start using this term found in the solution domain, **retaining nut**, to find the nearest store carrying this item. So, the term: **retaining nut** belongs to the solution domain.

Learning TDD

Learning by Coding Kata

Why coding Kata? Test Driven Development (TDD) is a difficult but learnable skill. So, in order to answer this question, we need to look at why TDD is difficult.

> *TDD is not a testing technique. It's an analysis technique, a design technique, really a technique for all activities of development.*

> —Kent Beck, *Test Driven Development by Example*

By using the small but precise nature of the coding kata to practice these skills separately, you can move past this difficulty and hone your TDD skills. So, coding kata is the best way to learn TDD. How do you practice a coding kata? You will work through a coding kata by following the five steps of TDD, which will be discussed in an upcoming section.

Learning Retrospective

After you complete a coding kata using TDD, reflect on the TDD practice session. Ask yourself the following questions:

- What went well during the TDD session?
- What went wrong during the TDD session?
- What can I do differently next time to improve?

The answers to these questions will tell you where you need to focus your efforts in your next practice session so as to improve your skills. It's a good idea to keep a journal that records the coding kata name and the answers to these questions for each practice session.

Intent vs. Implementation

In this section, we will discuss the intent and implementation, or the specification and implementation. We will look at examples to illustrate the differences between intent and implementation, why we need to separate them, and how to separate them in the code.

Intent

The dictionary definition of *intent* is *determined to do something*. If you want to travel in your car, your intent is to drive your car. You don't reach into the transmission and pull levers to drive. You can drive without knowing the details of the car engine. You use the visible parts of the car, such as the steering wheel, gas pedal, brake, and gears, to drive. You can express your intent by using the public interface of the car. In programming terms, the intent-revealing drive() method is used. The public interface would consist of things you can do to a car, such as start, stop, drive, turn, and so on.

Implementation

The things under the hood of the car make up the implementation. Only your car mechanic knows about the details of the car engine. You may be aware of the 3.0 liter V-6 engine, but you have no idea of how it works. There could be methods that are internal to the class, such as burn_fuel(), that are not part of the public interface of the car. This means the user does not directly invoke any private methods of the car.

Intent and Implementation

We will now see three examples of intent and implementation, the difference between them, and why we need to separate them.

Music

Music is composed by music composers. Music composers organize and develop the music to create a written score that can be interpreted by performers. Performers play the music using different musical instruments by referring the sheet music. Sheet music is not music. Sheet music is a visual abstraction of music. To be specific, it is a symbolic abstraction of music that can be read by anyone who knows how to read music notation. The composers communicate with other musicians across space and time using music notation. This is the **intent**, the **what**, the **logical design**. Figure 1-4 shows sheet music that communicates with other musicians.

Figure 1-4. *Sheet music is a symbolic abstraction of music*

Playing the music with a musical instrument is the **implementation**, the **how,** or the **physical design.** There are many physical designs for a given logical design. In this example, the same sheet music can be used to play the music using different musical instruments. Figure 1-5 shows music being performed by a musical instrument, achieved by interpreting the sheet music.

Figure 1-5. Music is played using a musical instrument

Lyrics

A lyricist writes the words for a song by organizing sections into one of the agreed upon structures. This provides the roadmap for the song. Let's consider the lyrics for the song "Come Together." John Lennon wrote this song. This is the *what*. The *how* in this case are the performances by The Beatles, Aerosmith, and Michael Jackson of the same song, "Come Together."

Home Plan

An architect gets requirements from the client. A hand-drawn sketch consisting of bubbles, squares, and rectangles captures the idea of where things are and how they interrelate. This diagram becomes architecture. Figure 1-6 shows the blueprint of a house that captures the design decisions made by the architect. This blueprint of a house is the *what*. It is a visual abstraction of the design. You can build many houses using the same blueprint.

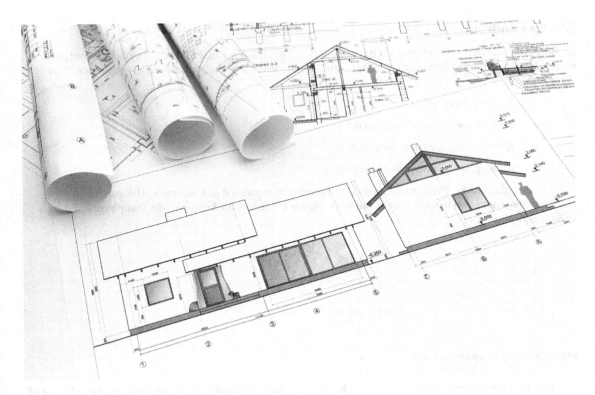

Figure 1-6. *Blueprint of a house*

Table 1-1 summarizes the intent and implementation of some common, everyday things that you encounter.

Table 1-1. *Intent vs. Implementation*

Intent	Implementation
Drive a car	Internal mechanism of a car that drives
Represent music	The process of playing music with a musical instrument
Lyrics of a song	The unique way of singing a song by a singer
Plan of a home	Houses that conform to the same blueprint but look different

Separate Intent from Implementation

We need to separate the intent from implementation. Why? Because it allows us to change the implementation without breaking the tests. The intent is the focus of the tests. The implementation is the focus of the production code. As long as the behavior is the same, the implementation changes should not break the tests.

Sheep Example

So, how do we separate the intent from implementation? We can use Chris Stevenson's TestDox (`https://en.wikipedia.org/wiki/TestDox`). TestDox expresses the subject in the code as part of a sentence. Here is an example:

- A sheep eats grass.

- A sheep bleats when frightened.

- A sheep produces delicious milk.

- A sheep moves away from sheep dogs.

In this example, the sheep is the subject. Its behavior is expressed in a sentence. This can be automatically converted to specifications in code. Figure 1-7 shows the behavior of a sheep expressed as specifications in code.

```
1 ▼ describe Sheep do
2      it 'eats grass'
3      it 'bleats when frightened'
4      it 'produces delicious milk'
5      it 'moves away from sheep dogs'
6 ▲ end
```

Figure 1-7. *Specifications in code*

In this example, we are using the spec style of the Minitest testing framework to describe the behavior of a sheep. Minitest ships with the Ruby language. When you think about a system from the outside, you focus on the intent. In this case, what does the sheep do?

Test API Example

For a realistic example, examine Figure 1-8 from the RSpec documentation that shows developers how the `eq()` method in RSpec (`http://rspec.info`) works.

○ compare using eq (==)

Given a file named "compare_using_eq.rb" with:

```
RSpec.describe "a string" do
  it "is equal to another string of the same value" do
    expect("this string").to eq("this string")
  end

  it "is not equal to another string of a different value" do
    expect("this string").not_to eq("a different string")
  end
end

RSpec.describe "an integer" do
  it "is equal to a float of the same value" do
    expect(5).to eq(5.0)
  end
end
```

When I run rspec compare_using_eq.rb

Then the output should contain "3 examples, 0 failures"

Figure 1-8. *Specification that shows RSpec API usage example*

The example is easy to read and shows how the eq() method can be used to compare two strings that are equal and not equal. (Source: https://www.relishapp.com/rspec/rspec-expectations/docs/built-in-matchers/equality-matchers)

Bowling Game Example

Let's look at an example that uses a bowling game scoring program to illustrate how to discover an intent-revealing interface.

```
it 'score is 10 for a strike - knocking down all ten pins' do
  game = BowlingGame.new
  10.times { game.roll(1) }

  assert_equal 10, game.score
end
```

This test does not reveal the intent of rolling ten times. We don't know why it invokes the roll method ten times, because the intent is hidden. We can make the intent explicit by asking the question: "What does it mean to hit all ten pins?" In the bowling game domain, it means a strike. So, we can express it directly in code as follows:

```
it 'score is 10 for a strike - knocking down all ten pins' do
  game = BowlingGame.new
  game.strike

  assert_equal 10, game.score
end
```

The strike method is intent-revealing and expresses the domain concept mentioned in the test name directly in the code. It clearly communicates the meaning of a strike in a bowling game to other developers.

Precision in Language and Meaning

An infant cries, and you don't know whether it is hungry or has tummy trouble. If you give it milk, it stops crying. As it grows, the request "Milk!" becomes "Me Milk!" and later "Please give me some milk to drink." Children learn as they grow and their language acquires more precise meaning. Similarly, as the software grows, the tests acquire more precise meaning.

A *proposition* in logic is a statement that expresses a concept that can be either true or false. For instance, we can make valid propositions about the concept of grass, as follows:

- Grass is green.

- Grass is a plant.

- Grass grows.

- Grass is a monocot.

And so on, leading to increased meaning and precision of meaning for the concept of grass. We can express this as specifications in code similar to the sheep example, as shown in Figure 1-9.

```
1  describe Grass do
2    it 'is green'
3    it 'is a plant'
4    it 'grows'
5    it 'is a monocot'
6  end
```

Figure 1-9. Specifications for grass

Now, consider the following:

- It has a wide opening to the water tank.

- It has a marked tank for exact water filling.

- It has two-hour auto-shutoff.

- It has a filter basket.
- It has a thermal carafe.
- It is usually in the kitchen.
- It has a sink.
- It maintains the temperature of the drink inside.

What is it? At some point in the sequence, you connected with the pattern and understood it was a description of a coffee maker. From that point, each statement confirmed your understanding. We can express these statements as specifications in code that describes the coffee maker. We will discuss this in more detail in an upcoming section on designing the sequence of test cases.

Tests Are Executable Documentation

Let's say you installed a gem and need to figure out how to use it. You should be able to look at the tests and see examples that show you how to use the library. It will answer questions such as:

- Which class should I instantiate?
- How do I instantiate the class?
- Which method should I invoke?
- What parameters does the method need?

And so on. However, you should not read the source code of the gem to figure out the answers to these questions. The developer of the gem has achieved the desired separation of intent and implementation only when one can write programs that use that gem by referring only to the tests that come with the gem. Tests are executable documentation and always tell the truth. Other forms of documentation, such as wiki, source code commenting, and so on, can get out of sync with the production code.

The tests are a way for the library developer to communicate with other developers about the library. Tests must be readable and easy to understand for someone who is new to the library.

Shift in Mental State

You focus on specifying what a system should do when you are reading the problem description. This is analysis. The mental state is the *what* during this activity. You will be looking at the problem domain. For *what*, you must focus on the input and output of the system, as illustrated in Figure 1-10. You will focus on what is visible outside of a system and ignore what is inside the system. You will ignore the details and treat the system under test as a black box.

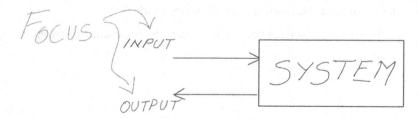

Figure 1-10. *Mental focus is on what*

From *what*, we move to *how*. The focus shifts from analysis to design. You will be looking at the solution domain. Your mental state is *how*. For *how*, you will focus on what is inside the system, as illustrated in Figure 1-11. You will consider the details of the system under test.

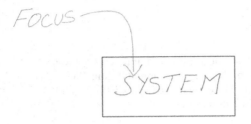

Figure 1-11. *Mental focus is on how*

A professional artist starts to draw a portrait with a general outline that gives the basic shape of the face, eyes, and so on. At this stage, the attributes of a person, such as eyes and lips, could be those of anyone. They don't look unique to the portrait subject. As the artist gradually adds more details and adds depth using shading, the drawing comes to life and resembles the subject. The final portrait fits the structure provided by the general outline drawn in the initial stages of the drawing. Software developers work in a similar way in order to write software to solve a given problem.

Overview of TDD

This section is a brief introduction to Test Driven Development. We will answer questions such as what, why, and how. We will discuss why we start with a failing test and are minimal when implementing the production code. We will also see how TDD separates the intent from implementation, how to get all the benefits of TDD, and, finally, what makes TDD difficult.

Test Driven Development

Test Driven Development is a software development practice where the test is written before the production code. The goal is clean code that works. It leads to better quality and fewer defects in code. It eliminates the need to spend days in a debugger to hunt down hard-to-find bugs. Thus, it reduces debugging efforts. Why have clean code that works as the goal?

> *Clean code that works gives you a chance to learn all the lessons that the code has to teach you. If you only slap together the first thing you think of, you never have time to think of a second, better thing. The intent is to learn and come up with a better solution.*

> —Kent Beck, *Test Driven Development by Example*

The Five Steps of TDD

Kent Beck is the creator of extreme programming, a software development methodology that avoids rigid formal specifications for a collaborative and iterative design process. Kent Beck sums up the fives steps of TDD as follows:

1. Quickly add a test.

2. Run all tests and see the new one fail. Since there is no code yet to make the test pass, this test will fail.

3. Make a little change to pass the test as quickly as possible.

4. Run all tests and see them all succeed.

5. Refactor to remove duplication.

Figure 1-12 shows how the red-green-refactor steps repeat to form the TDD cycle.

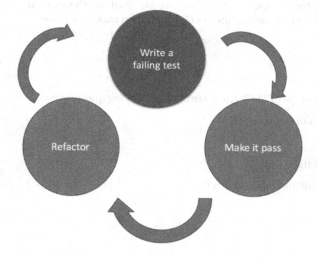

Figure 1-12. *The TDD steps repeat to form the TDD cycle*

In the first step, we write a test. In the second step, we record a requirement as a test. We also explicitly design the client API. Designing the API here means answering questions such as the following:

• Does the method name reveal the intent?

• Should this be an instance method or a class method?

• What are the parameters to this method?

• What are the required parameters?

• What are the optional parameters?

• Should this parameter be passed in to the constructor instead of being passed in to the method?

• Should the parameter have a default value?

The answers to these questions become your design decisions that you express in code. In the third step, we always write the simplest possible code that makes the test pass. This allows us to keep our options open and evolve our design. In the fourth step, the focus is on meeting the requirements. In the fifth step, the focus is on creating a good design.

Failing Test

Why start with a failing test? The following Kent Beck quote sums up the reason for writing the test before we write the production code:

> *Your goal as a programmer is running functionality. You will not test after coding a feature.*
>
> —Kent Beck, *Test Driven Development by Example*

Writing a failing test is a way of testing the test. If the tests are all passing, it gives us feedback that there are no known problems with our code. By writing a test to expose a deficiency, we are clarifying the problem. We are also sketching out the design. When we test first, we reduce the stress, which then makes us more likely to test.

Writing a Failing Test

Writing a failing test is steps one and two of the five steps of TDD. Ask yourself the following questions:

- What is the responsibility of our system under test (SUT)?
- What should it do?
- What is the API for making the SUT do this?
- What does the SUT need in order to fulfill its responsibility?
- What output are there to observe?
- How can we tell it worked correctly?
- How is correctness defined?

For the fourth question, the SUT may need data or collaborators to fulfill its responsibility.

Minimal Implementation

In step three of the TDD process, we make our test pass with the simplest code. Is it too hard to pass the test? Then we drop back to change our test and make it easier to pass. TDD has given us feedback that our test is forcing a big leap.

Is the implementation so trivial it has obvious flaws? TDD has just given us feedback to tell us what our next test should expose. Beginners find it difficult to make the implementation minimal. To overcome this difficulty, we can use a pair programming technique called Devil's Advocate. This pair programming technique is explained in an upcoming section.

If the test is already broken down into the smallest problem that you can tackle, and you still have problems making it pass, use the Autonomous Discovery Learning process. This is a simple three-step process that a learner can use to identify and select the information to be learned.

Autonomous Discovery Learning

Here is the process:

1. Write down your question.
2. Design an experiment to answer that question.
3. Run the experiment to learn.

Writing down the question makes you clarify your thoughts. The experiment must have minimal unknowns so that you can solve the problem easily. IRB console is very useful for experimenting and learning how something works. Once you figure out how it works, you can make the test pass by writing the production code. Instead of getting stuck and asking the question in an online forum when you don't know how to solve the problem, shift your mental focus to find the focus question, then ask yourself: "How can I design an experiment to answer the focus question?" Then, run the experiment to learn from your observations.

Devil's Advocate

According to the dictionary, a *Devil's advocate* is a person who expresses a contentious opinion in order to provoke debate or test the strength of the opposing arguments. Devil's Advocate in our case is a pair programming technique. In this context, it means the tests force you to write generic code. The first developer writes a failing test and passes the keyboard to the second developer. The second developer makes the test pass by using a minimal and incorrect implementation, then writes a failing test. The first developer makes the test pass by using an incorrect and minimal implementation. This cycle repeats till it becomes difficult to write anymore incorrect implementations and it is easier to pass all the tests by writing generic code. Once you familiarize yourself with this technique by working in a pair programming setting, you can use it when you are coding alone to critique your tests. Table 1-2 shows how developers use Devil's Advocate in a pair programming session.

Table 1-2. *Devil's Advocate*

Developer 1	Developer 2
Write a test	Pass the test by writing minimal production code Write a test
Pass all the tests with minimal production code	

Refactoring

The fifth step is the refactoring step. Our code works, but we have been focused on passing a very specific test that only shows a very small portion of the application. Now is our chance to zoom out and take in the entire application. If we have used a naïve implementation to get our test to pass, we can clean up the duplication and extract new classes or extract methods to make our code self-describing. TDD is a way of constraining a problem, encapsulating the process of design by using the abstraction of a test, and using rapid feedback to see how well the design is working. The process gives us a way to think about and do iterative design.

Separation of Intent from Implementation

TDD splits the design activity into two phases. First, we design the external, visible part of the code, the Application Programming Interface (API). Then, we design the internal organization of the code. The external, visible part of the code—the API—is the intent. The internal organization of the code is the implementation. This is a useful distinction because we can vary the implementation without breaking the tests. As long as the behavior is the same, change in implementation should not break any tests. For instance, if we improve the performance, the tests should not break. If we change the data structure, the tests should not break. If we change the implementation to use recursion instead of an iterative solution, the tests should not break. How can beginners learn to separate the intent from implementation? The Ping Pong pair programming technique is helpful for developing that skill.

Ping Pong Pair Programming Technique

Ping Pong is a pair programming technique. The first developer writes a failing test and passes the keyboard to the second developer. The second developer implements the production code so that the new test, together with all the existing tests, passes. Both developers can now collaborate on refactoring the code, but the keyboard stays with the second developer. When refactoring is over, the second developer writes a new failing test and passes the keyboard to the first developer. The first developer writes production code to make all tests pass. This cycle repeats till we complete the feature. Table 1-3 shows how developers use the Ping Pong pair programming technique.

Table 1-3. *Ping Pong Pair Programming*

Developer 1	Developer 2
Write a test	Pass the test Collaborate with developer 1 and refactor Write a test
Pass all the tests	

This technique makes it easier for beginners to separate the intent from implementation. The developer wears only one hat at a time. The focus is either on the *what* or *how*. A developer new to TDD who is working independently requires the ability to shift perspective in order to play both roles of the Ping Pong pair programming technique.

Black Box Perspective

Let's consider an example to demonstrate how you can develop the ability to focus on the intent. Imagine a system that takes a string input and returns either true or false. Table 1-4 shows the input and output of the system.

Table 1-4. *Input and Output of a System*

Input	Output
A	true
AB	false
ABA	true
ABBA	true
Anna	true
Eve	true

The first input returns true. You might come up with a hypothesis that any one-character input returns true. So, the next input could be AB, which returns false. Your hypothesis seems to be correct so far. The third data set ABA returns true, so your hypothesis was wrong. You create a new hypothesis that it could be a palindrome checker and provide it ABBA, which returns true. To confirm your hypothesis, you test it twice with different data: Anna and Eve. The result proves that your final hypothesis is correct. Figure 1-13 shows viewing the system from a black box perspective.

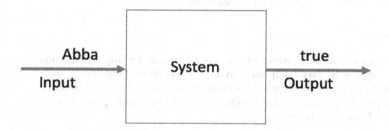

Figure 1-13. *Viewing the system as a black box*

As you observe the output for given input, you are not sure what the system does until you have sufficient examples from which to infer that it is a palindrome checker. You learn what it does, but you don't know or care how it processes the given input. You don't see what is inside the system. You only observe the input and output visible outside the system.

Shift in System and Mental States

The system under test is in a red state when you focus on the intent. From *what*, we can move to *how*. The system under test state is green when you focus on implementation. Figure 1-14 shows how the mental state and system state relate to each other.

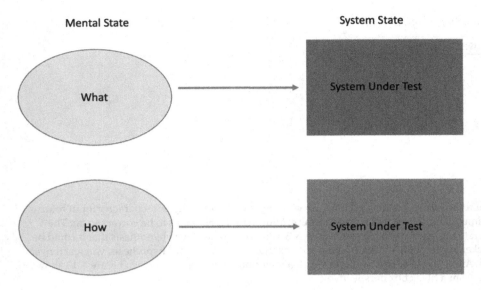

Figure 1-14. Red and green system states (red at the top, green at the bottom)

Importance of Discipline

TDD is a simple technique, as it only has a few steps to be followed. However, in practice the steps are not that easy to follow since programmers need to be very disciplined. In order to get all the benefits of TDD, programmers should follow each step. As an example, the second step states that programmers should watch the new test fail and the fifth step states that we need to refactor the code. Sometimes programmers just do not perform all the steps of Kent Beck's description of TDD.

> *I am not a great programmer, I am just a good programmer with great habits.*
>
> —Kent Beck, *Test Driven Development by Example*

The rest of this book is about how to do TDD and avoid common mistakes so that you can cultivate good habits.

Overcoming Difficulty

TDD is not a substitute for thinking. You as the developer make the design decisions. It is not a replacement for design skills. One way to make TDD easier to learn is to understand how it works. Start with a trivial one-class example (like implementing a stack) so as to learn the basics of the red-green-refactor process, then stop and think about what the process is doing. We will be discussing this in an upcoming chapter on katas.

Problem-Solving Skills

Software developers are in the business of solving problems. In TDD context, even if you know how to write the test, if you lack problem-solving skills you will not be able to complete coding the solution for a given problem.

If I had an hour to spend on a problem and my life depended on the solution, I would spend the first fifty-five minutes determining the proper question to ask for once I know the proper question, I could solve the problem in less than five minutes.

—Albert Einstein

Albert Einstein said he would spend fifty-five minutes defining the problem and alternatives and then find a way of solving the problem. So, you can see the importance of analyzing the problem. The question is, how do you analyze a given problem?

Four Phases of Problem Solving

In 1945, George Polya wrote the book *How to Solve It: A New Aspect of Mathematical Method.* This book discusses problem solving in the context of mathematics. The process he describes is applicable to software development. The four phases he describes in his book are as follows:

1. Understand the problem.
2. Devise a plan.
3. Carry out the plan.
4. Look back.

Understand the Problem

In this phase, you read the problem statement and draw a figure or table or introduce a suitable notation. You can do anything that helps you to understand the problem. In this book, we call this phase *Problem Domain Analysis.*

Devise a Plan

We have a plan when we know what needs to be done to solve the problem. The plan gives a general outline. This enables us to conceive the idea of the solution. In this book, we call this phase *Solution Domain Analysis.*

Carry Out the Plan

In this phase, we write the test first. The plan will consist of test cases ordered in the right sequence. The details of the plan will fit into the outline.

Look Back

In this phase, reconsider and reexamine the code. We can improve any solution by refactoring. The design becomes better at the end of this phase. We can also improve our understanding of the solution.

Subskills of Test Driven Development

In the book *The First 20 Hours: How to Learn Anything Fast*, Josh Kaufman says that in order to acquire a new skill you must break it down into subskills. So, the subskills needed for TDD are:

- Problem Domain Analysis

- Solution Domain Analysis

- Designing Test Cases

- Writing Tests First

- Refactoring

We can discuss and practice these subskills separately. This also helps when you get stuck in your TDD session. You can always step back and see which phase can help you get past an obstacle. We do problem domain analysis to gain an understanding of the problem. We do solution domain analysis to devise a plan. We test our plan by writing the test first and developing a solution that is driven by tests. We look back in the refactor step of the TDD process to improve the design.

So, when do we apply these tools? Before you start writing your code, you can apply the problem solving skills that will be explained in more detail in the upcoming sections. We use these tools just enough to give us a big-picture view and confidence to start writing the first test.

Problem Domain Analysis

Problem domain analysis is the process of creating a mental model that describes the problem. In this phase, you think about what you need to do. It is a reference for doing solution domain analysis and creating test cases. This step is important because we want to solve the given problem, not some other unrelated problem. We cannot solve the given problem if we don't understand it.

> *The formulation of the problem is often more essential than its solution, which may be merely a matter of mathematical or experimental skill.*
>
> —Albert Einstein

Experts spend more time on formulating the problem. They may seem to start slower, but they find the correct solution faster than novices do. Novices spend less time on formulating the problem. In the beginning, they may seem faster, but they end up starting over and spending more time than the experts do to solve the problem. For instance, expert physicists spend more time building a representation of the problem in terms of basic physics principles. After they understand the problem thoroughly, they construct the solution plan.

> *A problem well stated is a problem half-solved.*
>
> —Charles Kettering

Let's now look at an example. We begin with a problem statement. The problem statement could be: sum a list of numbers. The focus is on *what*. Ask yourself: What is the problem? Focus on understanding the problem. You focus on the inputs and output of the system. These are external to the system. You ignore what is inside the system. You ignore the implementation details. Ask yourself:

- Are there any assumptions?

- What are the assumptions?

Simplifying assumptions can define the scope of the problem. For instance, in our summing numbers problem, we can assume the list of numbers only contains numbers. This means the list does not contain any strings. So, we don't have to convert number in string format to numbers or deal with strings that are not numbers. Figure 1-15 shows that the numbers are assumed to be as shown in the first list; the second and third list are not handled by the system.

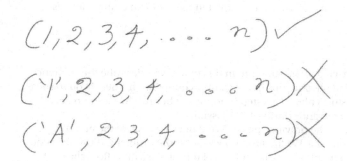

Figure 1-15. *Assumptions for summing a list of numbers*

Here are some tips for this phase:

- Do not solve the problem.

- Do not describe the steps needed to arrive at the solution.

- Draw diagrams that represent the problem in the problem domain.

- Use your own notation if necessary.

- You can also express the problem statement as an equation.

Let's now see the problem domain analysis in action. Consider a list of numbers: 1, 2, 3. We need to add 1 and 2 and 3, which will give us the total. Figure 1-16 shows the mental model of this problem.

Figure 1-16. *Mental model of summation problem*

Given numbers 1, 2, 3 and all the way up to n number of elements, we need to add the numbers from 1 all the way up to n. The final result is an unknown. Figure 1-17 shows the final artifact that describes the problem.

$$(1, 2, 3, \cdots n) \rightarrow (1 + 2 + 3 + \cdots n)$$

$$= result$$
$$= \, ?$$
$$unknown$$

Figure 1-17. *Final problem domain analysis artifact for summation problem*

We have now understood the problem statement. We have completed the problem domain analysis.

Solution Domain Analysis

Solution domain analysis is the process of arriving at the solution. In this phase, you describe the sequence of steps used to solve a given problem. You find abstractions in the solution domain. This helps you to solve problems elegantly. This phase is about devising a plan. This step is important because we want to get a big-picture view of the solution. This minimizes dead ends during TDD sessions.

We begin by taking a look at what we did in the previous phase. What did we create at the end of problem domain analysis? The focus here is on *how*. We focus on how to solve the problem. We look inside the system when we are focusing on the implementation. The artifacts of this phase can be flow charts. A flow chart is a diagram that shows the sequence of steps involved in an activity. It can be a sequence of steps for solving the problem. Figure 1-18 shows a flow chart.

Figure 1-18. *Flow chart*

It can be pseudo code. Pseudo code is a high-level description of a solution. It is the skeleton of the program. Figure 1-19 shows an example for pseudo code to create a CSV file from a food list.

Retrieve list of all foods
Create the csv file
Create the csv header
for each food in the list
 : create a row
save the csv file

Figure 1-19. *Pseudo code*

It can be an algorithm. An algorithm is a set of instructions for solving a problem. It can also be anything that describes how to arrive at a solution for a given problem. We stop when we have solved the entire problem. We will have described the steps needed to arrive at the solution. Figure 1-20 shows a high-level sequence of steps to export a food list as a CSV file.

1. Create a list of all foods
2. Create CSV header
3. Create a row for each food item
4. Save CSV file.

Figure 1-20. *Sequence of steps*

Let's now look at how to apply this to our summing a list of numbers problem. When you add numbers using a calculator, you first enter the number then press +, then enter another number, then press either +, if you want to continue adding, or press = to get the final result. You see the running total displayed. Figure 1-21 shows the running total of numbers that are added.

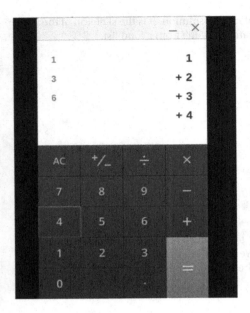

Figure 1-21. *Running total of numbers*

Hitting the equals button tells the calculator that there are no more numbers to be added. The final result is displayed on the screen. Figure 1-22 shows the final result of summing all the numbers displayed on the screen.

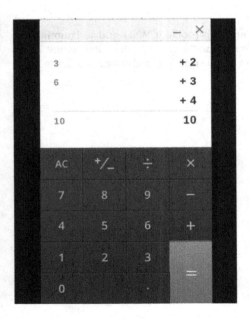

Figure 1-22. *Final total of numbers*

The terminating condition for our program is the processing of the last element. We also have a variable to track the running total. Let's say we are given a list of numbers consisting of 1, 2, and 3. The initial sum equals zero. This is the initial condition. The new sum equals the previous sum plus the first element. Next, the new sum equals the previous sum plus the second element and so on until we have new sum equals the previous sum plus the last element. Let's now develop an algorithm for this problem.

1. Take the list of numbers as an argument.

2. Initialize the running total to 0.

3. Initialize the index to 0.

4. While index < n, repeat the following:

   a. Read the number in the array at the specific index.

   b. Add the number to the running total.

   c. Go to the next element by incrementing the array index.

5. Return the sum of all the numbers as the final result.

This is the blueprint for our program. This can be implemented in any programming language. We have solved the given problem. This completes solution domain analysis. We looked at a simple problem so that we could focus on the process rather than being overwhelmed by the difficulty of the problem. The more difficult a problem, the more important these subskills become to solve the problem.

Alternative Representations

Alternative representations is a general problem-solving strategy. In this strategy, we describe the problem space in a different modality; for instance, visual instead of verbal. Everyone has a certain dominant mode for the representation of a problem. It could be visual abstraction, such as graphs or diagrams. Visual abstraction is a picture that represents the problem or solution space. It could be symbolic abstraction, such as equations. Symbolic abstraction is a mathematical expression that represents the problem or solution space. It can also be table of data consisting of the input and output of the system. It can be anything that helps us to reason about the system and tackle the problem.

It is easier to convert the problem representation from a dominant mode to a final solution in code. You must be capable of converting the given problem description from a non-dominant mode to your preferred dominant mode; for instance, converting a textual problem description to a graphical representation.

> *Written or spoken messages are linear sequences of concepts and propositions. Knowledge is stored in our minds in a hierarchical or holographic structure. When we generate written or spoken sentences, we must transform information from a hierarchical to a linear structure. Conversely, when we read or hear messages, we must transform linear sequences into a hierarchical structure in order to assimilate them into our minds.*
>
> —Novak & Govin, *Learning How to Learn*

A discussion about the conversion process is out of the scope of this book.

Divide and Conquer Strategy

Divide and conquer is a common problem-solving strategy. We reduce the complexity of a problem by dividing it into simpler sub-problems. There are two assumptions that must be true:

1. The problem can be divided into several sub-problems so that each sub-problem can be handled independently.

2. Solving each of the sub-problems and combining the solution is less complex than solving the whole problem.

We break a problem into sub-problems that are similar to the original problem, recursively solve the sub-problems, and finally combine the solutions to the sub-problems to solve the original problem. There are three parts: divide, conquer, and combine.

1. Divide the problem into a number of sub-problems that are smaller instances of the same type of problem.

2. Conquer the sub-problems by solving them recursively. If the sub-problem is small enough to be solved directly, solve it as the base case.

3. Combine the solutions to the sub-problems to solve the original problem.

This strategy often results in recursive algorithms. You will see it in action in Fibonacci and Factorial kata discussed in upcoming chapters.

Designing Test Cases

This section will cover designing test cases. We will discuss why we need them, when to design them, how to design them, and how many test cases are sufficient. Dead ends and most of the problems that arise during a TDD session can be avoided if you have the test cases in the right sequence before you start writing tests. Dead ends and problems lead to a long red time. *Red time* is the time taken to fix errors and failures in the tests. We expect some time in red, but we need to minimize it. Ideally, the only time the red system state is acceptable is when the test is failing for the right reason. We want to minimize the time spent in red so that we keep making progress, whether it is learning something about the code or completing a feature. We design test cases before we start writing tests.

Sum a List of Numbers

Let's look at an example to demonstrate how to design test cases for the summing a list of numbers problem. From our previous discussion on problem domain analysis and solution domain analysis, we already know the input and output for summing a list of numbers. So, for an empty list of numbers, we have 0 as the result. For a list that contains an element 1, we have 1 as the result. For list that contains two elements, 1 and 2, we have 1+2 as the result. For a list containing three elements, 1, 2, and 3, we have 1+2+3 as the result. Table 1-5 shows the sequence of test cases for summing a list of numbers.

Table 1-5. *Sequence of Test Cases*

Input	Output	Test Case
[ ]	0	Degenerate case
[1]	1	Simple one-element case
[1,2]	1+2	Extend the solution to two elements
[1,2...n]	1+2+...+n	Generalize to n elements

We are assuming a set of numbers is stored in an array. Degenerate is a limiting case in which a class of object changes its nature so as to belong to another, usually simpler, class. For example, the point is a degenerate case of the circle as the radius approaches 0. (Source: http://mathworld.wolfram.com/Degenerate.html)

In our example, the first row is the degenerate case. It is trivial and the simplest case. The second row is a simple one-element case. The third row extends the solution to two array elements. Finally, the fourth row generalizes to n array elements.

TDD's view of testing is pragmatic. In TDD, the tests are a means to an end. Kent Beck says that the end is the code in which we have great confidence. Confidence is a subjective thing and varies from one developer to another. It cannot be measured. So, here is a checklist that you can use:

1. Positive Case

2. Negative Case

3. Bad Inputs

4. Boundary Conditions

This is a systematic way to make sure you have a sufficient number of tests instead of depending on confidence. The test cases must be arranged in the right sequence, which must begin with the simplest one and gradually increase in complexity. We can add a fifth test case that takes nil as the input instead of an array.

Sequence of Test Cases

This section will discuss how to arrange the test cases in the right sequence. We will see where to begin and when to stop. Let's now discuss Kent Beck's testing patterns: Starter Test, Next Test, and Story Test.

Starter Test

Start by testing a variant of an operation that does not do anything. This is the degenerate case. If you write a realistic test first, then you will find yourself solving multiple problems at once. A realistic test will leave you too long without feedback. The Red-Green-Refactor loop should be completed in minutes. We aim to keep the feedback loop short to localize problems and fix them quickly. You can shorten the loop by choosing inputs and outputs that are easy to discover. If you are familiar with the problem and confident that you can get it working quickly, then you can write a realistic test.

Next Test

Which test should you pick next from the list? Pick a test that will teach you something about the system and that you are confident you can implement. Each test should represent one step toward your overall goal.

Story Test

You end with a story test. This is the acceptance test. We know we are done when this test passes. The code is generic enough and solves the entire problem.

Assertion

This section will cover the basics of assertion. In TDD, you write the test before you write the code. This section does not use TDD. The reason is that it is easier to learn something new when the discussion is focused on learning one new concept at a time. Introducing too many new concepts at once will result in confusion for beginners. Assertion is at the heart of a test. You cannot write a test without an assertion. We will work through a simple calculator program without TDD and discuss how we can verify automatically that the program works correctly.

Let's write a simple calculator program that can add two numbers. Create a file called `calculator.rb`. It has a `Calculator` class with an `add` method that takes two parameters, x and y. The add method returns the result of adding x and y. We create an instance of `Calculator` and then call the add method, passing in 1 for the value of x and 2 for the value of y. We then assign the result of adding those two numbers to a result variable and print the result.

```ruby
class Calculator
  def add(x, y)
    x + y
  end
end
calculator = Calculator.new
result = calculator.add(1, 2)
puts result
```

We can run this program by going to the terminal and typing:

```
ruby calculator.rb
```

This will print the result of 3 in the terminal. In this example, we print the result. We know that adding 1 and 2 equals 3, so we manually check that the printed result is equal to the expected value. If it is correct, we know that our calculator program works. Otherwise, we either debug our code using a debugger or add print statements to troubleshoot and fix the problem. This manual verification will become tedious when our programs grow and become big. So, the question is, how can we automate manual verification?

Let's slightly modify the program so that verifying the correct result is in code. We can check if the result is equal to the expected value, and, if it is, we can print `addition passed`. Otherwise, we print `addition failed`. The `if-else` statement automatically verifies the addition functionality.

```ruby
class Calculator
  def add(x, y)
    x + y
  end
end

calculator = Calculator.new
result = calculator.add(1, 2)

if result == 3
  puts 'Addition Passed'
else
  puts 'Addition Failed'
end
```

The expected result of 3 is in the code now. In the manual verification, 3 was inside our mind, and we did the comparison in our mind by looking at the printed value of the result.

Let's implement the subtract method that will subtract two numbers. This is similar to addition in that we have a condition that prints whether the subtraction passed or not. The code that follows shows the automated verification of the subtraction functionality.

```ruby
class Calculator
  def add(x, y)
    x + y
  end
  def subtract(x, y)
    x - y
  end
end

if result == 3
  puts 'Addition Passed'
else
  puts 'Addition Failed'
end

result2 = calculator.subtract(2, 1)
if result2 == 1
  puts 'Subtraction Passed'
else
  puts 'Subtraction Failed'
end
```

When we run this program, we now run both tests. So, we see the addition and subtraction tests passed. Figure 1-23 shows automated tests passing when we run calculator.rb.

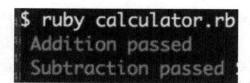

Figure 1-23. *Running the calculator program*

We see duplication in code, we can eliminate the code duplication by extracting a verify method. The code below shows the program re-written to use the verify method.

```ruby
# Calculator class code is same as before
def verify (expected, actual, message)
  if actual == expected
    puts "#{message} passed"
  else
    puts "Expected : #{expected} but got : #{actual}"
    puts "#{message} failed"
  end
end
```

```
calculator = Calculator.new
result = calculator.add(1, 2)
verify(3, result, 'Addition')
result2 = calculator.subtract(2, 1)
verify(1, result2, 'Subtraction')
```

In testing terminology, the `verify` method we have developed is called the assertion. According to the dictionary, *assertion* means *a confident or forceful statement of fact or belief*. An assertion we make in the code evaluates to either true or false; true for test passing and false for failure. The `verify` method we developed is very simple and does not distinguish between syntax errors and test failures. It does not provide the line number of the cause of failure. It does not have the summary of the number of tests that passed and tests that failed. That's where frameworks like Minitest and RSpec come into the picture. Testing frameworks provide such desired functionality, and we can avoid writing our own reusable testing methods from scratch. The assertion method is named `assert` in Minitest and expect in RSpec. We will be using the Minitest framework that comes with Ruby 2.0 and above in this book.

Test Driving Calculator

This section will cover the basic structure of a test and demonstrate its use by developing a simple calculator driven by tests. We will be using the Minitest framework as the testing framework. The reasons for this are that it is simple and very fast, with a short learning curve that makes learning easier for beginners. It is shipped with Ruby. Therefore, you don't need to install any gem.

Canonical Test Structure

According to the dictionary, the term *canonical* is defined as *relating to a general rule or standard formula*. The standard formula to write a test has three steps: given, when, and then.

Given

This is the first step. Given is the precondition. The system is in a known state in the given step.

When

This is the second step. We exercise a system under test in the when step.

Then

This is the third step. It is the post-condition. We check the outcome is as expected in the then step.

Arrange, Act, Assert

Given, when, and then is also called arrange, act, and assert, or Triple A. If you have difficulty writing a test, instead of thinking about how to write a test, ask yourself the following questions:

1. What is the given condition?

2. How do I exercise the system under test?

3. How do I verify the outcome?

The answers to these questions will help you write the test. These questions correspond to each step in the Canonical Test Structure. Question one corresponds to given. Question two corresponds to when. And question three corresponds to then. You can also work backward by writing the assertion first, then exercising the system, and finally writing the code for the precondition.

For example, if you have a Car class, you need to have fuel in order to drive the car. The given condition in this case is that it has fuel. The drive is the behavior that you are testing. So, you invoke the drive method on the car object in order to exercise the system under test. In our case, the SUT is the car. When you drive you expect to travel, so you can verify the outcome by checking the distance travelled on the odometer.

Calculator

Let's apply this testing structure to a calculator that can add two numbers. From the requirement, we could say that given two numbers, when we add them, we expect the result to be the sum of those two numbers. The breakdown of the requirement into Given-When-Then steps does not directly translate to the steps in the test. The structure for the test is as follows:

Given an instance of a calculator

When I add 1 and 2

Then the result should be equal to 3.

Why do we need an instance of a calculator? Why not make the add method a class method? In that case, we would not have a line of code for the given step in the test. These are the design decisions we consider when we write the test.

Addition

Let's create a test file called test_calculator.rb.

```
require 'minitest/autorun'

class TestCalculator < Minitest::Test
  def test_addition
    calculator = Calculator.new
    result = calculator.add(1,2)

    assert_equal 3, result
  end
end
```

We need to require minitest/autorun at the top of this file. We then define a TestCalculator class that is a sub-class of the Minitest::Test class provided by the Minitest framework. The first test will be called test_addition. Any method with a name that begins with test_ will be run automatically by the framework when we run the test file. We first create a Calculator object. We invoke the add method with two parameters, 1 and 2. The result of adding the numbers will be saved in the result variable. We will use the Minitest assertion method for equality, assert_equal, to check that the actual calculated value is equal to the expected result. Run the test in the terminal by executing the following command:

```
ruby test_calculator.rb
```

We will see an uninitialized constant error. Figure 1-24 shows the error when the calculator test is run.

```
$ ruby test_calculator.rb
Run options: --seed 24098

# Running:

E

Finished in 0.000747s, 1338.7114 runs/s, 0.0000 assertions/s.

  1) Error:
TestCalculator#test_addition:
NameError: uninitialized constant TestCalculator::Calculator
    test_calculator.rb:5:in `test_addition'

1 runs, 0 assertions, 0 failures, 1 errors, 0 skips
```

Figure 1-24. *Uninitialized constant error*

Now, define a Calculator class above the TestCalculator class.

```
require 'minitest/autorun'

class Calculator
end

class TestCalculator < Minitest::Test
  def test_addition
    # Code same as before
  end
end
```

Run the test again. The reason we are doing the minimal work is that we want to just get past the current error message, which we've just done. Now, we have an undefined method add error, shown in Figure 1-25.

```
$ ruby test_calculator.rb
Run options: --seed 2470

# Running:

E

Finished in 0.000712s, 1404.8456 runs/s, 0.0000 assertions/s.

  1) Error:
TestCalculator#test_addition:
NoMethodError: undefined method `add' for #<Calculator:0x007f80821ac6d8>
    test_calculator.rb:10:in `test_addition'

1 runs, 0 assertions, 0 failures, 1 errors, 0 skips
```

Figure 1-25. *Undefined method add error*

32

Let's define an add method in the Calculator class that takes two numbers, x and y.

```ruby
require 'minitest/autorun'

class Calculator
  def add(x, y)
  end
end

class TestCalculator < Minitest::Test
  def test_addition
    # Code same as before
  end
end
```

Run the test again. We now see the first failure. This is not an error. The test is now failing for the right reason. We have gotten past the syntax errors. Figure 1-26 shows the test failing for the right reason.

```
$ ruby test_calculator.rb
Run options: --seed 50497

# Running:

F

Finished in 0.002809s, 356.0182 runs/s, 356.0182 assertions/s.

  1) Failure:
TestCalculator#test_addition [test_calculator.rb:14]:
Expected: 3
  Actual: nil

1 runs, 1 assertions, 1 failures, 0 errors, 0 skips
```

Figure 1-26. Failing for the right reason

The failure message says that it expected 3 but it got nil. Let's implement the addition required to add those two numbers. It's simple and obvious to implement. So, we will add the two numbers.

```ruby
require 'minitest/autorun'

class Calculator
  def add(x, y)
    x + y
  end
end

class TestCalculator < Minitest::Test
  def test_addition
    # Code same as before
  end
end
```

If you run the test, it now passes. Figure 1-27 shows the first test passing.

```
$ ruby test_calculator.rb
Run options: --seed 48872

# Running:

.

Finished in 0.000783s, 1276.9940 runs/s, 1276.9940 assertions/s.

1 runs, 1 assertions, 0 failures, 0 errors, 0 skips
```

Figure 1-27. *First test passes*

Let's make the test output show color. Run the test with the -p option, as follows:

```
ruby test_calculator.rb -p
```

Figure 1-28 shows the output with one green dot just above the text Fabulous run for the passing test.

```
$ ruby test_calculator.rb -p
Run options: -p --seed 28675

# Running:

Fabulous run in 0.000732s, 1366.8802 runs/s, 1366.8802 assertions/s.

1 runs, 1 assertions, 0 failures, 0 errors, 0 skips
```

Figure 1-28. *Green color for passing tests*

Subtraction

Let's add the test for subtraction. The test is going to be similar to the one for addition.

```ruby
require 'minitest/autorun'

class TestCalculator < Minitest::Test
  def test_addition
    calculator = Calculator.new
    result = calculator.add(1,2)
    assert_equal 3, result
  end

  def test_subtraction
    calculator = Calculator.new
```

```
    result = calculator.subtract(3,2)
    assert_equal 1, result
  end
end
```

Define an empty subtract method in the Calculator class that takes two parameters.

```
require 'minitest/autorun'

class Calculator
  def add(x, y)
    # Code same as before
  end

  def subtract(x, y)

  end
end

class TestCalculator < Minitest::Test
  # Code same as before
end
```

Run the tests, which will now fail for the right reason. Figure 1-29 shows that using the -p switch displays red for test failures.

```
$ ruby test_calculator.rb -p -v
Run options: -p -v --seed 19042

# Running:

TestCalculator#test_addition = 0.00 s =
TestCalculator#test_subtraction = 0.00 s = █

Fabulous run in 0.000888s, 2252.9778 runs/s, 2252.9778 assertions/s.

   1) Failure:
TestCalculator#test_subtraction [test_calculator.rb:25]:
Expected: 1
  Actual: nil

2 runs, 2 assertions, 1 failures, 0 errors, 0 skips
```

Figure 1-29. *The minitest -p switch for color*

Implement the subtract method by subtracting y from x.

```
def subtract(x, y)
  x - y
end
```

The test will now pass. Figure 1-30 shows the name of the tests passing with the options -p for color output and -v for verbose output.

```
$ ruby test_calculator.rb -p -v
Run options: -p -v --seed 34780

# Running:

TestCalculator#test_addition = 0.00 s =
TestCalculator#test_subtraction = 0.00 s =

Fabulous run in 0.000772s, 2591.2409 runs/s, 2591.2409 assertions/s.

2 runs, 2 assertions, 0 failures, 0 errors, 0 skips
```

Figure 1-30. *Color and verbose output*

You can see the other options available in Minitest by running the test with the --help switch. Figure 1-31 shows the help output.

```
$ ruby test_calculator.rb --help
minitest options:
    -h, --help              Display this help.
    -s, --seed SEED         Sets random seed. Also via env. Eg: SEED=n rake
    -v, --verbose           Verbose. Show progress processing files.
    -n, --name PATTERN      Filter run on /regexp/ or string.

Known extensions: pride
    -p, --pride             Pride. Show your testing pride!
```

Figure 1-31. *Minitest help*

Now we have both tests passing. Move the Calculator class to a separate file called calculator.rb. We have now separated the production code from the tests.

```
class Calculator
  def add(x, y)
    x + y
  end

  def subtract(x, y)
    x - y
  end
end
```

Add require_relative 'calculator' to the top of the test_calculator.rb file. This tells Ruby where to find the Calculator class; in this case, the current directory.

```
require 'minitest/autorun'
require_relative 'calculator'
```

```ruby
class TestCalculator < Minitest::Test
  def test_addition
    calculator = Calculator.new
    result = calculator.add(1,2)
    assert_equal 3, result
  end

  def test_subtraction
    calculator = Calculator.new
    result = calculator.subtract(3,2)
    assert_equal 1, result
  end
end
```

The tests will still pass.

Common Mistakes

This section will cover the common mistakes that developers make in Test Driven Development. We will first discuss the common mistakes made in each step of the TDD Cycle before discussing some of the other mistakes such as code reflecting test data, multiple assertions, forgetting to test the negative case, and forgetting to handle boundary conditions.

Common Mistakes in the TDD Cycle

The five steps in TDD are as follows:

1. Quickly add a test.

2. Run all tests and see the new one fail.

3. Make a little change.

4. Run all tests and see them all succeed.

5. Refactor to remove duplication.

Let's now examine the mistakes in each of these steps.

Mistakes in Step One

Some of the common mistakes made in step one, quickly add a test, are the following:

- Not picking the simplest test case as the first test

- Not picking the next simplest test case as the simplest test and so on

Mistakes in Step Two

In step two, we need to run all tests and see the new one fail. Not watching the test fail is another common mistake. In this case, you directly implement the feature without watching the test fail. This is a mistake because when you write code and then run the test, you won't know whether the new code you added is the reason for the test passing. So, by making sure that the test fails before you write the code, you can be certain that the new code you added is responsible for making the test pass.

Mistakes in Step Three

Step three is to make a little change. A common mistake in this step is not implementing the simplest thing that makes the test pass. We learned about minimal implementation in an earlier section on the five steps of TDD.

Mistakes in Step Four

Step four is to run all tests and see them all succeed. The common mistake in step four is only running the current failing test. We run all tests to make sure we haven't broken anything. We also get a big-picture view of the overall design when we run all tests and they all pass.

Mistakes in Step Five

The last step is to refactor in order to remove duplication. The most common mistakes in this step are as follows:

- Forgetting the refactoring step
- Forgetting to refactor the test code for readability
- Refactoring when the tests are failing
- Refactoring some other piece of existing code that is unrelated to the feature that is currently being implemented
- Refactoring the test and the production code at the same time

When you refactor the code, you must run the test, and when you refactor the test, you must run the test. You cannot refactor both the tests and the production code without running the tests. You must either refactor the code then run all the tests or refactor the test and run all the tests. The reason is that if we change multiple things before running the tests, it will be difficult to isolate the cause of failure.

Base Conversion

This example will illustrate what happens when we skip the refactoring step and forget to clean up the production code.

Problem Statement

Convert a decimal integer to octal representation.

Problem Domain Analysis

For instance: (891) in base 10 = ? in base 8. Figure 1-32 shows the problem in symbolic form.

$$891 = (?)_8$$

Figure 1-32. *Model of the decimal-to-octal conversion problem*

Solution Domain Analysis

Divide the given number by the desired target radix, 8. Figure 1-33 shows the first step in the problem-solving process.

$$8\overline{\smash)891}$$

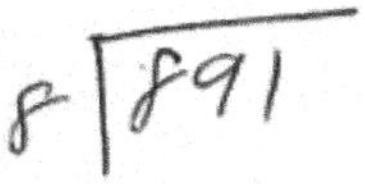

Figure 1-33. *Divide the given number to convert by 8*

Eight times one is eight. We get 0 when we subtract 8 from 8. We carry down the next digit, 9. Figure 1-34 shows the second step in the problem-solving process.

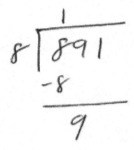

Figure 1-34. *Subtract and carry down 9*

Eight times one is eight. We get 1 when we subtract 8 from 9. Figure 1-35 shows the third step in the problem-solving process.

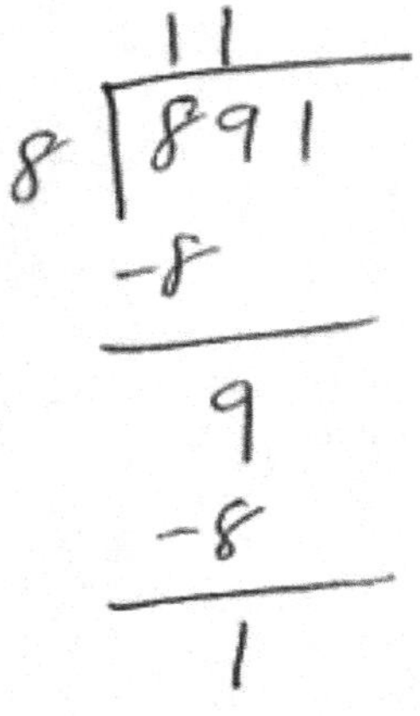

$$\begin{array}{r} 1\,1 \\ 8\,\overline{)8\,9\,1} \\ -8 \\ \hline 9 \\ -8 \\ \hline 1 \end{array}$$

Figure 1-35. *Subtract 8 from 9*

We carry down the last digit of 891, 1. Figure 1-36 shows the fourth step in the problem-solving process.

$$\begin{array}{r} 1\,1 \\ 8\,\overline{)8\,9\,1} \\ -8 \\ \hline 9 \\ -8 \\ \hline 1\,1 \end{array}$$

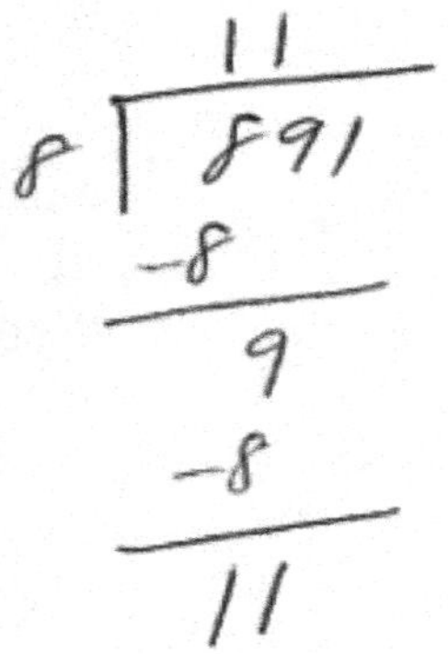

Figure 1-36. *Subtract and carry down the last digit of the given number*

So, we now have 11 that can be divided by 8. Eight times one is eight. We subtract 8 from 11 and get 3 as the remainder. This number 3 is the last digit of the result. Figure 1-37 shows the fifth step in the problem-solving process.

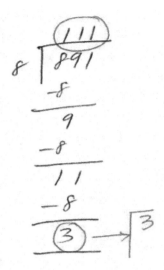

Figure 1-37. *Remainder 3 becomes last digit of the result*

We take 111 and continue this process by dividing it by 8. We get 3 as the remainder when we subtract 8 from 11. We carry down the 1 and we now have 31, which can be divided by 8. Eight times three is 24. We subtract 24 from 31 and we get 7 as the remainder. This number 7 becomes the next to last digit of the result. Figure 1-38 shows the sixth step in the problem-solving process.

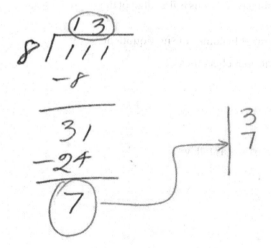

Figure 1-38. *Remainder 7 is the digit before the last digit of the result*

We take 13 and continue this process by dividing it by 8. We get 5 as the remainder when we subtract 8 from 13. The remainder 5 goes before the previous number 7. The final number 1 is less than 8 so we have reached the terminating condition. This number 1 becomes the first number of the result. So, the final result is 1573. Figure 1-39 shows the final step in the problem-solving process.

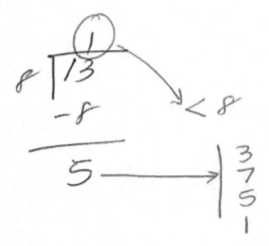

Figure 1-39. *Final result of converting 891 in decimal to octal 1573*

Algorithm

This will use the concept of reduction to reach the terminating condition. The terminating condition is reached when the remainder becomes less than 8. We will see an example to illustrate reduction in an upcoming chapter.

1. Find the remainder of the given number by using mod 8. This is first digit of the new base.

2. Divide the given number by 8; the reduced number becomes the new quotient.

3. The two steps are repeated until the reduced quotient becomes < 8.

Step 2 is the reduction step.

Code

Create a test_octal_converter.rb file and add the first two tests as follows:

```ruby
require 'minitest/autorun'
require_relative 'octal_converter'

describe OctalConverter do
  it 'should return 1 for 1' do
    converter = OctalConverter.new(1)
    result = converter.convert
    assert_equal 1, result
  end

  it 'should return 2 for 2' do
    converter = OctalConverter.new(2)
    result = converter.convert
```

```
    assert_equal 2, result
  end
end
```

Create an `octal_converter.rb` file. The implementation is trivial to make these two tests pass.

```ruby
class OctalConverter
  def initialize(number)
    @number = number
  end

  def convert
    @number
  end
end
```

Add the test to convert the number 8. Why did we skip numbers 3 through 7? The reason is that the test will pass without any modification to the current bogus implementation of `convert`.

```ruby
it 'should return 10 for 8' do
  converter = OctalConverter.new(8)
  result = converter.convert
  assert_equal 10, result
end
```

This test fails with the message:

```
Expected : 10, Actual: 8
```

The first attempt to make this test pass based on our algorithm is as follows:

```ruby
def convert
  if @number < 8
    @number
  else
    remainder = @number % 8
    @number = @number / 8
  end
end
```

This fails with a different error message:

```
Expected 10, Actual 1
```

This brings up a question: If the converter takes a decimal number as its argument, what is the base of the converted number? It should be 8. How do you return a value that is octal-based? Let's store the digits of the octal number in an array and return that as the result. Here is the implementation that works for the third test case:

```ruby
def convert
  if @number < 8
    @number
```

```
  else
    remainder = @number % 8
    @number = @number / 8
    octal = [@number, remainder]
  end
end
```

The current logic works until we hit a number that needs to generate three digits for the octal number. The fourth test that handles three-digit cases is shown here:

```
it 'should return 137 in octal for 95 decimal' do
  converter = OctalConverter.new(95)
  result = converter.convert
  assert_equal [1,3,7], result
end
```

The failure message is as follows:

```
Expected: [1,3,7] Actual: [11, 7]
```

After some print statements and thinking through the logic, here is the solution that works for the fourth test case:

```
class OctalConverter
  def initialize(number)
    @number = number
  end

  def convert
    octal = []
    if @number < 8
      octal << @number
    else
      if (@number % 8) == 0
        remainder = @number % 8
        @number = @number / 8

        octal << @number
        octal << remainder
      end

      until remainder == 0
        remainder = @number % 8
        @number = @number / 8
        octal << remainder unless remainder == 0

        octal.sort!
      end
      octal
    end
  end
end
```

It became difficult to make the fourth test pass. This is caused by not refactoring the solution. It did help us to find the right terminating condition. You have to work through this kata to experience this difficulty. The ugliness can be reduced by the following refactored solution:

```
def convert
  octal = []
  if @number < 8
    octal << @number
  else
    until @number == 0
      remainder = @number % 8
      @number = @number / 8
      octal.unshift(remainder)
    end
  end
  octal
end
```

Add the acceptance test to check if the code is generic enough to convert any decimal number to octal.

```
it 'should return 4000 for 2048' do
  converter = OctalConverter.new(2048)
  result = converter.convert
  assert_equal [4,0,0,0], result
end
```

This test passes without any changes to the existing solution. Cleaning up the code in the refactoring stage makes handling more complicated test cases easier. Here is the final refactored solution:

```
class OctalConverter
  def initialize(number)
    @number = number
  end

  def convert
    octal = []
    until finished?
      digit = extract_octal_digit
      reduce

      octal.unshift(digit)
    end
    octal
  end

  private

  def extract_octal_digit
    @number % 8
  end
```

```ruby
  def reduce
    @number = @number / 8
  end

  def finished?
    @number == 0
  end
end
```

The final version of the tests is as shown here:

```ruby
describe OctalConverter do
  it 'should return 1 in octal for 1 in decimal' do
    converter = OctalConverter.new(1)
    result = converter.convert
    assert_equal [1], result
  end

  it 'should return 2 in octal for 2 in decimal' do
    converter = OctalConverter.new(2)
    result = converter.convert
    assert_equal [2], result
  end

  it 'should return 10 in octal for 8 in decimal' do
    converter = OctalConverter.new(8)
    result = converter.convert
    assert_equal [1,0], result
  end

  it 'should return 137 in octal for 95 decimal' do
    converter = OctalConverter.new(95)
    result = converter.convert
    assert_equal [1,3,7], result
  end

  it 'should return 4000 for 2048' do
    converter = OctalConverter.new(2048)
    result = converter.convert
    assert_equal [4,0,0,0], result
  end
end
```

Code Reflecting Test Data

The code reflects the data set used in tests. We will be working through the Fibonacci problem in an upcoming chapter. Figure 1-40 illustrates production code that reflects test data for the Fibonacci problem.

```
if n == 0
  return 0
elsif n == 1
  return 1
elsif n == 2
  return 1
elsif n == 3
  return 2
elsif n == 4
  return 3
elsif n == 5
  return 5
elsif n == 6
  return 8
elsif n == 7
  return 13
elsif n == 8
  return 21
end
```

Figure 1-40. *Code reflecting test data*

Every test results in a conditional in the production code that hard codes the return value for that input value of n. As the number of tests goes up, the code does not generalize to solve the given problem. The data set you pick must be minimal and drive the evolution of code to become more generic.

Robert C. Martin came up with an axiom for this:

As the tests get more specific, the code gets more generic.

—Robert C. Martin

Martin says that programmers make specific cases work by writing code that makes the general case work. We need to keep this in mind as we write tests to drive the design. We will see this in action in chapter 2.

Multiple Assertions

The single assertion rule states that there should be only one assertion in a test. The test should be very focused and test only one thing. Having multiple assertions in a test is usually not a good idea.

You can quickly check if a test is focused by asking the question, "If this test breaks, is it due to one reason?" No other test should fail for the same reason. Why should the test break for only one reason?

Because ideally we want to achieve **defect localization**, which means being able to localize a defect so that we can trace a failing test to its cause and fix it quickly. This is critical because most of our time is spent on finding the cause of the problem than on fixing it. We want to prevent the undesirable situation where multiple tests fail due to the same bug and the amount of code we need to search through to find the cause of failure is large.

When can we break this rule? You can have multiple assertions if they are all logically related, they test only one thing, and they break for the same reason. We can also create an assertion utility method that raises the level of abstraction by combining the logically related assertions into one domain-specific assertion. This can be reused in all the tests.

Vowel Checker

Let's look at an example to illustrate the multiple assertion rule. We can reopen the String class and define a vowel? method to return true if the string is a vowel.

```ruby
class String
  def vowel?
    %w(a e i o u).include?(self)
  end
end
```

We can define a custom assertion that checks if a given letter is a vowel.

```ruby
module MiniTest::Assertions
  def assert_vowel(letter)
    assert %w(a e i o u).include?(letter), "Expected #{letter} to be a vowel"
  end
end
```

We open the MiniTest::Assertions module and define our custom assertion, assert_vowel. We can use Rspec-like syntax in Minitest to test if the letters in the array (a e i o u) are vowels or not.

```ruby
require 'minitest/autorun'

describe 'Vowel Checker' do
  %w(a e i o u).each do |letter|
    it "#{letter} is a vowel" do
      assert_vowel letter
    end
  end
end
```

The implementation detail buries the intent of the test. Run the test:

```
ruby test_vowel.rb --verbose
```

It passes with the following message:

```
Run options: --verbose --seed 7655
# Running:
Vowel Checker#test_0001_a is a vowel = 0.00 s = .
```

```
Vowel Checker#test_0002_e is a vowel = 0.00 s = .
Vowel Checker#test_0004_o is a vowel = 0.00 s = .
Vowel Checker#test_0005_u is a vowel = 0.00 s = .
Vowel Checker#test_0003_i is a vowel = 0.00 s = .
Finished in 0.000937s, 5333.8961 runs/s, 5333.8961 assertions/s.
5 runs, 5 assertions, 0 failures, 0 errors, 0 skips
```

You can see that there are five tests that are generated, and they show up in the test result. Vowel functionality is implemented with one line, so ideally we should have only one test that fails if that functionality breaks. We can fix the problem by using a data-driven test utility to write one test that fails to localize the defect.

```
module MiniTest::Assertions
  def data_driven_test(container)
    container.each do |element|
      yield element
    end
  end
end
```

The data_driven_test encapsulates the looping logic and yields one element at a time from the container that can be processed in the vowel test. The test can be rewritten as follows:

```
describe 'Vowel Checker' do
  it 'a, e, i, o, u are the vowel set' do
    data_driven_test(%w(a e i o u)) do |letter|
      assert_vowel letter
    end
  end
end
```

This test communicates the intent. We can run the test:

```
ruby test_vowel.rb --verbose
```

The test passes with the message:

```
Run options: --verbose --seed 5645
# Running:
Vowel Checker#test_0001_a, e, i, o, u are the vowel set = 0.00 s = .
Finished in 0.001040s, 961.5191 runs/s, 4807.5954 assertions/s.
1 runs, 5 assertions, 0 failures, 0 errors, 0 skips
```

We have five assertions, but only one test instead of five, before refactoring. The implementation details are now hidden behind a library call, data_driven_test. This demonstrates the **Communicate Intent Principle** discussed in the xUnit Test Patterns by Gerard Mezaros. This principle is also known as **Higher Level Language, Single Glance Readable**. If we have to squint our eyes when we look at the test, then it is harder to understand because we need to infer the big picture from all the details. You will see another example to illustrate the multiple assertion rule in an upcoming chapter on katas.

Forgetting to Test the Negative Case

Negative cases are the failure cases and abnormal cases. A negative case for a division method of a calculator would be that division by 0 must throw an exception. An example is shown in an upcoming chapter on katas using the fizz buzz kata. This is the missing test that is supposed to check for numbers that are not multiples of either 3 or 5. This is the case when the number does not require any transformation. The code example that follows tests the positive and negative cases.

```ruby
require 'minitest/autorun'

class User
  def assign_role(role)
    @role = role
  end

  def in_role?(role)
    @role == role
  end
end

describe User do
  it 'should be in any role assigned to it' do
    user = User.new
    user.assign_role('admin')
    assert user.in_role?('admin')
  end
  it 'should not be in a role that is not assigned to it' do
    user = User.new

    refute user.in_role?('admin')
  end
end
```

The tests are easy to read, and you can see we check that when the user is not in any role, they are not assigned to any role.

Not Testing the Boundary Conditions

Forgetting to write tests to exercise the limits of a system is a mistake. For instance, what should be the behavior when the maximum number of elements is added to a set? What happens when the input is 0, -1, maximum, or maximum + 1? By documenting the behavior for these inputs we communicate with other developers. This is useful when troubleshooting problems in software that uses libraries developed by others.

Not Updating the Tests

Another mistake is not updating the tests to reflect the current understanding of the system. Updating the tests means we could either delete or change an existing test to reflect our understanding of the system. As we implement the features, we will learn more about the domain. This knowledge must be expressed in the form of tests, so that other developers can gain that knowledge about the domain by reading the tests.

We will see an example of this mistake in an upcoming chapter, where we will work through the fizz buzz kata. Let's briefly discuss the fizz buzz kata example. Figure 1-41 shows the scaffold test for the fizz buzz kata.

```
def test_generate_numbers_from_1_to_100
  game = FizzBuzz.new

  result = game.numbers

  assert_equal((1..100).to_a, result)
end
```

Figure 1-41. *Scaffold test*

We will delete the test for creating numbers from 1 to 100 in the fizz buzz class and make the numbers method private. This test will give us the momentum to get started, but it's not required in the end. It's like the scaffold of a building. When the building is completed, the scaffold will go away. By making the numbers method private, we hide the implementation details in the fizz buzz class. Figure 1-42 shows the implementation details hidden behind a private method.

```
private

def numbers
  (1..100).to_a
end
```

Figure 1-42. *Private method in fizz buzz kata*

We will see an example of updating an existing test to reflect our new understanding in an upcoming chapter on Conway's Game of Life kata. In that kata, the initial test will look like this:

```
it 'two alive cells as neighbors will stay alive' do
  c1 = Cell.new(Location::CENTER)
  c2 = Cell.new(Location::NORTH)
  neighborhood = NeighborHood.new
  neighborhood.seed([c1,c2])

  neighborhood.tick

  assert_equal 2, neighborhood.alive_cells
end
```

Why are we counting the number of alive cells? We will realize that what the test says is not expressed in the assertion. We will update it as follows:

```
it 'a cell with two alive cells as neighbors will stay alive' do
  c1 = Cell.new(Location::CENTER)
  c2 = Cell.new(Location::NORTH)
  c3 = Cell.new(Location::SOUTH)
  neighborhood = NeighborHood.new
  neighborhood.seed([c1,c2,c3])

  neighborhood.tick

  assert c1.alive?
end
```

The test becomes semantically correct. It also expresses the meaning of the test in the assertion step as conveyed by the test name. We no longer use the number of alive cells as a way to check if a cell is alive. The relationship between the test name and the implementation of the test becomes consistent. We want to avoid code like the following:

```
it 'Dog should wag the tail when it sees the owner' do
  owner = Person.new
  dog = Dog.new
  result = dog.see(owner)

  assert_equal 'bark', result
end
```

This example seems obvious, but developers make this very common mistake. We can fix this code as follows:

```
it 'Dog should wag the tail when it sees the owner' do
  owner = Person.new
  dog = Dog.new
  result = dog.see(owner)

  assert_equal 'wagging my tail', result
end
```

The mistake is often caused by a lack of knowledge about the domain, as the developer is unfamiliar with the domain. So, instead of blindly adding new tests, during the refactoring step we must review the existing tests and make decisions about deleting or updating the tests to reflect our growing knowledge about the domain. By doing so, we as developers make the transition from "Me Milk" to "Please give me some milk to drink."

■ **Note** A test must be syntactically and semantically correct. Ruby interpreter enforces the syntactic correctness of a test. It is the developer's responsibility to enforce the semantic correctness of a test.

Implementation-Aware Tests

One of the most common mistakes is writing tests that are aware of the implementation details. It could be data structure used in the code. For instance, in the example that follows, the test is aware of the fact that the concept of color is represented as a string.

```ruby
require 'minitest/autorun'

class Grass
  attr_reader :color

  def initialize
    @color = 'green'
  end
end

describe Grass do
  it 'is green' do
    grass = Grass.new
    result = grass.color
    assert_equal 'green', result
  end
end
```

The design decision of how to represent color could change to RGB values, Struct, etc. In this case, the client code would like this:

```ruby
grass = Grass.new
if grass.color == 'green'
  puts "Well maintained lawn"
else
  puts "Grass is brown"
end
```

If we do not hide the design decisions from the clients; we will break them when we change our design decision. We can hide the design decision by rewriting our test and implementation as shown below:

```ruby
require 'minitest/autorun'


class Grass
  def initialize
    @color = 'green'
  end

  def green?
    @color == 'green'
  end
end
```

```ruby
describe Grass do
  it 'is green' do
    grass = Grass.new
    result = grass.green?
    assert result
  end
end
```

In this case, our class does not expose its internal data representation to its clients. It provides a higher level, well-defined interface green? that encapsulates the data to provide a service to its clients. In this case, contrast the client code shown next with the previous version of the client code.

```ruby
grass = Grass.new
if grass.green?
  puts "Well maintained lawn"
else
  puts "Grass is brown"
end
```

The client has no knowledge about whether the color is a string, Struct, or RGB value. It does not ask for data and then process the data to make a decision. It uses the boolean return value of the green? method in the conditional. This makes it immune to any changes to the way the color is represented inside the Green class. We will see another example in an upcoming chapter that demonstrates that if you change the data structure from an array to a hash, the tests coupled to implementation details will break.

It could also be other implementation details, such as private data or private methods. One of the common questions that beginners ask me is: Do we test methods? We test methods that are part of the public API. We do not write tests for private methods. If you are not confident and feel like testing the private methods, then it is a good idea to see if all the private methods are operating on the same data and if they can be moved to a new class. This new class captures the missing abstraction and becomes a collaborator of the old class. The private methods in the old class will become the public methods in the new class. So, the new class can be tested separately. The private section of the class should not become a place for abstractions to hide.

Summary

In this chapter, you learned about coding kata, why we use them to learn TDD, and also basic terminology such as domain, problem domain, and solution domain. We also briefly discussed how to apply continuous improvement to improve your TDD skills over time. You learned about intent and implementation. We saw examples to illustrate the difference between them, why you need to separate them, and how to separate them in code.

We briefly discussed the basics of Test Driven Development, how beginners can learn to separate the intent from implementation, and how to overcome difficulty in Test Driven Development. We discussed how problem-solving skills fit into Test Driven Development. We saw that the focus shifts from *what* to *how* when doing problem domain analysis and solution domain analysis. We learned why we need these tools and the artifacts that are created at the end of these phases.

We discussed designing test cases, why we need them before we write a test, how many test cases are sufficient, and how to come up with the right sequence for the test cases.

We used a trivial calculator example to explain how we can automate manual verification of any program. We saw that assertion is at the heart of a test and that we cannot write a test without using an assertion. We also saw why we need testing frameworks.

We discussed the Canonical Test Structure. If you have difficulty writing a test, you can use the three questions we discussed to guide you in writing a test. We took baby steps. We wrote the test first and then the production code. Initial error messages were syntax errors. Once we got past that, we made the test fail for the right reason. Then, we implemented the code to make the test pass. Once you get to green you can clean up the test and the production code. This is called refactoring. We will discuss more about refactoring in an upcoming chapter.

You learned about the common mistakes developers make in each step of the TDD cycle. You also saw other common mistakes and how to avoid them. You learned why these mistakes must be avoided.

EXERCISES

Multiply Given List of Numbers

Given a list of numbers, perform problem domain analysis and solution domain analysis to multiply them all.

Design test cases for multiplying a given list of numbers. The sequence of the test cases must be from simplest to the most complex.

Calculator

Implement multiplication and division of two given numbers. Use the verify method we have developed to test.

Implement multiplication and division of two given numbers driven by tests. You must write the test first.

CHAPTER 2

■ ■ ■

Katas

In this chapter, we will work through katas and apply constraints to our solution. Constraints are a way to force developers to write code in a different way. Developers learn new coding techniques by enforcing the constraints. The constraints are applied so as to build on the existing solution. We will discuss the order of the test cases, implementation independent tests, testing random behavior, testing time-dependent behavior, difference reduction, using mocks as a design technique, the open-closed principle, and testing guidelines such as testing precisely and concretely.

Fibonacci Sequence

This section will put together everything we have discussed so far to develop a solution for generating a Fibonacci sequence driven by tests. The Fibonacci sequence appears in nature. You can find it in the leaf arrangement of a plant, the pattern of florets on a flower, the scales of a pineapple, and so on. The size of the leaf grows in size but maintains the same shape. Figure 2-1 shows the spirals in the leaf arrangement of a plant exhibiting the Fibonacci sequence.

Figure 2-1. *Fibonacci sequence in nature*

© Bala Paranj 2017
B. Paranj, *Test Driven Development in Ruby*, DOI 10.1007/978-1-4842-2638-4_2

Problem Statement

Generate a Fibonacci sequence for a given number. The sequence goes like this: 0, 1, 1, 2, 3, 5, 8, 13, and so on. We need to understand the problem. Therefore, we need to quickly do problem domain analysis. Figure 2-2 shows the visual representation of the Fibonacci sequence as a spiral when we make squares with widths corresponding to the numbers in the sequence.

Figure 2-2. *Visual representation of Fibonacci sequence*

Problem Domain Analysis

Let's tabulate the input and output to our system. The output for the first two inputs are known values. We don't need to compute those values. Figure 2-3 shows the first two data sets: (0, 0), (1, 1) are given and are known values.

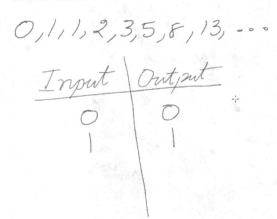

Figure 2-3. *First two in the Fibonacci sequence are not calculated*

We can represent the problem in an equation form like this:

```
f(0) = 0
f(1) = 1
f(2) = 1
f(3) = 2
```

and so on.

We now understand the Fibonacci sequence problem. How do we transform the input to the given output? Let's now do solution domain analysis to figure out how the function $f(n)$ transforms the input to produce the output. Figure 2-4 shows mathematical notation as the header of a table with the Fibonacci sequence for a given term.

F_0	F_1	F_2	F_3	F_4	F_5	F_6	F_7	F_8	F_9	F_{10}	F_{11}	F_{12}	F_{13}	F_{14}	F_{15}
0	1	1	2	3	5	8	13	21	34	55	89	144	233	377	610

Figure 2-4. *Tabular representation of Fibonacci sequence*

Solution Domain Analysis

Let's now discuss how to generate the Fibonacci sequence. From the problem domain analysis, we already know that the initial conditions are given. So, the first two numbers in the sequence are given and not calculated. Let's tabulate the input and output to our system. The output for the first two inputs are known values. We don't need to compute those values.

The value for input 2 in the sequence is computed by adding 0 and 1, and the result is 1. Figure 2-5 shows how we arrive at the third value in the Fibonacci sequence.

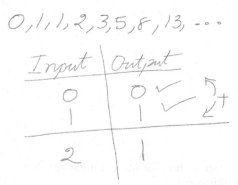

Figure 2-5. *Calculating the third value in the Fibonacci sequence*

For an input of 3, we add 1 and 1, so we get 2. Figure 2-6 shows how we arrive at the fourth value in the Fibonacci sequence by adding the output of the second and third inputs.

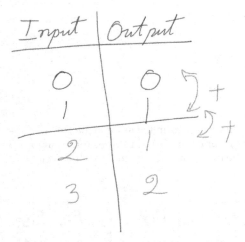

Figure 2-6. *Calculating the fourth value in the Fibonacci sequence*

When you add 2 and 1 you get 3, which is the value for input 4. Figure 2-7 shows how we arrive at the fifth value in the Fibonacci sequence by adding the output of the third and and fourth inputs.

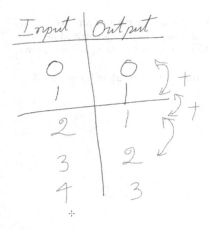

Figure 2-7. *Calculating the fifth value in the Fibonacci sequence*

For 5, we add 2 and 3, which gives us the output of 5. Figure 2-8 shows how we arrive at the sixth value in the Fibonacci sequence by adding the output of the fourth and fifth inputs.

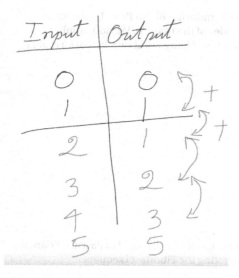

Figure 2-8. *Calculating the sixth value in the Fibonacci sequence*

The first two rows have the known output values for the given input. So, we have (0, 0), (1, 1), (2, 1), (3, 2), (4, 3) and (5, 5). When you reflect on the process of generating the sequence, you can see a pattern emerge. We add the previous two output values to generate the next output in the sequence. We have seen:

```
f(0) = 0
f(1) = 1
f(2) = f(1) + f(0)
```

We can see a pattern. We can now generalize the transformation function f(n) as:

```
f(n) = f(n - 1) + f(n - 2)
```

Table 2-1 tabulates the input and output for the Fibonacci sequence.

Table 2-1. *Fibonacci Sequence*

Input	Output
0	0
1	1
2	1
3	2
4	3
5	5

The input is f(n) and the output is f(n-1) + f(n-2). We can think about the terminating condition in this phase. The terminating condition in our case is reaching the Fibonacci value for 0.

Pascal's Triangle is a number pattern named after French mathematician Blaise Pascal. Imagine a triangle, with the number one at the top and ones at the slanting sides of the triangle. We add numbers directly above each row to get the value for numbers within the triangle. Figure 2-9 shows Pascal's Triangle.

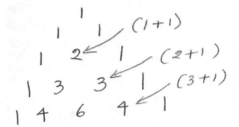

Figure 2-9. *Pascal's Triangle*

We can generate the Fibonacci sequence by summing the numbers in the diagonal of Pascal's Triangle as shown in Figure 2-10, which shows the visual summary of generating the Fibonacci sequence.

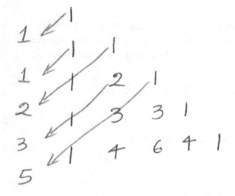

Figure 2-10. *Visual summary of generating Fibonacci sequence*

Pascal's Triangle and its relation to Fibonacci is a just an interesting mathematical fact. It is not a required for solution domain analysis of this problem.

Assumptions

We do not need to worry about performance issues, huge numbers that can throw errors, or bad user input in this kata.

Test-Driven Fibonacci

We are now ready to generate the Fibonacci sequence driven by tests. Create a fibonacci.rb file with an empty Fibonacci class as shown here:

```
class Fibonacci
end
```

Create another file called `test_fibonacci.rb` with the first test for the first test case from the Table 2-1 we have created. The code that follows shows the test file `test_fibonacci.rb`.

```ruby
require 'minitest/autorun'
require_relative 'fibonacci'

class TestFibonacci < Minitest::Test
  def test_fibonacci_of_zero_is_zero
    result = Fibonacci.of(0)

    assert_equal 0, result
  end
end
```

We have a `require_relative` statement to include the `Fibonacci` class in the test file. `Fibonacci` of zero is zero, zero is passed to a class method called `of()` in the `Fibonacci` class, and the test method name is test_fibonacci_of_zero_is_zero. We then check that the result is the expected value, zero, using `assert_equal`. Run the test by running the command: `ruby -rminitest/pride test_fibonacci.rb --verbose`. It's failing because it does not have the `of()` method. Let's declare this method that takes a number:

```ruby
class Fibonacci
  def self.of(n)
  end
end
```

Run the test again. It fails with the failure message: `Expected zero actual nil`. Figure 2-11 shows the first failing test.

```
$ ruby -rminitest/pride test_fibonacci.rb --verbose
Run options: --verbose --seed 51169

# Running:

TestFibonacci#test_fibonacci_of_zero_is_zero = 0.00 s = F

Fabulous run in 0.001398s, 715.3076 runs/s, 715.3076 assertions/s.

  1) Failure:
TestFibonacci#test_fibonacci_of_zero_is_zero [test_fibonacci.rb:9]:
Expected: 0
  Actual: nil

1 runs, 1 assertions, 1 failures, 0 errors, 0 skips
```

Figure 2-11. First failing test

Let's return zero. That's the quickest way to get to green. The simplest implementation to make the first test pass is as follows:

```ruby
class Fibonacci
  def self.of(n)
    0
  end
end
```

Run the test again; it will pass. Figure 2-12 shows the first test passing.

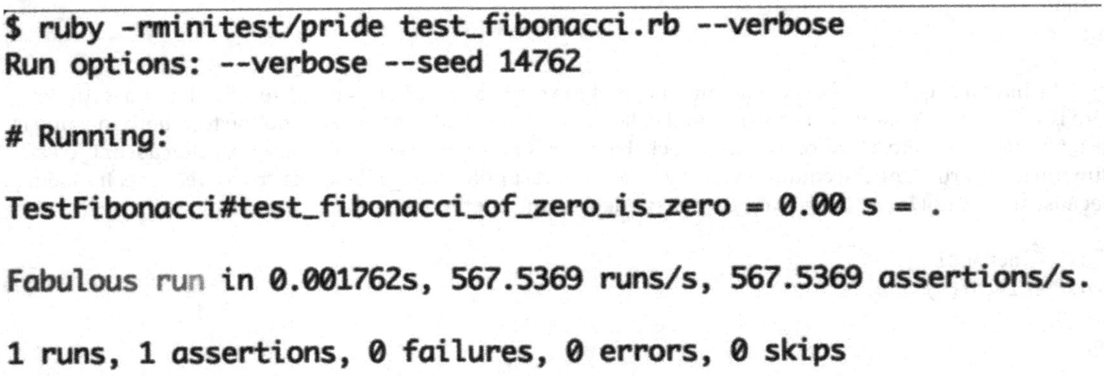

```
$ ruby -rminitest/pride test_fibonacci.rb --verbose
Run options: --verbose --seed 14762

# Running:

TestFibonacci#test_fibonacci_of_zero_is_zero = 0.00 s = .

Fabulous run in 0.001762s, 567.5369 runs/s, 567.5369 assertions/s.

1 runs, 1 assertions, 0 failures, 0 errors, 0 skips
```

Figure 2-12. First test passes

Let's add the second test, Fibonacci of one is one:

```ruby
def test_fibonacci_of_one_is_one
  result = Fibonacci.of(1)

  assert_equal 1, result
end
```

The assertion checks if the result is the expected value of one. Let's run the test again; it fails with this message: Expected 1, Actual 0.

Figure 2-13 shows the test failure for the second test.

```
$ ruby -rminitest/pride test_fibonacci.rb --verbose
Run options: --verbose --seed 24474

# Running:

TestFibonacci#test_fibonacci_of_one_is_one = 0.00 s = F
TestFibonacci#test_fibonacci_of_zero_is_zero = 0.00 s = .

Fabulous run in 0.001596s, 1253.1328 runs/s, 1253.1328 assertions/s.

  1) Failure:
TestFibonacci#test_fibonacci_of_one_is_one [test_fibonacci.rb:15]:
Expected: 1
  Actual: 0

2 runs, 2 assertions, 1 failures, 0 errors, 0 skips
```

Figure 2-13. *Second test fails*

The quickest way to get this working is to just return the value that was given to us. The code to make the second test pass quickly is as follows:

```
class Fibonacci
  def self.of(n)
    n
  end
end
```

Let's run the test again. Both tests pass. Figure 2-14 shows two tests passing.

```
$ ruby -rminitest/pride test_fibonacci.rb --verbose
Run options: --verbose --seed 51686

# Running:

TestFibonacci#test_fibonacci_of_one_is_one = 0.00 s = .
TestFibonacci#test_fibonacci_of_zero_is_zero = 0.00 s = .

Fabulous run in 0.001516s, 1319.2612 runs/s, 1319.2612 assertions/s.

2 runs, 2 assertions, 0 failures, 0 errors, 0 skips
```

Figure 2-14. *First and second tests pass*

Let's add the third test. The third test is Fibonacci of two is one:

```ruby
def test_fibonacci_of_two_is_one
  result = Fibonacci.of(2)

  assert_equal 1, result
end
```

We check if the result is the expected value of one via the assertion. Let's run the tests. This test fails with the following message:

```
Expected 1, Actual 2.
```

Figure 2-15 shows the third test failure.

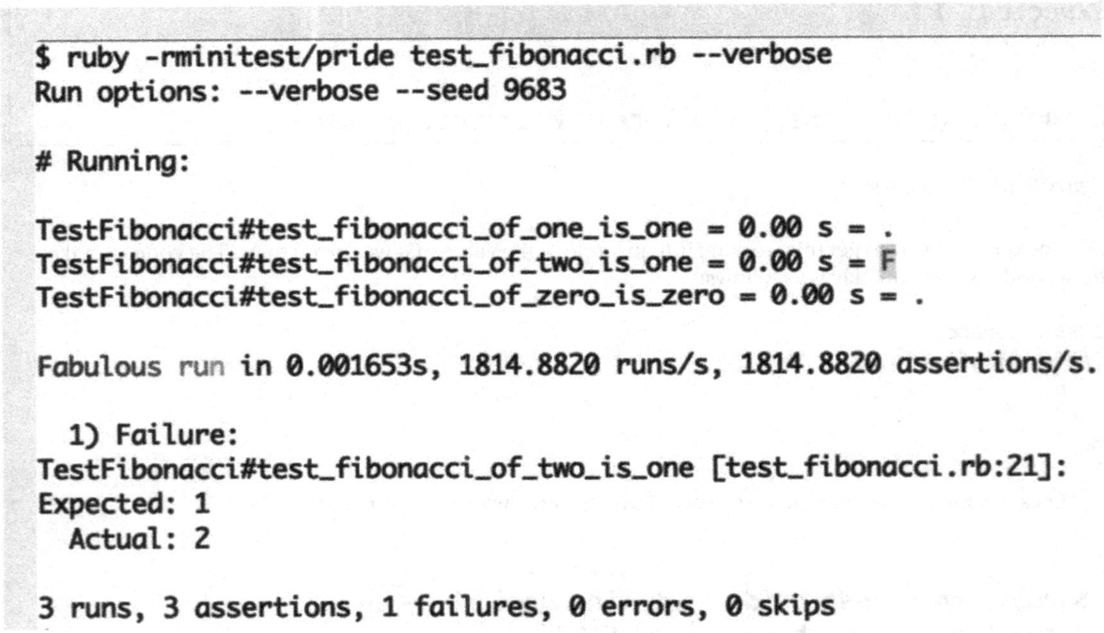

```
$ ruby -rminitest/pride test_fibonacci.rb --verbose
Run options: --verbose --seed 9683

# Running:

TestFibonacci#test_fibonacci_of_one_is_one = 0.00 s = .
TestFibonacci#test_fibonacci_of_two_is_one = 0.00 s = F
TestFibonacci#test_fibonacci_of_zero_is_zero = 0.00 s = .

Fabulous run in 0.001653s, 1814.8820 runs/s, 1814.8820 assertions/s.

  1) Failure:
TestFibonacci#test_fibonacci_of_two_is_one [test_fibonacci.rb:21]:
Expected: 1
  Actual: 2

3 runs, 3 assertions, 1 failures, 0 errors, 0 skips
```

Figure 2-15. *Third test failure*

We can have a conditional that checks if the given number is zero, and, if so, we return zero. Otherwise, we return one. The code shows the if-else statement that splits the execution path to satisfy the requirement stated in the third test.

```ruby
class Fibonacci
  def self.of(n)
    if n == 0
      0
    else
      1
```

```
      end
    end
end
```

Let's run all the tests; they will pass. Figure 2-16 shows that all three tests pass now.

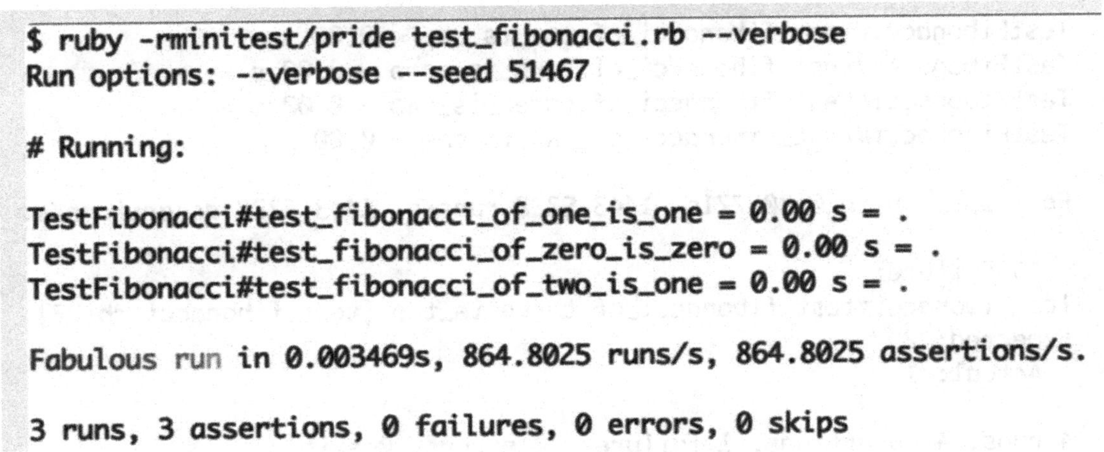

```
$ ruby -rminitest/pride test_fibonacci.rb --verbose
Run options: --verbose --seed 51467

# Running:

TestFibonacci#test_fibonacci_of_one_is_one = 0.00 s = .
TestFibonacci#test_fibonacci_of_zero_is_zero = 0.00 s = .
TestFibonacci#test_fibonacci_of_two_is_one = 0.00 s = .

Fabulous run in 0.003469s, 864.8025 runs/s, 864.8025 assertions/s.

3 runs, 3 assertions, 0 failures, 0 errors, 0 skips
```

Figure 2-16. *All three tests pass*

Let's add the fourth test. The fourth test is Fibonacci of three is two. The following code shows the fourth test, which expresses the intent for the fourth data set from our table:

```
def test_fibonacci_of_three_is_two
  result = Fibonacci.of(3)

  assert_equal 2, result
end
```

We check if the result is the expected value of two via the assertion. Run all the tests; the fourth test fails. Figure 2-17 shows the fourth test failure.

```
$ ruby -rminitest/pride test_fibonacci.rb --verbose
Run options: --verbose --seed 28952

# Running:

TestFibonacci#test_fibonacci_of_one_is_one = 0.00 s = .
TestFibonacci#test_fibonacci_of_zero_is_zero = 0.00 s = .
TestFibonacci#test_fibonacci_of_three_is_two = 0.00 s = F
TestFibonacci#test_fibonacci_of_two_is_one = 0.00 s = .

Fabulous run in 0.002771s, 1443.5222 runs/s, 1443.5222 assertions/s.

  1) Failure:
TestFibonacci#test_fibonacci_of_three_is_two [test_fibonacci.rb:27]:
Expected: 2
  Actual: 1

4 runs, 4 assertions, 1 failures, 0 errors, 0 skips
```

Figure 2-17. *Fourth test failure*

We know from the solution domain analysis that f(n)= f(n - 1) + f(n - 2). We can use that fact here. The code that follows shows the quick and dirty implementation to make all four tests pass.

```
class Fibonacci
  def self.of(n)
    if n == 0
      0
    elsif n <= 2
      1
    else
      return of(n-1) + of(n-2)
    end
  end
end
```

So, in this case we handle the second and third tests by checking that *n* is less than or equal to two. Otherwise, we can just return f(n - 1) +f(n - 2).

Let's run the tests. Figure 2-18 shows all four tests passing.

```
$ ruby -rminitest/pride test_fibonacci.rb --verbose
Run options: --verbose --seed 44651

# Running:

TestFibonacci#test_fibonacci_of_two_is_one = 0.00 s = .
TestFibonacci#test_fibonacci_of_zero_is_zero = 0.00 s = .
TestFibonacci#test_fibonacci_of_three_is_two = 0.00 s = .
TestFibonacci#test_fibonacci_of_one_is_one = 0.00 s = .

Fabulous run in 0.001677s, 2385.2117 runs/s, 2385.2117 assertions/s.

4 runs, 4 assertions, 0 failures, 0 errors, 0 skips
```

Figure 2-18. *All four tests pass*

Let's see if this will work for a much larger number. Let's add a test for Fibonacci of ten is fifty-five. The following code shows the test for a larger number:

```
def test_fibonacci_of_ten_is_fifty_five
  result = Fibonacci.of(10)

  assert_equal 55, result
end
```

The test checks if the result is the expected value of fifty-five via the assertion. Figure 2-19 shows that all the tests passed. We did not have to modify or add any new code to make this test pass.

```
$ ruby -rminitest/pride test_fibonacci.rb --verbose
Run options: --verbose --seed 27353

# Running:

TestFibonacci#test_fibonacci_of_one_is_one = 0.00 s = .
TestFibonacci#test_fibonacci_of_ten_is_fifty_five = 0.00 s = .
TestFibonacci#test_fibonacci_of_two_is_one = 0.00 s = .
TestFibonacci#test_fibonacci_of_three_is_two = 0.00 s = .
TestFibonacci#test_fibonacci_of_zero_is_zero = 0.00 s = .

Fabulous run in 0.001722s, 2903.6005 runs/s, 2903.6005 assertions/s.

5 runs, 5 assertions, 0 failures, 0 errors, 0 skips
```

Figure 2-19. *All tests pass*

The test we just added is called a story test because it tells us whether we are done or not. It's an acceptance criterion. So, we are confident enough that our algorithm will work for any given number. Let's refactor this solution to a better solution.

```ruby
class Fibonacci
  def self.of(n)
    return 0 if n == 0
    return 1 if n <= 2

    return of(n-1) + of(n-2)
  end
end
```

Let's run all the tests. They will still pass. So, we use the existing tests as a safety net. They provided us with a regression test so that if we had introduced any bugs in the refactoring phase, our tests would have caught it. The complete code for all the tests is shown here:

```ruby
require 'minitest/autorun'
require_relative 'fibonacci'

class TestFibonacci < Minitest::Test
  def test_fibonacci_of_zero_is_zero
    result = Fibonacci.of(0)
    assert_equal 0, result
  end
  def test_fibonacci_of_one_is_one
    result = Fibonacci.of(1)
    assert_equal 1, result
  end
  def test_fibonacci_of_two_is_one
    result = Fibonacci.of(2)
    assert_equal 1, result
  end
  def test_fibonacci_of_three_is_two
    result = Fibonacci.of(3)
    assert_equal 2, result
  end

  def test_fibonacci_of_four_is_three
    result = Fibonacci.of(4)
    assert_equal 3, result
  end
  def test_fibonacci_of_five_is_five
    result = Fibonacci.of(5)
    assert_equal 5, result
  end
  def test_fibonacci_of_ten_is_fifty_five
    result = Fibonacci.of(10)
    assert_equal 55, result
  end
end
```

Fizz Buzz

This section will cover the topic of how to order test cases. Having the test cases in the right order helps us to make the tests pass quickly. It is less likely that we will get stuck, and we will make progress toward coding the final solution. In the subsequent sections of this kata, the code examples will build on each other.

Problem Statement

Write a program that prints the numbers from 1 to 100. But for multiples of three print "Fizz" instead of the number and for the multiples of five print "Buzz". For numbers which are multiples of both three and five print "FizzBuzz". We need to understand the problem. Therefore, we need to quickly do problem domain analysis.

Problem Domain Analysis

Let's consider the numbers from 1 to 20. Table 2-2 summarizes the input and output for the FizzBuzz problem.

Table 2-2. *FizzBuzz*

Input	Output
1	1
2	2
3	Fizz
4	4
5	Buzz
6	Fizz
7	7
8	8
9	Fizz
10	Buzz
11	11
12	Fizz
13	13
14	14
15	FizzBuzz
16	16
17	17
18	Fizz
19	19
20	Buzz

We have now understood the Fibonacci sequence problem. How do we transform the input to the given output? Let's now do solution domain analysis to figure out how to transform the input to produce the output shown in the table.

Solution Domain Analysis

Let's discuss how to generate the FizzBuzz sequence. What does it mean when a number is a multiple of 3? Let's experiment in the IRB console:

```
> 1 % 3
 => 1
> 2 % 3
 => 2
> 3 % 3
 => 0
> 4 % 3
 => 1
> 5 % 3
 => 2
> 6 % 3
 => 0
> 7 % 3
 => 1
> 8 % 3
 => 2
> 9 % 3
 => 0
> 10 % 3
 => 1
```

You can see that when a number is a multiple of 3, the remainder is zero when we divide that number by 3. Similarly, when a number is multiple of 5, the remainder is zero when we divide that number by 5. We applied the simple three-step process that we discussed in first chapter section on minimal implementation. The focus question in this case is: What does it mean when a number is a multiple of 3? The experiment we designed took numbers from 1 through 10 and divided them all by 3. We observed the pattern that emerged in the result and concluded that the remainder is zero when it is a multiple of 3.

Test-Driven FizzBuzz

We are now ready to generate the FizzBuzz sequence driven by tests. Create a file called `fizz_buzz.rb` with an empty `FizzBuzz` class.

```ruby
class FizzBuzz
end
```

Create a test file, `test_fizzbuzz.rb`, that has a test for printing fizz for multiples of 3.

```ruby
require 'minitest/autorun'
require_relative 'fizz_buzz'

class TestFizzBuzz < Minitest::Test
  def test_print_fizz_for_multiples_of_3
    fb = FizzBuzz.new
    # We are stuck here
  end
end
```

We create an instance of the FizzBuzz class and assign it to variable fb. Now, how do I verify that we print fizz for multiples of 3? We have to think really hard about writing this test. The very first test needs to be something easy that you can quickly write and get working with a quick and dirty implementation. So, if you have difficulty writing the very first test, it means that you are solving a much bigger problem, which you don't want to do at this stage. This test is providing us feedback.

■ **Note**   We can come up with a better design by applying good design principles. We must separate sequence-generation logic from displaying the sequence to the user.

Why should the sequence-generation logic be tied to how it is displayed to the user? We don't want to check whether the output is printed on a terminal or displayed on a graphical user interface. What if we applied good design principles and separate displaying the sequence to the user from sequence-generation logic? You could also argue that if we add a series of test cases that gradually increase in complexity, we will not have this problem.

Let's simplify our problem and write a simpler test. Delete the first test and add a new test that solves a smaller problem that is easier to solve. By doing so, we are applying the Starter Test that we learned in the earlier chapter.

This new test is called test_generate_numbers_from_1_to_100. We create an instance of FizzBuzz and invoke the numbers method on the fizz buzz instance fb.

```ruby
require 'minitest/autorun'
require_relative 'fizz_buzz'

class TestFizzBuzz < Minitest::Test
  def test_generate_numbers_from_1_to_100
    fb = FizzBuzz.new
    result = fb.numbers
    assert_equal (1..100).to_a, result
  end
end
```

The assertion method checks whether we are generating a list of numbers from 1 to 100. Run the test. We get an undefined method numbers error. Define and implement the numbers method.

```ruby
class FizzBuzz
  def numbers
    (1..100).to_a
  end
end
```

Run the test again. The test now passes. Add the second test, test_generate_fizz_for_multiples_of_3.

```ruby
def test_generate_fizz_for_multiples_of_3
  fb = FizzBuzz.new
  result = fb.sequence
  assert_equal 'Fizz', result[2]
end
```

We create an instance of the FizzBuzz class and invoke the sequence method on it. We expect the third element in the array to be Fizz. Since the array is zero based, the index is 2 to check the third element in the array. Run the test. It will fail because the sequence method is not defined yet. Let's implement the sequence method.

```
class FizzBuzz
  def numbers
    (1..100).to_a
  end

  def sequence
    numbers.collect do |n|
      if (n % 3 == 0)
        'Fizz'
      end
    end
  end
end
```

Run the test. It will now pass. Let's add a third test, test_generate_buzz_for_multiples_of_5. In this test, we check that the fifth element in the array is Buzz. Run the test, and it will fail.

```
def test_generate_buzz_for_multiples_of_5
  fb = FizzBuzz.new
  result = fb.sequence
  assert_equal 'Buzz', result[4]
end
```

Add the logic to handle the Buzz case.

```
class FizzBuzz
  def numbers
    (1..100).to_a
  end

  def sequence
    numbers.collect do |n|
      if (n % 3 == 0)
        'Fizz'
      elsif (n % 5 == 0)
        'Buzz'
      end
    end
  end
end
```

The test will now pass. Next, write a test for numbers that are multiples of 3 and 5.

```
def test_generate_fizzbuzz_for_multiples_of_3_and_5
  fb = FizzBuzz.new
  result = fb.sequence
  assert_equal 'FizzBuzz', result[14]
end
```

This test will fail with the following failure message: `Expected: FizzBuzz Actual: Fizz`. What is the reason for this failure? The clue is in the name of the test. Add the logic to make the test pass.

```ruby
class FizzBuzz
  def numbers
    (1..100).to_a
  end

  def sequence
    numbers.collect do |n|
      if (n % 3 == 0) and (n % 5 == 0)
        'FizzBuzz'
      elsif (n % 3 == 0)
        'Fizz'
      elsif (n % 5 == 0)
        'Buzz'
      end
    end
  end
end
```

All the tests will now pass. Do you think we can change the order of the conditionals without breaking any of the tests? Why so? Let's refactor to clean up our quick and dirty implementation by extracting a private method that checks for the multiple of a given number.

```ruby
class FizzBuzz
  def numbers
    (1..100).to_a
  end

  def sequence
    numbers.collect do |n|
      if (n % 3 == 0) and (n % 5 == 0)
        'FizzBuzz'
      elsif multiple_of(3, n)
        'Fizz'
      elsif (n % 5 == 0)
        'Buzz'
      end
    end
  end

  private

  def multiple_of(x, n)
    n % x == 0
  end
end
```

We use this new private method only for the Fizz case. Run the test. It passes. Let's make the similar change for the Buzz case.

```ruby
class FizzBuzz
  def numbers
    # Code same as before
  end

  def sequence
    numbers.collect do |n|
      if (n % 3 == 0) and (n % 5 == 0)
        'FizzBuzz'
      elsif multiple_of(3, n)
        'Fizz'
      elsif multiple_of(5, n)
        'Buzz'
      end
    end
  end

  private

  def multiple_of(x, n)
    # Code same as before
  end
end
```

Run the tests again. It will still pass. Change the conditional for multiple of 3 and 5 to use the private method.

```ruby
class FizzBuzz
  def numbers
    # Code same as before
  end

  def sequence
    numbers.collect do |n|
      if (multiple_of(3, n) and multiple_of(5, n))
        'FizzBuzz'
      elsif multiple_of(3, n)
        'Fizz'
      elsif multiple_of(5, n)
        'Buzz'
      end
    end
  end

  private

  def multiple_of(x, n)
    # Code same as before
  end
end
```

The tests still pass. Let's make the private method expressive by making the variable names and the implementation self-describing.

```ruby
def multiple_of(divisor, number)
  number.modulo(divisor).zero?
end
```

Run all the tests; they will still pass. The concept of modulo is in the solution domain; it is not found in the problem domain. If you have enough domain knowledge, you can translate the requirement to abstractions in code. Otherwise, you have to collaborate with a domain expert to translate the requirement to abstractions in the solution domain.

We began our TDD session with a Starter Test and ended it with a Story Test. The complexity of the test cases gradually increased as we added more tests. If the sequence of the tests is not in the right order, we will have difficulty writing tests and making the tests pass. Difficulty in testing can also arise due to bad design. We experimented in the IRB console to do solution domain analysis to figure out what it means when a number is a multiple of a given number. The knowledge we gained helped us in writing the production code. The sequence of test cases is important because it makes it easier to pass the test quickly.

No if-else Constraint

In this section, we will improve the FizzBuzz kata solution by applying the no if-else constraint. You will also learn that when you discover a bug you write a failing test to expose the bug and then fix the bug to make the test pass. Let's refactor the solution to not use any if-else statements.

Create a new file, fizz_buzz_engine.rb, with a FizzBuzzEngine class. It has a constructor that takes a parameter for the number. This number is passed in when we initialize an instance of the FizzBuzzEngine class. It is saved in the instance variable @number. It has a value method that returns Fizz as the value if the given number is a multiple of 3.

```ruby
class FizzBuzzEngine
  def initialize(number)
    @number = number
  end

  def value
    return 'Fizz' if multiple_of(3)
  end

  private

  def multiple_of(divisor)
    @number.modulo(divisor).zero?
  end
end
```

Let's change the implementation of the FizzBuzz class for the elsif condition, multiple of 3 case, to use the new FizzBuzzEngine class.

```ruby
require_relative 'fizz_buzz_engine'

class FizzBuzz
  def numbers
    # Code same as before
  end

  def sequence
    numbers.collect do |n|
      if (multiple_of(3, n) and multiple_of(5, n))
        'FizzBuzz'
      elsif multiple_of(3, n)
        fbe = FizzBuzzEngine.new(n)
        fbe.value
      elsif multiple_of(5, n)
        'Buzz'
      end
    end
  end

  private

  def multiple_of(number, divisor)
    number.modulo(divisor).zero?
  end
end
```

We create an instance of the FizzBuzzEngine class with a number *n* and then invoke the value method on the FizzBuzzEngine object. Run all the tests. They will pass. We can now make a similar change for a number that is multiple of 5.

```ruby
class FizzBuzzEngine
  def initialize(number)
    # Code same as before
  end

  def value
    return 'Fizz' if multiple_of(3)
    return 'Buzz' if multiple_of(5)
  end

  private

  def multiple_of(divisor)
    # Code same as before
  end
end
```

The `FizzBuzz` class can now use the `FizzBuzzEngine` to handle the multiple of 5 case.

```ruby
require_relative 'fizz_buzz_engine'

class FizzBuzz
  def numbers
    # Code same as before
  end

  def sequence
    numbers.collect do |n|
      if (multiple_of(3, n) and multiple_of(5, n))
        'FizzBuzz'
      elsif multiple_of(3, n)
        fbe = FizzBuzzEngine.new(n)
        fbe.value
      elsif multiple_of(5, n)
        fbe = FizzBuzzEngine.new(n)
        fbe.value
      end
    end
  end

  private

  def multiple_of(number, divisor)
    # Code same as before
  end
end
```

Run all the tests; they will pass. Let's now handle the case for multiples of 3 and 5. Modify the FizzBuzzEngine class to handle the FizzBuzz case.

```ruby
class FizzBuzzEngine

  def initialize(number)
    # Code same as before
  end

  def value
    return 'FizzBuzz' if multiple_of(3) and multiple_of(5)
    return 'Fizz' if multiple_of(3)
    return 'Buzz' if multiple_of(5)
  end

  private

  def multiple_of(divisor)
    # Code same as before
  end
end
```

Modify the `FizzBuzz` class to use the `FizzBuzzEngine` class for multiples of 3 and 5.

```ruby
require_relative 'fizz_buzz_engine'

class FizzBuzz
  def numbers
    # Code same as before
  end

  def sequence
    numbers.collect do |n|
      if (multiple_of(3, n) and multiple_of(5, n))
        fbe = FizzBuzzEngine.new(n)
        fbe.value
      elsif multiple_of(3, n)
        fbe = FizzBuzzEngine.new(n)
        fbe.value
      elsif multiple_of(5, n)
        fbe = FizzBuzzEngine.new(n)
        fbe.value
      end
    end
  end

  private

  def multiple_of(number, divisor)
    # Code same as before
  end
end
```

The tests will still pass, but we have ugliness in the code. If we make our code similar for all cases, we can reduce the amount of code and make it elegant. How can we make all three cases similar? The ugliness is the result of expressing the requirement for multiple of 3 and 5 directly in the code. If a number is a multiple of 3 and 5, it means it is a multiple of 15. This insight translates English to math and can simplify our code and make it elegant.

■ **Note**   A number that is multiple of 3 and 5 means it is a multiple of 15. Collaborating with domain experts will tease out inferences about the requirements that can simplify the code.

The basic math we learn in school provides us a way to translate words in English language to math. Table 2-3 shows some of the words translated to math.

Table 2-3. *Translating English Language to Math*

English	Math
Sum, Total, Combine, More	+
Difference, Decrease, Less, Fewer	-
Product, Times, Per, Double	*
Quotient, Per, Share, Split	%

In our case, the words *of* and *and* give us an implicit clue for coming up with our insight. FizzBuzzEngine can be modified to make the code symmetric and express this insight.

```
class FizzBuzzEngine
  def initialize(number)
    # Code same as before
  end

  def value
    return 'FizzBuzz' if multiple_of(15)
    return 'Fizz' if multiple_of(3)
    return 'Buzz' if multiple_of(5)
  end

  private

  def multiple_of(divisor)
    # Code same as before
  end
end
```

We can change the FizzBuzz class to use this modified version of the FizzBuzzEngine class.

```
require_relative 'fizz_buzz_engine'

class FizzBuzz
  def numbers
    # Code same as before
  end

  def sequence
    numbers.collect do |n|
      if multiple_of(15, n)
        fbe = FizzBuzzEngine.new(n)
        fbe.value
      elsif multiple_of(3, n)
        fbe = FizzBuzzEngine.new(n)
        fbe.value
      elsif multiple_of(5, n)
        fbe = FizzBuzzEngine.new(n)
        fbe.value
```

```
      end
    end
  end

  private

  def multiple_of(n, x)
    # Code same as before
  end
end
```

Run all the tests; they will still pass. Let's eliminate the redundant checks and duplication in the sequence method of the FizzBuzz class.

```
require_relative 'fizz_buzz_engine'

class FizzBuzz
  def numbers
    # Code same as before
  end

  def sequence
    numbers.collect do |n|
      fbe = FizzBuzzEngine.new(n)
      fbe.value
    end
  end

  private

  def multiple_of(number, divisor)
    # Code same as before
  end

end
```

Run all the tests. They will still pass. We can also delete the private method multiple_of in the FizzBuzz class. It is no longer used.

```
require_relative 'fizz_buzz_engine'

class FizzBuzz
  def numbers
    # Code same as before
  end

  def sequence
    numbers.collect do |n|
      fbe = FizzBuzzEngine.new(n)
      fbe.value
    end
  end
end
```

The tests will still pass. Let's do exploratory testing in the IRB console.

```
> load 'fizz_buzz.rb'
=> true
> fb = FizzBuzz.new
=> #<FizzBuzz:0x007fda5996d760>
> fb.sequence
=> [nil, nil, "Fizz", nil, "Buzz", "Fizz", nil, nil, "Fizz", "Buzz", nil, "Fizz", nil, nil,
"FizzBuzz", nil, nil, "Fizz", nil, "Buzz", "Fizz", nil, nil, "Fizz", "Buzz", nil, "Fizz",
nil, nil, "FizzBuzz", nil, nil, "Fizz", nil, "Buzz", "Fizz", nil, nil, "Fizz", "Buzz", nil,
"Fizz", nil, nil, "FizzBuzz", nil, nil, "Fizz", nil, "Buzz", "Fizz", nil, nil, "Fizz",
"Buzz", nil, "Fizz", nil, nil, "FizzBuzz", nil, nil, "Fizz", nil, "Buzz", "Fizz", nil, nil,
"Fizz", "Buzz", nil, "Fizz", nil, nil, "FizzBuzz", nil, nil, "Fizz", nil, "Buzz", "Fizz",
nil, nil, "Fizz", "Buzz", nil, "Fizz", nil, nil, "FizzBuzz", nil, nil, "Fizz", nil, "Buzz",
"Fizz", nil, nil, "Fizz", "Buzz"]
```

We are able to see the entire data set of the result. This gives a big-picture view of the application.

■ **Note** You can visually see the big picture of the application by experimenting in the IRB console. When you run all the tests, it also provides a big picture view of the application but you can only see which requirements are being met by the test pass/fail report, you cannot see any missing requirement or missing tests.

As you can see, the current implementation does not return anything if the number does not have to be transformed. This is one of the common mistakes that we discussed in Chapter 1–forgetting to test the negative case. Let's write a failing test for this scenario. We are going to expose the bug by writing the test first and letting it fail, and then we will fix the bug so that the test passes.

Add a new test for the case where the generated number is not a multiple of 3, 5, or 15. Create an instance of FizzBuzz and call the sequence method. The assertion checks that the first element is equal to 1.

```
def test_generate_number_is_not_multiple
  fb = FizzBuzz.new
  result = fb.sequence
  assert_equal 1, result[0]
end
```

This test fails. We have exposed the bug via a failing test. Let's make the test pass by fixing the bug in the value method.

```
def value
  return 'FizzBuzz' if multiple_of(15)
  return 'Fizz' if multiple_of(3)
  return 'Buzz' if multiple_of(5)
  @number
end
```

Let's look at the final solution. The value method in the FizzBuzzEngine class encapsulates all the logic required to look up the string for a given multiple of some number.

```ruby
class FizzBuzzEngine
  def initialize(number)
    @number = number
  end

  def value
    return 'FizzBuzz' if multiple_of(15)
    return 'Fizz' if multiple_of(3)
    return 'Buzz' if multiple_of(5)
    @number
  end

  private

  def multiple_of(divisor)
    @number.modulo(divisor).zero?
  end
end
```

The key to eliminating if-else statements is to encapsulate the logic behind a well-defined interface. In this case, it is the value method. The numbers method in the FizzBuzz class is now private. By making the numbers method private, we hide the implementation details within the FizzBuzz class.

```ruby
require_relative 'fizz_buzz_engine'
```

```ruby
class FizzBuzz
  def sequence
    numbers.collect do |n|
      fbe = FizzBuzzEngine.new(n)
      fbe.value
    end
  end

  private

  def numbers
    (1..100).to_a
  end
end
```

The test for the generation of numbers from 1 to 100 can now be deleted; we no longer need this test. It provided us with the initial momentum to get started when we began our TDD session. It is like a scaffold of a building, as shown in Figure 2-20. The scaffold is useful during the construction of the building and is not needed when the building construction is over.

Figure 2-20. *Initial implementation-specific tests are like scaffold of a building*

```ruby
require 'minitest/autorun'
require_relative 'fizz_buzz'

class TestFizzBuzz < Minitest::Test
  def test_generate_fizz_for_multiples_of_3
    fb = FizzBuzz.new
    result = fb.sequence

    assert_equal 'Fizz', result[2]
  end

  def test_generate_buzz_for_multiples_of_5
    fb = FizzBuzz.new
    result = fb.sequence

    assert_equal 'Buzz', result[4]
  end

  def test_generate_fizz_buzz_for_multiples_of_3_and_5
    fb = FizzBuzz.new
    result = fb.sequence
```

```
    assert_equal 'FizzBuzz', result[14]
  end
  def test_generate_number_is_not_multiple
    fb = FizzBuzz.new
    result = fb.sequence

    assert_equal 1, result[0]
  end
end
```

We have three similar lines of code in the value method. We can eliminate the code duplication by looping through a hash to check if the given number is a multiple of any of the numbers in the requirement and return the corresponding string. The refactored solution would look like this:

```
class FizzBuzzEngine
  LOOKUP = {15 => 'FizzBuzz', 3 => 'Fizz', 5 => 'Buzz'}

  def initialize(number)
    @number = number
  end

  def value
    LOOKUP.keys.each do |key|
      return LOOKUP[key] if multiple_of(key)
    end
    @number
  end

  private

  def multiple_of(divisor)
    @number.modulo(divisor).zero?
  end
end
```

The aim of TDD is simplicity, knowing when to stop refactoring requires judgement about whether you have achieved simplicity in your code. If our requirements grow and we add more lines of code to the value method, we can consider using a hash to look up the string from a given multiple of a number. For now, we will stick with the existing solution, since it results in less code.

No if Constraint

We are going to apply the no if statement constraint to our solution. This means we cannot use any if statements in our solution. We will not change the existing tests. Our aim is to modify the solution to satisfy the constraint without breaking any existing tests. We will start from where we left off in the previous section on the no if-else constraint. Create a new file called fixnum_extensions.rb.

```
module FixnumExtensions
  refine Fixnum do
    def fizz_buzz
      self.modulo(15).zero? && (return 'FizzBuzz')
      self.modulo(3).zero? && (return 'Fizz')
```

```
      self.modulo(5).zero? && (return 'Buzz')
      self
    end
  end
end
```

We use the refinements feature of Ruby to add the `fizz_buzz` method to the `Fixnum` class. The implementation checks whether the current number that is receiving the `fizz_buzz` message is a multiple of 15. If so, it returns FizzBuzz. Similarly, we check for mulitples of 3 and 5 and return Fizz and Buzz respectively. We can use this module in the `FizzBuzz` class by using the keyword ***using***.

```
require_relative 'fixnum_extensions'


class FizzBuzz
  using FixnumExtensions

  def sequence
    numbers.collect do |n|
      n.fizz_buzz
    end
  end

  private

  def numbers
    (1..100).to_a
  end
end
```

In the sequence method, we send the message `fizz_buzz` to the `Fixnum` object *n*. Run the tests; they will pass. We can clean up the `FixnumExtensions` class by extracting a `multiple_of` method to eliminate the duplication in the `fizz_buzz` method.

```
module FixnumExtensions
  refine Fixnum do
    def fizz_buzz
      multiple_of(15) && (return 'FizzBuzz')
      multiple_of(3) && (return 'Fizz')
      multiple_of(5) && (return 'Buzz')
      self
    end

    def multiple_of(number)
      self.modulo(number).zero?
    end
  end
end
```

We can remove the `require_relative 'fizz_buzz_engine'` in the fizz_buzz.rb file, since we are not using it anymore. We can also delete `fizz_buzz_engine.rb`. Run all the tests. They will still pass. The test code was not modified. We refactored the implementation to be more message-centric. The key takeaway of this section is that in order to eliminate the if statement in our code we used the && operator in combination with return, thus making our code message-centric.

Implementation-Independent Tests

Tests must focus on intent and should be implementation independent. One way to check if they are implementation indendent is to change a design decision, such as the data structure used. Let's change the implementation of the sequence method in the FizzBuzz class to use hash instead of an array.

```
def sequence
  pairs = {}
  (1..100).each do |n|
    pairs[n] = n
  end
  result = {}
  pairs.keys.each do |key|
    result[key] = key.fizz_buzz
  end
  result
end
```

Run all the tests; they all fail. The current tests are tied to the implementation details; in this case, the data structure. The choice of data structure is a design decision. We must hide this design decision from the clients, which will allow us to change our decision without breaking them. Modify the test to focus on the intent rather than the implementation.

```
def test_generate_fizz_for_multiples_of_3
  fb = FizzBuzz.new
  result = fb.transform(3)
  assert_equal 'Fizz', result
end
```

We now have a transform method that passes the number to be processed and checks the result for the expected value. It does not have any knowledge about the data structure used in the implementation. Implementation details do not leak into the tests. Revert the sequence method to the working version.

```
def sequence
  numbers.collect do |n|
    n.fizz_buzz
  end
end
```

We retain the old implementation to avoid the existing tests from failing. We gradually make use of the new interface by changing one test at a time. Run the tests. The test that uses transform method will fail. Let's implement the transform method.

```
def transform(number)
  pairs = {}
  (1..100).each do |n|
    pairs[n] = n
  end
```

```
    result = {}
    pairs.keys.each do |key|
      result[key] = key.fizz_buzz
    end
    result[number]
  end
```

The tests now pass. Let's modify the test for multiples of 5 to use the new intent-revealing transform method.

```
def test_generate_buzz_for_multiples_of_5
  fb = FizzBuzz.new
  result = fb.transform(5)
  assert_equal 'Buzz', result
end
```

Run the tests, and they will still pass. We can use the transform method for all the tests.

```
def test_generate_fizzbuzz_for_multiples_of_15
  fb = FizzBuzz.new
  result = fb.transform(15)
  assert_equal 'FizzBuzz', result
end
```

```
def test_generate_number_is_not_multiple
  fb = FizzBuzz.new
  result = fb.transform(1)
  assert_equal 1, result
end
```

The tests will pass. We have tests that are focused on intent. We can verify that fact by changing the transform method to use array as the data structure.

```
def sequence
  numbers.collect do |n|
    n.fizz_buzz
  end
end
```

```
def transform(n)
  sequence[n-1]
end
```

The tests will still pass. This means our tests are not tied to the implementation details. Since our tests are only focused on testing the behavior, we were able to hide the implementation. This is ideal because tests that depend on implementation will break whenever the implementation changes, even if the behavior did not change. Brittle tests are hard to maintain and offer no value. Tests should break only if the behavior changes, which acts as a safety net protecting us from regression bugs.

Crossing the System Boundary

Let's consider the first test `test_print_fizz_for_multiples_of_3` in the beginning of the FizzBuzz kata. It was our very first test, and we got stuck. We found it difficult to test the printing of Fizz for the number 3 to the standard output. We now have enough momentum to tackle this test. We can use the `assert_output` assertion to check whether, when we use 3 as the argument, it prints the Fizz string to the standard output.

```ruby
require 'minitest/autorun'
require_relative 'fizz_buzz'

class TestFizzBuzz < Minitest::Test
  def test_print_fizz_for_multiples_of_3
    fb = FizzBuzz.new

    assert_output('Fizz') { fb.output(3) }
  end
end
```

This test fails with the error message: `"NoMethodError: undefined method 'output' for FizzBuzz"` class. Add an empty output method that takes an argument to the `FizzBuzz` class.

```ruby
def output(n)

end
```

The test now fails with the failure message: `"Expected: "Fizz" Actual: ""`. Implement the output method as follows:

```ruby
def output(n)
  result = transform(n)

  print result
end
```

The test will now pass. The test is tied to the standard output. For instance, if you need to output to a file, the design and the test must be modified. We do not want to speculate on future requirements. For now, we will stop at this simple implementation.

Mocking as a Design Technique

The future has arrived. We have a new requirement where we need to handle writing the result to a file. We need to be able to switch the output device so that it could be a standard terminal or a file. In order to discover the interface of the new object, we can use a mock.

Mocks are pre-programmed with expectations which form a specification of the calls they are expected to receive. They can throw an exception if they receive a call they don't expect and are checked during verification to ensure they got all the calls they were expecting.

—Martin Fowler

The FizzBuzz class will no longer be responsible for interfacing with the user by printing to the terminal. Delete the existing test, test_print_fizz_for_multiples_of_3. Create a new test, test_write_fizz_for_multiples_of_3.

```
def test_write_fizz_for_multiples_of_3
  mock = MiniTest::Mock.new
  mock.expect(:write, nil, ['Fizz'])

  fb = FizzBuzz.new(mock)
  fb.output(3)

  mock.verify
end
```

We create an instance of MiniTest::Mock. We expect the mock to receive the write message–with the argument Fizz and nil as the return value–from the write method. We then create a FizzBuzz object and invoke the output method with 3 as the argument. We then verify that the mock receives the write message. Run the test. It fails with the following failure message:

```
ArgumentError: wrong number of arguments (given 1, expected 0).
```

We need to change the constructor of the FizzBuzz class to take an argument for the output.

```
def initialize(output)
  @output = output
end
```

Add skip to the new test so that we can fix the existing tests that fail because of this change. The existing tests do not provide an argument to the constructor. We can fix this problem by providing a default value for the output in the constructor.

```
def initialize(output = $stdout)
  @output = output
end
```

Remove the skip statement for the new test and run it. It now fails with the following error message:

```
MockExpectationError: expected write("Fizz").
```

Modify the output method:

```
def output(n)
  result = transform(n)
  @output.write result
end
```

We are now using standard output as the default output device. All the tests will now pass.

We can separate the sequence-generation logic from the logic used to display the sequence to a user. This makes the class focus on only one purpose. We can also add logic to read from the standard console to the class that is responsible for interfacing with the user. Let's move the code related to printing to a new class, StandardConsole, that will implement the print functionality. Create test_standard_console.rb.

```
require 'minitest/autorun'
require_relative 'standard_console'

class TestStandardConsole < Minitest::Test
  def test_print_message
    console = StandardConsole.new

    assert_output('testing') { console.write('testing') }
  end
end
```

Create standard_console.rb and implement the write method in the StandardConsole class.

```
class StandardConsole
  def write(message)
    print message
  end
end
```

Run the test for the standard console; it will pass. A boundary object encapsulates the interaction with the boundary of the system. Figure 2-21 shows the boundary object, in our case a StandardConsole object, which interacts with the terminal of the operating system (the internal boundary of the system). The domain object, in this case FizzBuzz object, now depends on the standard interface defined in the boundary object to write messages.

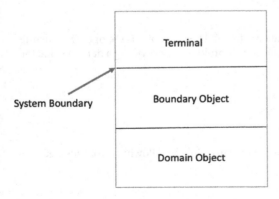

Figure 2-21. *Domain objects interact indirectly with the terminal via boundary objects*

The IRB session that follows shows how the standard console defaults to standard output when you don't provide an output device in the constructor. FizzBuzz objects depend on the standard interface, which is defined and implemented in the boundary object, in this case standard_console.rb, to print the output to standard output.

```
> load 'standard_console.rb'
 => true
> load 'fizz_buzz.rb'
 => true
> fb = FizzBuzz.new
 => #<FizzBuzz:0x007ff7e0 @output=#<IO:<STDOUT>>>
> fb.output(1)
1 => 1
> fb.output(3)
Fizz => 4
> fb.output(5)
Buzz => 4
```

Let's now tackle writing the output to a file. Create a file called test_virtual_file.rb.

```ruby
require 'minitest/autorun'
require_relative 'virtual_file'

class TestVirtualFile < Minitest::Test
  def test_write_message
    file = VirtualFile.new
    file.write('testing')

    result = file.read

    assert_equal 'testing', result
  end
end
```

We create an instance of the VirtualFile class and write the string, 'testing'. We then read back the string that was written and assert that it should be 'testing'. Test code is the first client of our code, and it needs a way to read the contents to verify the behavior. By making the class we are developing testable, we have discovered the new interface, the read method. Run the test, and it will fail. Create a file called virtual_file.rb. The implementation of VirtualFile is as follows:

```ruby
class VirtualFile
  def initialize
    @file = StringIO.new
  end

  def write(message)
    @file.write(message)
  end

  def read
    @file.string
  end
end
```

This example illustrates using the Ruby built-in class StringIO as a fake file object. File accessing is involved. It requires using the right read or write mode. If you do not use the block version of the File, it also requires the closing and opening of the file at the appropriate times. StringIO is a Ruby built-in class that mimics the interface of the file. This test will run faster than if we were to access the file system. If we were to use a real file in the test, the test would no longer be a unit test and would also slow down our tests. The `VirtualFile` is an in-memory version of a file.

Abstraction Levels in a System

Sequence-generation logic and user-interface logic are abstractions at different levels of our system. One is at the domain level and the other is at the user-interface level. The abstraction captured by a class must be consistent, as you cannot mix different levels of abstraction into one class. How can we use the tools to help us maintain a consistent level of abstraction? The Minitest test framework allows you to use spec syntax to describe the purpose of the class in the second argument, as follows:

```
describe ClassName, 'here you can state the purpose of the class' do
end
```

If the class is focused on doing one thing really well, this second argument will be short. It will *not* have words such as *and* and *or*. When you use those words, the class has more than one purpose. We can now describe the purpose of the `FizzBuzz` class as `Generate FizzBuzz sequence`. Before this refactoring, it was `Generate FizzBuzz sequence and interface with a user`.

```
describe FizzBuzz, 'Generate FizzBuzz sequence' do
end
```

```
describe StandardConsole, 'Inteface with a user' do
end
```

> *A class should capture one and only one key abstraction.*
>
> —Arthur Riel, *Object Oriented Design Heuristics*

In this section, we split the `FizzBuzz` class into two classes that are each focused on one purpose. We discovered the API for the new boundary object that interacts with a user. We separated the boundary object from the domain object. In any system, we need to identify the core of the system and separate it from the objects found at the system boundary.

The boundary object `StandardConsole` is domain agnostic. It can be reused in other applications. The `StandardConsole` class interacts with a user whereas the `VirtualFile` class mimics the file system's interaction with the operating system. The operating system boundary is the internal boundary of the system. Similarly, if we were to develop a `NetworkConsole` class that communicates with a server, it would be part of the external boundary of our system. The implementation details are hidden behind the well-defined read/write methods. Our software is now capable of adapting to change to different implementations of read/write methods. The final solution now has the proper allocation of responsibilities to the objects. The figure 2-22 shows how the clients depend on the console abstraction and not on any of the concrete implementation of console.

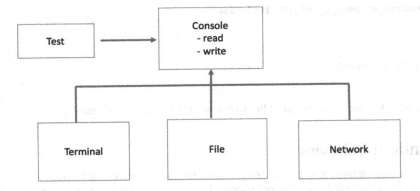

Figure 2-22. *Clients depend on console abstraction*

Testing Random Behavior

We have a new requirement that states we need to generate a random number between 1 and 100 for the FizzBuzz generation. It is difficult to write a test for non-deterministic behavior. Your first attempt at writing a test might look like this:

```
def test_generate_random_number_between_1_and_100_inclusive
  fb = FizzBuzz.new
  result = fb.random

  assert_kind_of Fixnum, result
end
```

The implementation of random in the FizzBuzz class is as follows:

```
def random
  numbers.sample
end
```

This test will pass, but it is not specific or precise enough for the requirement expressed in the test name. Another issue with this test is that we can make this test pass by returning a hardcoded 0 or a negative number. Your second attempt may be something like this:

```
def test_generate_random_number_between_1_and_100_inclusive
  fb = FizzBuzz.new
  lots_of_rolls = 100.times.map { fb.random }
  assert_equal lots_of_rolls.uniq.sort, (1..100).to_a
end
```

This test will never pass, since the random numbers generated will have duplicates and uniq will reduce the generated number list to less than 100. Even if this test passes, it is an example of over specification in tests. There is a solution that is a middle ground between these two extremes. We can assert that the generated number is within the given range.

```ruby
def test_generate_random_number_between_1_and_100_inclusive
  fb = FizzBuzz.new
  result = fb.random

  assert_includes (1..100).to_a, result
end
```

This test uses `assert_includes` to check that the result lies within the range of 1 to 100 inclusive.

Testing Time-Dependent Behavior

We have a new requirement that states we need to append a 'Morning' string to the `Fizz` string, but only in the mornings. Otherwise, the `Fizz` string's behavior will not change. We cannot rely on the system clock provided by the operating system for our test. We will not be able to run our test, because we cannot force the system clock to be in the morning to test the new requirement at night. We need a `VirtualClock` that will give us control over time.

```ruby
class VirtualClock
  attr_accessor :hour

  def morning?
    hour <= 12
  end
end
```

We can set the hour to anything in the test and the `morning?` method will tell us whether the time is morning or not. We can now instantiate a `VirtualClock` class and pass it to the constructor of `FizzBuzz` class. The assertion checks if `Fizz Morning` is printed.

```ruby
def test_generate_fizz_morning_for_mornings
  clock = VirtualClock.new
  clock.hour = 10
  fb = FizzBuzz.new nil, clock
  result = fb.transform(3)

  assert_equal 'Fizz Morning', result
end
```

Modify both the constructor and the `transform` method in the `FizzBuzz` class to append the `Morning` string.

```ruby
class FizzBuzz
  def initialize(output=$stdout, clock)
    @output = output
    @clock = clock
  end

  def transform(n)
    result = sequence[n-1]
    if @clock && @clock.morning?
     result = "#{result} Morning"
```

```
    end
    result
  end
end
```

To prevent the existing tests from breaking, we need to pass a `VirtualClock` object that has an hour value greater than 12. The tests will now pass.

```
def test_generate_fizz_for_not_morning
  clock = VirtualClock.new
  clock.hour = 14
  fb = FizzBuzz.new nil, clock
  result = fb.transform(3)

  assert_equal 'Fizz', result
end
```

Why did the existing tests fail when we introduced a new requirement? The time and output mechanisms are two different dimensions of the program. The current solution has dependency on both time and output device. The inability of the solution to vary them independently causes the existing tests to fail. In a real application, we can design a solution that allows us to vary the different aspects independent of each other. Composition is a way to achieve this level of flexibility. For our kata, that level of flexibility would be overkill.

Simulating User Input

This section will discuss developing functionality that requires user input. We cannot expect a user to enter input when we run a test. This is not possible when we run the tests on a build server with no human intervention. We will see how to write a test for a feature that requires user input. First, we need to discuss seams in a system.

Seams in a System

You can use the electrical outlet to plug in a lamp, a laptop adapter, TV, and so on, as long as the device can handle the voltage and frequency rating. There is one outlet, but different devices connect to it that have different functionality. Seams in a software system are similar to electrical plugin points. Figure 2-23 shows the electrical plugin point for connecting different electronic devices.

Figure 2-23. Seams in a software system are similar to electrical plugin points

Why do we care about seams? Seams make the code testable and flexible.

> *Seam is a place where you can alter behavior of your program without editing in that place. Every seam has an enabling point; a place where you can make the decision to use one behavior or another.*

—Michael C. Feathers, Working Effectively with Legacy Code

If you build a system with flexibility where it is needed, it becomes easy to test. You will also recognize that when it is difficult to test, it is a symptom of bad design. In such cases, you need to think hard about improving the design.

Dealing with User Input

We now have to deal with getting input from the user. The new requirement states that we need to prompt the user for the input number by displaying "Please enter a number from 1 to 100" and then read the user-entered number from the terminal. We have to test drive the development of FizzBuzz. We are now getting to the system boundary, where we need to interact with users to get input. The way we interact with users is likely to change at a different rate than that at which the sequence-generation requirements will change. This means that we have found a seam in our system. This is a plugin point to our system where we could have different ways of getting user input. So, the question is: How can we abstract the standard input and standard output?

We can combine the standard input and standard output into a console object. By definition, a console is a monitor or keyboard in a multiuser computer system. We can call this new class StandardConsole. We need to prevent the StandardConsole class from prompting for user input when we run the test. Thus, the test can be run without any human intervention. We can use StringIO for this purpose.

```ruby
def test_prompt_user_for_number
  input = StringIO.new('10')
  output = StringIO.new
  console = StandardConsole.new(input, output)
  console.prompt

  assert_equal "Please enter a number from 1 to 100\n", output.string
  assert_includes (1..100).to_a, input.string.to_i
end
```

The test creates input and output streams using StringIO objects that mimick the operating system IO. We create an instance of StandardConsole and inject the dependencies for the input and output. We then assert the prompt string and that the value entered by the user lies within the expected range. Modify the StandardConsole class to define a constructor that takes input and output streams and the prompt method.

```ruby
class StandardConsole
  def initialize(input = $stdin, output=$stdout)
    @input = input
    @output = output
  end

  def prompt
    @output.puts "Please enter a number from 1 to 100\n"
    @input.gets.chomp.to_i
  end
end
```

```
  def write(message)
    print message
  end
end
```

The prompt method prints the instruction, gets the user input, removes the new line, and converts the input string to an integer. The constructor defaults the input and output to the standard input and output stream, which allows them to be customized for testing purposes. The input and output are the seams of this class. This StandardConsole class encapsulates the interaction with the standard input and standard output (monitor and keyboard). Run test_standard_console.rb; it will pass. You can also do exploratory testing in the IRB console.

```
> load 'standard_console.rb'
 => true
> c = StandardConsole.new
 => #<StandardConsole:0x00a4cb8 @input=#<IO:<STDIN>>, @output=#<IO:<STDOUT>>>
> c.prompt
Please enter a number from 1 to 100
98
 => 98
```

The StandardConsole class now has become specific to our application. We can no longer say that it can be used in other applications. We can refactor the StandardConsole class by extracting the read method from the prompt method.

```
class StandardConsole
  def initialize(input = $stdin, output=$stdout)
    @input = input
    @output = output
  end

  def prompt
    @output.puts "Please enter a number from 1 to 100\n"
    read.to_i
  end

  def write(message)
    print message
  end

  def read
    @input.gets.chomp
  end
end
```

We can also refactor the first test for writing a message so it is similar to the second test.

```
def test_print_message
  input = StringIO.new
  output = StringIO.new
```

```
console = StandardConsole.new(input, output)
console.write('testing')

assert_equal 'testing', output.string
end
```

To make this test pass, we need to change the `write` method implementation in StandardConsole as follows:

```
def write(message)
  @output.print message
end
```

Our FizzBuzz program is extensible to different user-interfacing code as long as it conforms to our console interface. We can now have different implementations of the console object, such as `NetworkConsole`, `GraphicalConsole`, and so on.

Open Closed Principle

Modules should be both open (for extension and adaptation) and closed (to avoid modification that affect clients).

—Bertrand Meyer, *Object-Oriented Software Construction*

The term *module* used by Bertrand Meyer is not the Ruby language construct module. You can think of the module in this context as an object or a group of objects that provide a specific functionality. To apply the Open Closed Principle, we must identify things that are likely to change and create a stable interface around them. We can use D.L. Parnas' idea of information hiding that he discusses in his paper *"On the Criteria To Be Used in Decomposing Systems Into Modules"* as a guiding design principle.

We have tried to demonstrate by these examples that it is almost always incorrect to begin the decomposition of a system into modules on the basis of a flowchart. We propose instead that one begins with a list of difficult design decisions or design decisions which are likely to change. Each module is then designed to hide such a decision from the others.

—D.L. Parnas, *On the Criteria to Be Used in Decomposing Systems into Modules*

We will now see how to apply the Open Closed Principle. Define classes to implement the requirements, as shown below. Each class will be in its own file, which are named `fizz.rb`, `buzz.rb`, and `fizz_buzz.rb`.

```
class Fizz
  def value(n)
    if n % 3 == 0
      'Fizz'
    end
  end
end
```

```
class Buzz
  def value(n)
    if n % 5 == 0
      'Buzz'
    end
  end
end

class FizzBuzz
  def value(n)
    if n % 15 == 0
      'FizzBuzz'
    end
  end
end
```

One of the requirements is implicit, because numbers that are not multiples of 3, 5, or 15 should not be transformed. Therefore we need a NoOp class, included in the no_fizz_buzz.rb file with the following code:

```
class NoFizzBuzz
  def value(n)
    n
  end
end
```

So far, we have the concrete classes that implement the FizzBuzz logic. Notice that we have a uniform interface value(n) that allows clients to program to an interface and not to an implementation. You will see this in action in upcoming steps. Define a FizzBuzzGenerator class that will delegate the FizzBuzz generation to the concrete classes. Add the require_relative statement for every class we previously created in this class.

```
class FizzBuzzGenerator
  def initialize(objects, list)
    @list = list
    @objects = objects
  end

  def generate
    result = []
    @list.each do |num|
      @objects.each do |l|
        v = l.value(num)
        unless v.nil?
          result << v
          break
        end
      end
    end
    result
  end
end
```

101

Notice that the dependency is on the message value(n). There is no dependency on the name of a class, so we don't have any references to the Fizz, Buzz, FizzBuzz, or NoFizzBuzz classes. The FizzBuzzGenerator class is open for extension and closed for modification. This means we can add more concrete classes—such as Fazz, which returns multiples of 7 as Fazz if such a new requirement arises—without modifying the FizzBuzzGenerator class, and thus we can extend the functionality. The test for the sequence generator would be as follows:

```
require 'minitest/autorun'
require_relative 'fizz_buzz_generator'

class TestFizzBuzzGenerator < Minitest::Test
  def test_fizz_buzz_sequence
    objects = [FizzBuzz.new, Fizz.new, Buzz.new, NoFizzBuzz.new]
    g = FizzBuzzGenerator.new(objects, (1..20).to_a)
    result = g.generate
    expected = [1, 2, "Fizz", 4, "Buzz", "Fizz", 7, 8, "Fizz", "Buzz", 11, "Fizz", 13, 14,
"FizzBuzz", 16, 17, "Fizz", 19, "Buzz"]

    assert_equal expected, result
  end
end
```

The list of concrete classes (objects), needs to change only when new concrete classes are added. Deploying a new feature requires additive changes. This means we add a new concrete class and an instance of that object to the objects array. The generator class does not require any modification to the existing code. This results in a flexible and easy-to-maintain code base. In our solution, notice that we don't have any if-elsif-else statements. If our solution used if-elsif-else then it would require localized changes and it would not be an additive change.

There is a subtle dependency between the FizzBuzzGenerator class and the order of the objects in the test run's code. The correct generation of the FizzBuzz sequence depends on the order of objects. This is a quick-and-dirty implementation of the Chain of Responsibility pattern. However, this example was chosen to illustrate the Open Closed Principle. If the concrete classes have business logic that can be implemented by passing through a chain of handlers independent of the order in which they are executed, this solution would shine. Because, in that case, there would be no dependency on the order of the handlers in the objects array.

Difference Reduction

We have code duplication in the conditional of the value method. We can refactor the existing solution by gradually reducing the differences and reshape the solution to increase the similarities. In this case, we can gradually reduce the differences between the classes by increasing the similarities. We can stop when we have reduced the duplication and have discovered the uniform interface for the object. The final solution now uses procs to eliminate duplication in the conditionals.

```
class Fizz
  def value(n, proc)
    if proc.call(n, 3)
      'Fizz'
    end
  end
end
```

```ruby
class Buzz
  def value(n, proc)
    if proc.call(n, 5)
      'Buzz'
    end
  end
end

class FizzBuzz
  def value(n, proc)
    if proc.call(n, 15)
      'FizzBuzz'
    end
  end
end

class NoFizzBuzz
  def value(n, proc)
    n
  end
end
```

The FizzBuzzGenerator class now initializes the modulo proc in the constructor and passes it to the value method of the concrete classes that generate the sequence in the generate method.

```ruby
class FizzBuzzGenerator
  def initialize(objects, list)
    @list = list
    @objects = objects
    @modulo_proc = ->(number, divisor) { number % divisor == 0 }
  end

  def generate
    result = []
    @list.each do |num|
      @objects.each do |l|
        v = l.value(num, @modulo_proc)
        unless v.nil?
          result << v
          break
        end
      end
    end
    result
  end
end
```

The difference-reduction process can be difficult, if you separate things that change at different rates from each other, it can make the process less daunting. The decision to initialize the modulo proc in the constructor was made using this guideline. Since this new solution involves refactoring of the production code only, no modifications are required for the test file.

Defect Localization

A unit test that tests only a single behavior will enable us to find the cause of a bug quickly. The failure of a particular unit test will tell us where to look in the code base to find the cause of the problem. This is called *defect localization*. We can deliberately introduce known defects and check if the test messages tell us where the defect is located.

Mutation Testing

Mutation testing is the process of rewriting code to flush out ambiguities in the code. These ambiguities can cause failures. Since these faults are often very subtle, the code can easily pass testing and debugging and end up in production.

> *It is a good idea to test your tests. You can verify that they detect the errors you think they detect by inserting those errors into the production code. Make sure they report errors in a meaningful way. You should also verify that your tests speak clearly to a person trying to understand your code. The only way to do this is to have someone who isn't familiar with your code read your tests and tell you what they learned.*
>
> —Gerard Meszaros, 97 *Things a Programmer Should Know*

For our purposes of demonstrating the concept of defect localization, we will comment out a line in the NoFizzBuzz class that contains the implementation of the value(n) method. We will see if the test failure messages are meaningful or not. Let's comment out the logic for the NoFizzBuzz class and run the test.

```
class NoFizzBuzz
  def value(n)
    # n
  end
end
```

```
TestFizzBuzzGenerator#test_fizz_buzz_sequence [test_fizz_buzz_generator.rb:12]:
--- expected
+++ actual
@@ -1 +1 @@
-[1, 2, "Fizz", 4, "Buzz", "Fizz", 7, 8, "Fizz", "Buzz", 11, "Fizz", 13, 14, "FizzBuzz", 16,
17, "Fizz", 19, "Buzz"]
+["Fizz", "Buzz", "Fizz", "Fizz", "Buzz", "Fizz", "FizzBuzz", "Fizz", "Buzz"]
```

The error message shows the line number 12 in the test, which is the assertion line. Ideally, we want the message to tell us where exactly a regression bug cropped up. In this case, it is the value method of the NoFizzBuzz class. We must write a separate test for each of these classes so that the test indicates the cause of failure.

```
def test_no_fizz_buzz_sequence
  fb = NoFizzBuzz.new
  result = fb.value(1, ->{})

  assert_equal 1, result
end
```

We pass in a no-op proc as the second parameter to the value method. The no-op proc has no functionality. Now, the test failure localizes the defect and shows that NoFizzBuzz is the cause of the regression bug.

```
TestFizzBuzzGenerator#test_no_fizz_buzz_sequence [test_fizz_buzz_generator.rb:19]:
Expected: 1
  Actual: nil
```

We can also improve the failure message by providing a custom message as the third parameter to the assert_equal method.

```
def test_no_fizz_buzz_sequence
  fb = NoFizzBuzz.new
  result = fb.value(1, ->{})

  assert_equal 1, result, 'Failure in the NoFizzBuzz value method'
end
```

The failure message is now meaningful and helps other developers working on the same code base isolate and fix the regression bug quickly. We can now revert the implementation of the value method to return the number. The test will now pass.

Stack

This section will cover two guidelines for writing good tests: test precisely and concretely and make your code robust. We will develop a simple stack that we can work through in this section to illustrate these testing guidelines.

Basic Stack

Create a test_stack.rb file that has the test test_should_push_a_given_item. Create an instance of the Stack class and invoke the push method with 2 as the parameter, and then check that the stack size is equal to the expected value of 1.

```
require 'minitest/autorun'
require_relative 'stack'

class TestStack < Minitest::Test
  def test_should_push_a_given_item
    stack = Stack.new
    stack.push(2)
    assert_equal 1, stack.size
  end
end
```

Create a `Stack` class with a `push` method that takes an element as the argument.

```
class Stack
  def push(element)
  end
end
```

Run the test, and it will fail with the following error: `Undefined method size for stack`. Define a `size` method.

```
class Stack
  def push(element)
  end

  def size
  end
end
```

Run the test. We get a failure with the following message: `Expected 1, actual nil`. Let's just hardcode one to make the test pass quickly.

```
class Stack
  def push(element)
  end

  def size
    1
  end
end
```

The test will now pass.

Add the second test, `test_should_pop_a_given_item`. We create a `stack` object and push an element 2 by invoking the push on the `stack` object. We then invoke the pop method and check whether the result is 2 or not.

```
def test_should_pop_a_given_item
  stack = Stack.new
  stack.push(2)
  result = stack.pop
  assert_equal 2, result
end
```

Run all the tests. We get the error `Undefined method pop for stack`. Define the pop method and run the test again. The second test fails with the message `Expected 2, actual nil`.

```
class Stack
  def push(element)
  end

  def pop
  end
```

```
    def size
    end
end
```

This gives us enough permission to implement the real stack implementation that's going to delegate the functionality to an array. We initialize an empty array in the constructor. We push the new element into the array in push, and pop will delegate the call to the array's pop method. Run the tests, and both tests will now pass.

```
class Stack
  def initialize
    @elements = []
  end

  def push(element)
    @elements << element
  end

  def pop
    @elements.pop
  end

  def size
    @elements.size
  end
end
```

We got rid of the bogus implementation of size and delegate the size to the array's size method. We now have a basic stack implementation that we will continue to work on in this section. We have multiple assertions in the test. Since they are logically related, it is not an issue. They will break for the same reason. For instance, if one of the assertions for the pop test fails, we know it is a regression bug in the pop functionality. We can also define a custom assertion, assert_pop, that will encapsulate the multiple assertions.

Test Precisely and Concretely

We will now discuss how to test precisely and concretely.

In specifying behavior, tests should not simply be accurate. They must also be precise.

—Kevlin Henney, *97 Things Every Programmer Should Know*

The result of adding an item to an empty collection is not simply that it is not empty. It is that the collection now has a single item and that the single item held is the item added. Two or more items would also qualify the collection as not empty and would also be wrong. A single item of a different value would also be wrong.

So, for the stack example, if we push an element, 2, the size is 1 and the item held in the stack is now 2. In the second case, if you push an item, 2, and there are two elements, 2 and something else, it is wrong. If you push an element, 2, onto the stack and it results in some other element 'x' to be pushed onto the stack, it is wrong. So, the second and third cases are not correct behavior. The first case is the right behavior.

The stack implementation we developed in the previous section does not follow the "test precisely and concretely" guideline. The reason is that we implemented the push operation first. So, we did not have the pop to check the value that was pushed. Let's update the first test so that it uses pop to make the test more precise.

```
def test_should_push_a_given_item
  stack = Stack.new
  stack.push(2)
  assert_equal 1, stack.size
  assert_equal 2, stack.pop
end
```

Let's run the test now. It will pass. Let's make the second test also precise. When you pop, the element is returned and the size is reduced by 1. So, the stack size must be 0.

```
def test_should_pop_a_given_item
  stack = Stack.new
  stack.push(2)
  result = stack.pop
  assert_equal 2, result
  assert_equal 0, stack.size
end
```

Run the test. It will pass. Let's delete the second assertion in the first test. Let's run the test. We are still green.

```
def test_should_push_a_given_item
  stack = Stack.new
  stack.push(2)
  assert_equal 1, stack.size
end
```

Since the pop operation is destructive, we have another option where we can implement a top() method that will leave the element in place and will return the value that is on top of the stack.

```
def test_should_push_a_given_item
  stack = Stack.new
  stack.push(2)
  assert_equal 1, stack.size
  assert_equal 2, stack.top
end
```

Let's run all the tests. They will fail with the undefined method error message. Let's define a top() method that looks at the last element. Run all the tests; we are now green.

```
class Stack
  def initialize
    @elements = []
  end
```

```ruby
  def push(element)
    @elements << element
  end

  def pop
    @elements.pop
  end

  def size
    @elements.size
  end

  def top
    @elements.last
  end
end
```

You can experiment in the IRB console to see how the pop and last methods differ. If you have an array a that contains 1 and 2, the last will be the second element, and a is not modified. If I do a pop it returns 2, but array a has been modified.

```
> a = [1,2]
=> [1, 2]
> a.last
=> 2
> a
=> [1, 2]
> a.pop
=> 2
> a
=> [1]
```

In this section, we looked at a simple implementation of stack and discussed a few solutions. We picked a solution that required the least amount of code, but still satisfied the "test precisely and concretely" testing guideline.

Make Your Code Robust

In this section, we will discuss how to make your code robust. In the previous section, we worked on a simple stack implementation that dealt with normal cases. To make the code robust, it is time to think about cases such as the following: extreme cases like 0, negative, nil, maximums, and so on. What happens if the user passes in bad data such as nil or negative values? For the stack example, we have the following test cases:

- A stack is empty on construction.

- Popping from an empty stack throws an exception.

- Peeking from an empty stack throws an exception.

- After n pushes to an empty stack, where $n > 0$, the stack is not empty and its size is n.

- If the size is n, then after n pops, the stack is empty and has a size of 0.

Let's now tackle these cases. Add a new test, test_stack_should_be_empty_on_construction. We create an instance of stack and assert that the stack should be empty.

```
def test_stack_should_be_empty_on_construction
  stack = Stack.new

  assert stack.empty?
end
```

Run the test. We get an error: undefined method empty? Add the empty? method to the stack.rb file and delegate the functionality to the empty? method of the array class.

```
  def empty?
    @elements.empty?
  end
```

Run the test; it will now pass.

Add the next test, named test_after_n_pushes_to_an_empty_stack_the_stack_is_not_empty. We create an instance of stack. We can push two elements into the stack (2 and 4 in this case), and we can assert that the stack is not empty.

```
def test_after_n_pushes_to_an_empty_stack_the_stack_is_not_empty
  stack = Stack.new
  stack.push(2)
  stack.push(4)

  assert !stack.empty?
end
```

Let's run the test. It passes. We can change assert to refute. So, we can take the negation out and have the code refute that the stack is empty.

```
def test_after_n_pushes_to_an_empty_stack_the_stack_is_not_empty
  stack = Stack.new
  stack.push(2)
  stack.push(4)

  refute stack.empty?
end
```

Run the tests; we are still green. Let's add the next test, test_after_n_pushes_to_an_empty_stack_stack_size_is_n. Create an instance of stack and push two elements onto the stack; stack size should be two.

```
def test_after_n_pushes_to_an_empty_stack_stack_its_size_is_n
  stack = Stack.new
  stack.push(2)
  stack.push(4)

  assert_equal 2, stack.size
end
```

Let's run the test. We are green.

Let's add the next test, test_stack_with_n_elements_becomes_empty_after_n_pops. We create an instance of stack and push two elements (2 and 4) onto the stack. We then pop two items from the stack by calling pop twice. We expect the size to be 0.

```
def test_stack_with_n_elements_becomes_empty_after_n_pops
  stack = Stack.new
  stack.push(2)
  stack.push(4)

  stack.pop
  stack.pop

  assert_equal 0, stack.size
end
```

Run the test, it will pass. There is a relationship between the test name and the steps of a test. If you read the name of the test, it says "Stack with *n* elements becomes empty after *n* pops." So, it is more expressive if you change the test to match what the test name is by doing the following:

```
assert stack.empty?
```

```
def test_stack_with_n_elements_becomes_empty_after_n_pops
  stack = Stack.new
  stack.push(2)
  stack.push(4)

  stack.pop
  stack.pop

  assert stack.empty?
end
```

We just refactored the test. Run it. It will pass. Let's add the next test, test_popping_from_an_empty_stack_throws_an_exception. We create an instance of stack and then use assert_raises within the block we pop from the stack, which should throw an exception.

```
def test_popping_from_an_empty_stack_throws_an_exception
  stack = Stack.new

  assert_raises do
    stack.pop
  end
end
```

Run the test; it will fail with the following message:

```
Exception expected but nothing was raised.
```

Modify the `stack.rb` file to raise an exception with the message `Cannot pop an empty stack`.

```
def pop
  if empty?
    raise 'Cannot pop an empty stack'
  end
  @elements.pop
end
```

Now we run the test again. It will pass. In this section, we applied Bertrand Meyer's guideline when deciding about exceptions: When a contract is broken either by a client or supplier, throw an exception. This helps us to determine whether the bug is in the client code or the supplier code. In our case, the "contract" is that as long as the client invokes the pop operation when at least one element exists, the supplier will return the element in the last position of the stack.

> *A program must be able to deal with exceptions. A good design rule is to list explicitly the situations that may cause a program to break down.*
>
> —Jorgen Knudsen, *Object Design: Roles, Responsibilities, and Collaborations*

We must explicitly document the behavior of our API by writing contract tests. This will help other developers understand and use our library as intended.

The Sieve of Eratosthenes

The Sieve of Eratosthenes will be used in the Prime Factors kata in the next section. This section will discuss the basics of the Sieve of Eratosthenes and how to apply it to find all the small primes for a given list of numbers. It is the most efficient way to find primes. From a high level, it has two steps:

1. Make a list of all the integers $<= n$ and > 1

2. Strike out the multiples of all primes $<= \mathrm{sqrt}(n)$. The numbers that are left are the primes.

Let's now consider an example. We need to find all the primes up to a given number n. For 30 the result is 2, 3, 5, 7, 11, 13, 17, 19, 23, 29. Let's find all the primes $<= 30$. The first step is to list the numbers from 2 to 30, as shown in Figure 2-24.

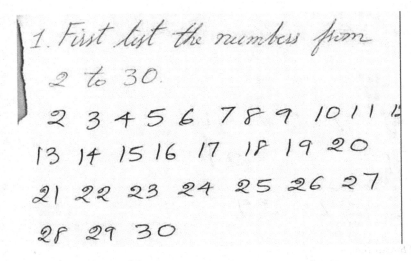

Figure 2-24. *Step one of Sieve of Erastosthenes*

The second step is to keep the first number, as it is prime. The third step is to cross out multiples of 2, as shown in Figure 2-25.

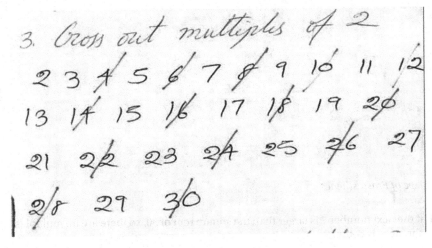

Figure 2-25. *Step three of Sieve of Erastosthenes*

In step four, we look at the first number left. It is 3, and it is the first odd prime, so we keep it. Step five is to cross out all multiples of 3, as shown in Figure 2-26.

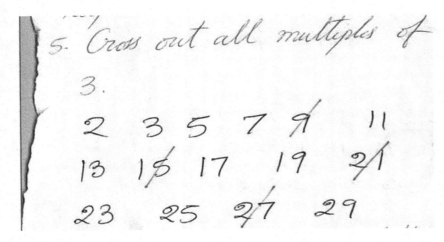

Figure 2-26. *Step five of Sieve of Erastosthenes*

In step six, we see the first number left is 5, which is the second odd prime, so we keep it. In step seven, cross out all multiples of 5, as shown in Figure 2-27.

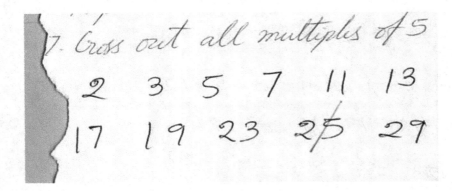

Figure 2-27. *Step seven of Sieve of Erastosthenes*

In step eight, we see that the next number 7 is larger than the square root of 30, so there are no multiples of 7 to eliminate. Therefore, the sieve is complete.

Algorithm

We can now write the general outline in the form of pseudo code for the Sieve of Eratosthenes. We apply the sieve till we reach the terminating condition, as shown here:

```
while square root of(current_prime) >= n
  apply the sieve
end
```

The terminating condition is when the square root of(current_prime) <= n. Let's write the test for step one of the example. Create an eratosthenes_test.rb file with the following content:

```
require 'minitest/autorun'

class Erastostenes
  def initialize(limit)
    @limit = limit
  end

  def number_list

  end
end

describe Erastostenes do
  it 'makes a list of all integers <= 30 and greater than 1' do
    e = Erastostenes.new(30)
    result = e.number_list
    expected = [2, 3, 4, 5, 6, 7, 8, 9, 10, 11, 12, 13, 14, 15, 16, 17, 18, 19, 20, 21, 22,
23, 24, 25, 26, 27, 28, 29, 30]
    assert_equal expected, result
  end
end
```

This test will fail. Implement the number_list as follows:

```
def number_list
  (2..@limit).to_a
end
```

This test passes. Let's add the test for the second step in the example, as follows:

```
it 'should cross out multiples of 2' do
  e = Erastostenes.new(30)
  result = e.cross_out_multiples_of_two
  expected = [2,3,5,7,9,11,13,15,17,19,21,23,25,27,29]
  assert_equal expected, result
end
```

This test fails. Here is the implementation that passes the test:

```
def cross_out_multiples_of_two
  number_list.reject do |x|
    unless x == 2
      x % 2 == 0
    end
  end
end
```

Let's write the test for the next step as follows:

```
it 'should cross out multiples of 2 and 3' do
  e = Erastostenes.new(30)
  result = e.cross_out_multiples_of_three
  expected = [2,3,5,7,11,13,17,19,23,25,29]
  assert_equal expected, result
end
```

We are not just testing step two by itself. We are developing the algorithm incrementally, so it needs to build on top of the previous step. The following implementation passes the test:

```
def cross_out_multiples_of_three
  list = cross_out_multiples_of_two
  list.reject do |x|
    unless x == 3
      x % 3 == 0
    end
  end
end
```

Add the next test:

```
it 'should cross out multiples of 2, 3, and 5' do
  e = Erastostenes.new(30)
  result = e.cross_out_multiples_of_five
  expected = [2,3,5,7,11,13,17,19,23,29]
  assert_equal expected, result
end
```

The following implementation passes the test:

```
def cross_out_multiples_of_five
  list = cross_out_multiples_of_three
  list.reject do |x|
    unless x == 5
      x % 5 == 0
    end
  end
end
```

There is a relationship between the doc strings used in the it() method and the test. In our tests, the doc strings say the right thing, but the test names are not expressing what the doc string conveys. The semantics must be revealed by the method names. We will address this issue later. Let's first refactor to eliminate the duplication in the Eratosthenes class. The number_list method is used only once, by the cross_out_multiples_of_two method. We can initialize an instance variable @list in the constructor. Once we get the new implementation working, we can delete the number_list method. We see duplication in the cross_out_multiples_of_two, cross_out_multiples_of_three, and cross_out_multiples_of_five methods. We can extract a new generic method that parameterizes the number to cross out. This method, cross_out_multiples_of(number), is made private because it is not part of the public API.

```ruby
class Erastostenes
  def initialize(limit)
    @limit = limit
    @list = (2..@limit).to_a
  end

  def number_list
    (2..@limit).to_a
  end

  def cross_out_multiples_of_two
    cross_out_multiples_of(2)
  end

  def cross_out_multiples_of_three
    @list = cross_out_multiples_of(2)
    cross_out_multiples_of(3)
  end

  def cross_out_multiples_of_five
    list = cross_out_multiples_of_three
    list.reject! do |x|
      unless x == 5
        x % 5 == 0
      end
    end
  end

  private

  def cross_out_multiples_of(number)
    @list.reject! do |x|
      unless x == number
        x % number == 0
      end
    end
  end
end
```

Let's now address the semantics issue we briefly discussed earlier. Add the story test, as follows:

```ruby
it 'should calculate the prime numbers for 30' do
  e = Erastostenes.new(30)
  result = e.calculate
  expected = [2,3,5,7,11,13,17,19,23,29]
  assert_equal expected, result
end
```

We now have a calculate method that is meaningful. By looking at our discussion in the algorithm section and at the terminating condition we came up with, we know what the real implementation will be like.

```ruby
def calculate
  list = number_list
  list.each do |x|
    unless x >= Math.sqrt(@limit)
      cross_out_multiples_of(x)
    end
  end
  @list
end
```

This passes all our tests. Let's clean up. Here is the listing after deleting unnecessary code and tests:

```ruby
require 'minitest/autorun'

class Erastostenes
  def initialize(limit)
    @limit = limit
    @list = (2..@limit).to_a
  end

  def number_list
    (2..@limit).to_a
  end

  def calculate
    list = number_list
    list.each do |x|
      unless x >= Math.sqrt(@limit)
        cross_out_multiples_of(x)
      end
    end
    @list
  end

  private

  def cross_out_multiples_of(number)
    @list.reject! do |x|
      unless x == number
        x % number == 0
      end
    end
  end
end

describe Erastostenes do
  it 'makes a list of all integers <= 30 and greater than 1' do
    e = Erastostenes.new(30)
    result = e.number_list
```

```
    expected = [2, 3, 4, 5, 6, 7, 8, 9, 10, 11, 12, 13, 14, 15, 16, 17, 18, 19, 20, 21, 22,
23, 24, 25, 26, 27, 28, 29, 30]
    assert_equal expected, result
  end

  it 'should calculate the prime numbers for 30' do
    e = Erastostenes.new(30)
    result = e.calculate
    expected = [2,3,5,7,11,13,17,19,23,29]
    assert_equal expected, result
  end
end
```

The deleted tests were necessary in the beginning to get us moving in the right direction to solve the problem. Now, they are no longer required. We can also make the number_list method private and delete the corresponding test. Remember to modify either the test code or the production code and run the tests. Do not modify both at the same time without running the tests. If you do, you will have difficulty in figuring out whether the problem is the result of production code or the tests.

Prime Factors

In number theory, the prime factors of a positive integer are the prime numbers that divide that integer exactly. The prime factorization of a positive integer is a list of the integer's prime factors together with their multiplicities; the process of determining these factors is called *integer factorization* (Source: https://en.wikipedia.org/wiki/Prime_factor). This kata is used to illustrate how to evaluate whether the amount of test code to production code is reasonable or not. The Ensure Commensurate Effort and Responsibility principle states that the amount of effort it takes to write or modify tests should not exceed the effort it takes to implement the corresponding functionality. This principle is discussed in *xUnit Test Patterns* by Gerard Meszaros.

Problem Statement

Factorize a positive integer number into its prime factors.

Problem Domain Analysis

Table 2-4 shows some sample input and output for the prime factors problem.

Table 2-4. Sample Input and Output for Prime Factors

Input	Expected Output
2	[2]
3	[2,3]
4	[2,2]
6	[2,3]
8	[2,2,2]
9	[3,3]
10	[2,5]

Solution Domain Analysis

Start with the divisor 2 and repeatedly reduce n by a factor of 2 until 2 is no longer an exact divisor. We then try 3 as a divisor and again repeat the reduction process and so on until n has been reduced to 1. Consider n = 60. Figure 2-28 shows the unsuccessful attempts to divide by marking the number with an asterisk.

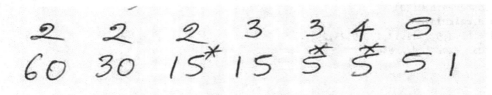

***Figure 2-28.** Asterisks mark unsuccessful attempts to divide*

The successful divisors are 2, 2, 3, and 5. That is, 60 = 2 x 2 x 3 x 5, and those numbers are primes. Create a prime_factor_test.rb file with one test for the first test case and an empty calculate implementation.

```ruby
require 'minitest/autorun'

class PrimeFactor
  def initialize(number)
    @number = number
  end

  def calculate

  end
end

describe PrimeFactor do
  it 'should return 2 for input of 2' do
    prime_factorial = PrimeFactor.new(2)
    result = prime_factorial.calculate
    assert_equal [2], result
  end
end
```

Hardcode the result to make the test pass quickly.

```ruby
def calculate
  [2]
end
```

Add the next test.

```ruby
it 'should return 3 for input of 3' do
  prime_factorial = PrimeFactor.new(3)
  result = prime_factorial.calculate
  assert_equal [3], result
end
```

Change the calculate method as follows:

```
def calculate
  [@number]
end
```

Both tests will now pass. Add the next test.

```
it 'should return [2,2] for input of 4' do
  prime_factorial = PrimeFactor.new(4)
  result = prime_factorial.calculate
  assert_equal [2,2], result
end
```

This test fails. Add the following quick and dirty implementation:

```
def calculate
  result = []
  remainder = @number / 2
  result << 2
  result << remainder if Prime.prime?(remainder)
  result
end
```

We are using Ruby's builtin Prime class. We need to add the require statement before we can use it. So, add require 'prime' at the top. The new test now passes, but it breaks the second test. We will make it pending for now by using the skip method.

```
it 'should return 3 for input of 3' do
  skip 'pending for now'
  prime_factorial = PrimeFactor.new(3)
  result = prime_factorial.calculate
  assert_equal [3], result
end
```

If n = 12, we can divide it by 2 to get 6 as the remainder. Is 12 evenly divisible by 2? Yes, so add 2 to the result list. The remainder 6 is not a prime number, so we need to continue processing. Try 2 again: 6 / 2 = 3. 6 is evenly divisible by 2, so add 2 to the result list. Is the remainder 3 a prime? Yes. Add it to the result list and stop. Using this as the reference, here is the implementation that passes all three tests:

```
def calculate
  result = []
  until Prime.prime?(@number)
    if (@number % 2) == 0
      result << 2
      @number = @number / 2
    elsif (@number % 3) == 0
      result << 3
      @number = @number / 3
    end
  end
```

```
    result << @number
    result
end
```

This implementation uses reduction to reduce the problem size. Add the next test:

```
it 'should return [3,7,7] for input of 147' do
  prime_factorial = PrimeFactor.new(147)
  result = prime_factorial.calculate
  assert_equal [3,7,7], result
end
```

This test will fail, because the algorithm does not consider the multiple of 7 yet. Here is the quick and dirty implementation that makes all the tests pass.

```
def calculate
  result = []
  until Prime.prime?(@number)
    if (@number % 2) == 0
      result << 2
      @number = @number / 2
    elsif (@number % 3) == 0
      result << 3
      @number = @number / 3
    elsif (@number % 7) == 0
      result << 7
      @number = @number / 7
    end
  end
  result << @number
  result
end
```

We see that we need to continuously look for whether the given number is evenly divisible by a series of prime numbers. Let's not delete any code; we will make the transition gradual by running the tests frequently and refactoring as the tests pass for each refactoring change. We have already discussed how to generate primes using the Sieve of Eratosthenes in a previous kata. Let's adapt that function so that, given a number, the Eratosthenes function will give us the next prime for us to use in the "divisible by prime" check condition. After experimenting in the IRB, here is a function that assumes we only need a list of primes up to 100. It takes a number and gives the next prime in the list. This next class method is added to our existing Eratosthenes class.

```
def self.next(n)
  e = Erastosthenes.new(100)
  primes = e.calculate
  primes.detect{|x| x > n}
end
```

Let's refactor our code so that it uses the Sieve of Eratosthenes for the evenly divisible check. Here is a partial refactoring:

```
def calculate
  result = []
  current_prime = 2
  until Prime.prime?(@number)
    if (@number % current_prime) == 0
      result << current_prime
      @number = @number / current_prime
    elsif (@number % 3) == 0
      result << 3
      @number = @number / 3
    elsif (@number % 7) == 0
      result << 7
      @number = @number / 7
    end
  end
  result << @number
  result
end
```

All tests pass, so let's continue the refactoring. Add the require_relative 'Eratosthenes' statement to the top of the prime_factors.rb file.

```
def calculate
  result = []
  current_prime = 2
  until Prime.prime?(@number)
    if (@number % current_prime) == 0
      result << current_prime
      @number = @number / current_prime
    else
      current_prime = Erastosthenes.next(current_prime)
    end
  end
  result << @number
  result
end
```

This version uses the next method in the Eratosthenes class to find the next prime number. All the tests still pass after refactoring. Write tests for the following test cases:

```
it 'should return [2,3] for input of 6'
it 'should return [2,2,2] for input of 8'
it 'should return [2,7] for input of 14'
```

These tests will pass without any modification to the solution. Add the story test to confirm that our solution can handle any number.

```
it 'should handle any number' do
  prime_factorial = PrimeFactor.new(168)
  result = prime_factorial.calculate
  assert_equal [2, 2, 2, 3, 7], result
end
```

The tests still pass; therefore, our solution is generic enough to handle any number. We have 20 lines of production code and almost 70 lines of test code. Ideally, we want the minimal number of tests that gives us enough confidence in our code. After you write the story test, do some exploratory testing and write some tests based on those exploratory tests, evaluating whether the test-to-code ratio is reasonable. We made a simplifying assumption in generating a prime factors list by limiting it to 100.

EXERCISES

Change in Requirement

Instead of printing Fizz for multiples of 3, change the program to print Fizz for multiples of 7. Write a failing test first.

Replace Recursive Solution with Iterative Solution

Instead of using recursion, use iteration to solve the Fibonacci problem. You don't need to modify the tests. You will only modify the production code. All the tests should pass at the end of the refactoring phase.

Summary

In this chapter, we put everything that was discussed in the previous chapter together. We developed a solution for the Fibonacci sequence problem driven by tests. It is much easier to write tests and code the solution when we have done problem domain analysis and solution domain analysis.

We discussed how the sequence of test cases can affect a TDD session. We saw how to expose a bug using a test and add a regression test for the bug. We also discussed how to make the test focus on the intent rather than on the implementation and how to test when you cross the system boundary, such as interfacing with standard output. We discussed how to make your code robust to handle extreme cases and bad user input. We also saw how to test precisely and concretely. We applied the Ensure Commensurate Effort and Responsibility guideline to the prime factors kata.

CHAPTER 3

Techniques in TDD

This chapter will cover three approaches to making a test work cleanly: Obvious Implementation, Fake It Till You Make It, and Triangulation. We will also discuss the use of the Transformation Priority Premise and the Reduction process when coding the solution to a given problem. We will revisit solution domain analysis to gain a deeper understanding of the problem-solving process.

Obvious Implementation

In Obvious Implementation, we type in real implementation if it is obvious and can quickly make the test pass. This is what we did in the calculator addition implementation by adding the two numbers in the arguments to the add method. The solution was obvious to us, so we added the numbers to make the test pass quickly. If we end up in red, we take smaller steps. This probably means you are solving the *clean code* part at the same time as you are solving the *it works* part. If you find that it is too much to do at once, go back to solving *it works* first and then solve *clean code*.

We want to maintain the red-green-refactor rhythm. Be prepared to solve smaller problems if you are not getting to green quickly. Create a test file called test_calculator.rb. Add a new test, test_multiplication. Create a new instance of calculator and invoke multiply on it, passing 2 and 3. We expect the result to be 6. Run the test, and it will fail.

```
require 'minitest/autorun'

class Calculator
end

class TestCalculator < Minitest::Test
  def test_multiplication
    calculator = Calculator.new
    result = calculator.multiply(3, 2)
    assert_equal 6, result
  end
end
```

Define the multiply method, which takes two arguments, x and y, to be multiplied. Run the test, and it fails with the following failure message:

```
Expected 6, actual nil.
```

© Bala Paranj 2017
B. Paranj, *Test Driven Development in Ruby*, DOI 10.1007/978-1-4842-2638-4_3

It is obvious that to implement multiplication, we need to multiply x and y. Run the test again. It will pass.

```
class Calculator
  def multiply(x, y)
    x * y
  end
end
```

Let's look at another example that is not so trivial. Create a test file called test_swap.rb with the test test_swap. Create an instance of Swapper by passing 1 and 2 to the constructor. Then, invoke the swap method on the swapper object. The swap method will swap the values of a and b. So, if a is 1 and b is 2, after the swap, a will be 2 and b will be 1.

```
require 'minitest/autorun'

class TestSwapper < Minitest::Test
  def test_swap
    swapper = Swapper.new(1, 2)
    swapper.swap
    assert_equal 2, swapper.a
    assert_equal 1, swapper.b
  end
end
```

Run the test, and it will fail with the following error:

```
Uninitialized constant Swapper.
```

Define the Swapper class with the swap method. The constructor will initialize the values for instance variables a and b. The swap method will swap the values held in a and b. We declare an attr_reader to read the values of a and b.

```
require 'minitest/autorun'

class Swapper
  attr_reader :a, :b

  def initialize(a, b)
    @a = a
    @b = b
  end

  def swap
    @a, @b = @b, @a
  end
end

class TestSwapper < Minitest::Test
  def test_swap
    swapper = Swapper.new (1, 2)
    swapper.swap
```

```
    assert_equal 2, swapper.a
    assert_equal 1, swapper.b
  end
end
```

Run the test; it will pass. You also need to make sure the negative condition also works. So, write another test called test_no_swap. In this case, the values will not be swapped. The assertion asserts the value of a is 1 and the value of b is 2.

```
def test_no_swap
  swapper = Swapper.new(1, 2)

  assert_equal 1, swapper.a
  assert_equal 2, swapper.b
end
```

Run the test; it will pass. So, we have seen two examples of Obvious Implementation. You can use this technique when you are confident that you can get to green quickly.

Fake It Till You Make It

In Fake It Till You Make It, you initially hard code constants to make the tests pass and gradually generalize code using variables. This technique is used when the solution is not obvious and you need to focus on one problem at a time. This allows you to control the scope of the problem. Starting with one concrete example and generalizing from there helps you to focus on one problem at a time. When you implement the next test case, you can focus on that one too, knowing that the previous test is guaranteed to work. Create a new file called test_calculator.rb that has a test for addition, test_addition, and a Calculator class with an empty add method.

```
require 'minitest/autorun'

class Calculator
  def add(addend, augend)
  end
end

class TestCaculator < Minitest::Test
  def test_addition
    calculator = Calculator.new
    result = calculator.add(1, 2)
    assert_equal 3, result
  end
end
```

▪ **Note** You can see the arguments to the add method are expressive, with names such as addend and augend instead of the meaningless x and y. Domain experts will be familiar with terms that can be expressed in the code. Developers must communicate with the domain experts to find the domain-specific terms to express in the code.

Running the test, we get the following failure message:

```
Expected 3, got nil.
```

There are two core things that we need to pay attention to when using this technique:

- Start with the simplest possible implementation, which is usually returning a constant. Then, gradually transform the code of both the test and the implementation to use variables.

- When doing it, rely on your sense of duplication between test and fake implementation.

The simplest implementation to make this test pass is to return a constant, 3.

```ruby
class Calculator
  def add(addend, augend)
    3
  end
end
```

Run the test again, and it will now pass. We know the implementation is obviously wrong, but the TDD cycle is not over yet. Remember that as soon as the test is passing, the refactoring phase kicks in. We can use the refactoring phase to remove any duplication between the test and the production code. We can see that the duplication is not in the logic of the code, but rather is in the data. We can see the data duplication of 3 in both the add method of the Calculator class and the assertion in the test_addition test method. So, we have the number 3 duplicated between test and implementation. The implementation returns it and the test asserts on it. To reduce this duplication, let's break 3 in the implementation into a sum. So, it will become 1 + 2.

```ruby
class Calculator
  def add(addend, augend)
    1+2
  end
end
```

Run the test; it will still pass. So, we changed the duplication from being between implementation and expected result to being between implementation and the input values of the test. We now have 1 + 2. Data of 1 and 2 is the same as what we have in the calculator's add step in the test_addition method of the test. The duplication is now in the arguments to the add method. This kind of duplication is different in that it can be removed using variables. So, let's eliminate the duplication of the number 1 first by replacing 1 with the variable addend. There is no more duplication between the test and the implementation for the number 1.

```ruby
class Calculator
  def add(addend, augend)
    addend + 2
  end
end
```

Run the test again, and it will pass. Now we only have the 2 duplicated, because we used a variable to transfer the value of 1 from the test method to the add implementation. We have it in one place now. Let's do the same with 2. We can replace 2 with augend.

```
class Calculator
  def add(addend, augend)
    addend + augend
  end
end
```

Run the test, and it will still pass. We no longer have duplication of 1 and 2 or even the number 3 between the test data and the actual implementation of the addition logic. We picked a trivial problem because it allows us to focus on the technique rather than being distracted by the complexity of the problem. You can find an advanced example of this technique in the book *Test Driven Development by Example* by Kent Beck.

Triangulation

Triangulation is a term used in trigonometry. It is defined as follows:

> *The tracing and measurement of a series or network of triangles in order to determine the distances and relative positions of points spread over a territory or region, especially by measuring the length of one side of each triangle and deducing its angles and the length of the other two sides by observation from this baseline.*

It is the process of pinpointing a certain object or location by taking bearings to it from two remote points. In the context of TDD, in triangulation we only abstract when we have two or more examples. We briefly ignore the duplication between test and production code. When the second example demands a more general solution, then, and only then, we generalize. This technique is the most conservative way to drive abstraction with tests because it involves the tiniest possible steps to arrive at the right solution.

> *As the tests get more specific, the code gets more generic.*

—Robert C. Martin

This technique is used when you are unsure about the correct abstraction or when you are unsure about how to refactor. Triangulation gives you a chance to think about the problem from a slightly different direction. What axis of variability are you trying to support in your design? Make some of them vary, and the answer may become clearer.

Addition

Create a new test file, test_calculator.rb, with one test, test_addition_of_1_and_2_is_3. Create an instance of Calculator and invoke the add method, then pass 1 and 2 as the parameters. Then, assert that the result should be 3. The Calculator class has an empty add method.

```
require 'minitest/autorun'

class Calculator
  def add(addend, augend)
  end
end
```

```ruby
class TestCaculator < Minitest::Test
  def test_addition_of_1_and_2_is_3
    calculator = Calculator.new
    result = calculator.add(1, 2)
    assert_equal 3, result
  end
end
```

Run the test. It will fail with the following failure message:

```
Expected 3, actual nil.
```

The simplest thing we can do to get this working is to hard code the result.

```ruby
class Calculator
  def add(addend, augend)
    3
  end
end
```

The test will now pass. Add the second test, test_addition_of_2_and_2_is_4. This test is similar to the first test.

```ruby
  def test_addition_of_2_and_2_is_4
    calculator = Calculator.new
    result = calculator.add(2, 2)
    assert_equal 4, result
  end
```

Run the test. It will fail with the following failure message:

```
Expected 4, actual 3.
```

Now you have two examples expressed by the two tests. You can add those two numbers and return the result.

```ruby
class Calculator
  def add(addend, augend)
    addend + augend
  end
end
```

The tests will now pass. The second test forces the production code to be generic so that it can add a different set of numbers. Since the second test does not really document anything other than what the first test covers, we can delete it. We can also change the name of the first method to test_addition. The test should pass after refactoring the test.

Sum a List of Numbers

Let's take a look at another example for triangulation.

Problem Domain Analysis

Let's consider a set of numbers.
    Numbers = $(1, 2, 3, \ldots n)$

Sum $s = 1 + 2 + 3 + \ldots + n$

Let's formulate an algorithm that takes into account that computers can add two numbers at a time. The algorithm needs to be repetitive to sum all the given numbers.

$s = a1 + a2$
$s = s + a3$
$\ldots$
$s = s + (a)n$

All sums for $n >= 1$ can be generated iteratively.

Solution Domain Analysis

In Ruby, this problem can be solved in just one line by using the inject method. We must implement our own version of the inject method. The reason for this is twofold. First, we will learn new concepts that we can use to program in any language. Second, we will come up with an algorithm that can be used to implement the summing function in any language. This gives us one logical design with many physical design possibilities.

Initial Condition

We observe that for $n = 0$ and $n = 1$, the initial condition is $s = 0$.

Steps to Solve the Problem

1. Compute first sum ($s = 0$) as a special case.

2. Build each of the n remaining sums from its predecessor by an iterative process.

3. Return the sum of n numbers.

Algorithm Description

1. Take the list of numbers to be summed.

2. Initialize sum for 0 numbers.

3. while < n numbers have been summed, repeatedly do the following:

    a. Read the number.

    b. Compute current sum by adding the number read to the most recent sum.

    c. Go to the next number.

4. Return the result.

We have solved the problem by giving the stupid computer specific steps to find the sum.

131

Assumptions

- Numbers in the list are whole numbers.

- Numbers will not cause stack-overflow issues when added.

Test Cases

- Pick a degenerate case first.

- Simple one-element case.

- Extend the solution to two elements.

- Generalize to *n* elements.

We will see why we chose the test cases in this order as we work through the problem. Create a `summer.rb` file with a Summer class that will add a list of numbers. The `sum` method will take an array as the argument, sum the list of numbers in that array, and return the sum as the result. The first test is thus `test_sum_list_of_numbers_with_no_elements`. That's the degenerate case. That's the easiest test to get working quickly.

```
require 'minitest/autorun'

class TestSum < Minitest::Test
  def test_sum_list_of_numbers_with_no_elements
    summer = Summer.new
    result = summer.sum([])
    assert_equal 0, result
  end
end
```

Run the test. We will get the error message `uninitialized constant summer`. Let's define a `sum` method in the Summer class that takes a list as its argument.

```
class Summer
  def sum(list)

  end
end
```

Let's run the test again. We get the failure message `Expected 0 got nil`. The easiest way to get this working is hard code 0 as the return value.

```
require 'minitest/autorun'

class Summer
  def sum(list)
    0
  end
end
```

The test passes.

Now, let's pick another test that will be a little bit more complicated than the previous one. Looking at our test case list, we see we now have a simple, one-element case. If we take a list that contains just one element, 0, we know that the existing fake implementation will pass. What is the next simplest value that will force the fake implementation to go away? How about a list that contains 1? Let's handle the one-element case. Add the second test name: test_sum_list_of_numbers_with_one_element. The list will contain one element, 1, and we will assert the result is 1.

```
def test_sum_list_of_numbers_with_one_element
  summer = Summer.new
  result = summer.sum([1])
  assert_equal 1, result
end
```

The test will fail with the following failure message:

```
Expected 1, result is 0.
```

We want to return 0 if it's empty. Otherwise, we will just return the element that is in the one-element list.

```
class Summer
  def sum(list)
    if list.empty?
      0
    else
      list[0]
    end
  end
end
```

Both tests will now pass.

According to our test case list, next we have to extend the solution to a two-element case. What should be the values of these two elements? We could choose any two numbers, but I am choosing [1,1]. Why use [1,1] instead of a set of larger numbers? Because the simplest set of numbers is sufficient to make our production code evolve toward an abstract solution. We have an if-else statement for the fake implementation version. Remember this, because this is going to evolve into another programming construct; we will discuss *why* when it happens. Let's now handle the two-element case. Add the new test, test_sum_list_of_numbers_with_two_elements. The list elements are 1 and 1, and the sum should be 2 in this case.

```
def test_sum_list_of_numbers_with_two_elements
  summer = Summer.new
  result = summer.sum([1,1])
  assert_equal 2, result
end
```

Run the test. It fails with the following failure message:

```
Expected 2, actual 1.
```

Let's make the production code handle the two-element case. Replace the `else` condition with the algorithm we developed earlier.

```
class Summer
  def sum(list)
    if list.empty?
      0
    else
      index = 0
      result = 0

      while index < list.size
        result += list[index]
        index += 1
      end
      result
    end
  end
end
```

The tests will now pass. Now we have three examples.

Let's see if we can make this code more generic. We can refer to our algorithm to guide our cleaning up of the implementation. The first step is the argument to the `sum()` method. The second step is the initial condition before we enter the iterative construct, which processes the elements one by one until all elements in the list have been processed. In order for us to go to the next number in step 3c of the algorithm, we must increment the index. We do this every time an element is processed successfully. This makes us reach the terminating condition, which is evaluated in the beginning of the loop, so that we can terminate the loop and return the final result. So, we know what needs to be initialized before we enter the loop, the index of the array that will be incremented within the loop, and the result. Let's define a `result` variable that's initialized to 0; the index will also be initialized to 0.

```
class Summer
  def sum(list)
    index = 0
    result = 0

    while index < list.size
      result += list[index]
      index += 1
    end
    result
  end
end
```

Did you see how the first `if` conditional that was handling the boundary case disappeared? It is now handled by the initial conditions that initialize the index and result variables. It's now clear why the degenerate test case is the first test case in our test cases list. Degenerate test cases establish initial conditions for loops. We establish index and result values that handle degenerate cases. The `if-else` construct has been replaced by a `while` loop to generalize the solution.

We have evolved our code from `if-else` to a more generic `while` loop. We did incremental algorithm design by going one by one through the test cases list, starting from the top. We made simplifying assumptions to delineate the scope of the problem. We know under which conditions our solution is valid by looking at the assumptions. The tests will still pass. Let's add the story test by adding another test for *n* number of elements–let's say five elements. We'll have 1, 2, 3, 4, and 5. We expect that adding these numbers should produce 15 as the result.

```
def test_sum_list_of_numbers_with_5_elements
  summer = Summer.new
  result = summer.sum([1,2,3,4,5])
  assert_equal 15, result
end
```

The new test passes, along with all the existing tests. We did not have to make any modifications to the production code. Since the last test doesn't add much value to our test suite, we can just delete it. We know that if we can handle one element or two elements, we can extend the solution to *n* number of elements. We can delete the test so that we have a minimum number of tests, but we still have the same generic production code. This is an example of triangulation, where you have two or more examples that gradually force the code to become generic enough to handle any number of cases.

Solution Domain Analysis Redux

A problem has many solutions. Most often, the first solution is not the best solution. The human mind thinks in a sequential manner. We need to break this tendency of sequential thinking to find better solutions. The solution in the previous section on triangulation to sum a list of numbers is not the best.

Carl Gauss is one of the greatest mathematicians of all time. He lived during the time before computers were invented. During his lifetime, he made significant contributions to almost every area of mathematics, as well as physics, astronomy, and statistics. When he was just eight years old, Gauss' teacher asked his students to add all the numbers from 1 to 100, assuming that this task would occupy them for quite a while. He was shocked when young Gauss, after only a few minutes, wrote down the answer: 5050. Figure 3-1 shows a portrait of the mathematician Carl Friedrich Gauss.

Figure 3-1. Mathematician Carl Friedrich Gauss

If you look at the process behind his thinking, what he did was solution domain analysis. Gauss took a big-picture view. He saw the forest, the entire data set, instead of looking at one tree at a time, which is one number at a time. He found the relationship between data by analyzing the solution domain. He recognized patterns by working through concrete examples and generalized a solution.

Given a series of numbers from 1 to 100, how do you go about solving this problem? If you add 1 and 100, you get 101. If you add 2 and 99 you get 101. If you add 3 and 98 you get 101. So, we have 50 of these pairs that add up to 101. If you multiply these numbers, you get the final answer, which is 5050. Figure 3-2 shows the big-picture view of summing a list of numbers.

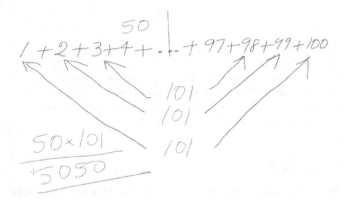

Figure 3-2. Big-picture view of the solution to summing a list of numbers

Thus, we need to take a big-picture view of the problem to find better solutions. Instead of just looking at one number at a time, Gauss took in the entire data set, found relationships between them, and derived an equation to solve the problem. Figure 3-3 shows the equation for solving the summation problem.

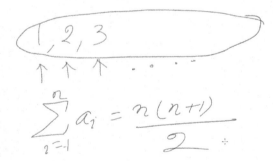

Figure 3-3. Equation to solve the summation problem

Reduction

Reduction is a process by which the original problem is reduced to a smaller problem in each iteration until the given problem is solved. It is the basis for the divide and conquer problem-solving strategy. It's like the shrinking charm *Reducio* in the Harry Potter series, which enables a wizard to decrease the physical size of the target. Let's now see how to apply the Reduction process to solve problems.

Problem Statement

Given two positive non-zero integers *n* and *m*, find their greatest common divisor (GCD). The GCD of two integers is the largest integer that will divide exactly into the two integers with no remainder.

Example 1

Figure 3-4 shows a worked-out example of the GCD of 8 and 12. In the second division, we can divide both numbers without any remainder. So, the GCD of 8 and 12 is 4. Figure 3-4 shows how the GCD of 8 and 12 can be calculated by hand.

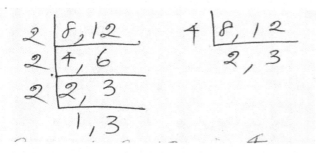

Figure 3-4. *Working out the GCD of 8 and 12 by hand*

Example 2

Let's consider the GCD of 54 and 24. The number 54 can be expressed as a product of two other integers in several different ways.

54 x 1 = 27 x 2 = 18 x 3 = 9 x 6

Thus, the divisors of 54 are 1, 2, 3, 6, 9, 18, 27, and 54.
Similarly, the divisors of 24 are 1, 2, 3, 4, 6, 8, 12, and 24.
The numbers that these two lists share are the common divisors of 54 and 24. In this case, they are 1, 2, 3, and 6. The greatest of these is 6. That is the GCD of 54 and 24.

Steps to Solve the Problem

The basic strategy for computing the GCD of two numbers is as follows:

1. Divide the larger of the two numbers by the smaller number.

2. If the smaller number exactly divides into the larger number, then the smaller number is the GCD; else, remove from the larger number the part common to the smaller number and repeat the whole procedure with the new pair of numbers.

Let's apply the preceding steps to calculate GCD(18,30). Figure 3-5 shows the Reduction process with three smaller problems that are similar.

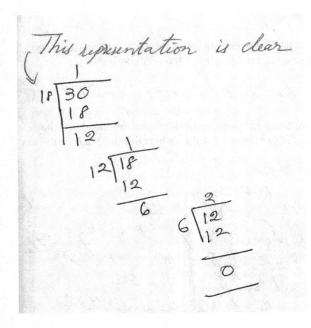

Figure 3-5. *Reduction process that shows three smaller problems*

Figure 3-6 shows the iterative construct that occurs in the Reduction process.

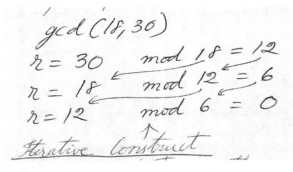

Figure 3-6. *Discovery of iterative construct during the Reduction process*

Iterative Construct

With each reduction in the problem size the smaller integer assumes the role of the larger integer and the remainder assumes the role of the smaller integer. The reduction in problem size and the role-changing steps change the divisor, dividend, and the remainder. The exact division will correspond to a 0 remainder.

```
while non-zero remainder do
  continue search for gcd
end
```

Initial Conditions

Before entering the loop, we need a remainder for the terminating-condition check, so we must do the following:

1. Compute remainder for original pair of integers.

2. Search for GCD until there is a 0 remainder.

```
while non-zero remainder
  continue search for gcd
end
```

Euclidean Algorithm

1. Take the two positive non-zero integers, smaller and larger.

2. Repeat the following:

    a. Get the remainder from dividing the larger integer by the smaller integer.

    b. Let the smaller integer assume the role of the divisor until a 0 remainder is obtained.

3. Return the GCD.

Figure 3-7 shows the how the variables change during the Reduction process.

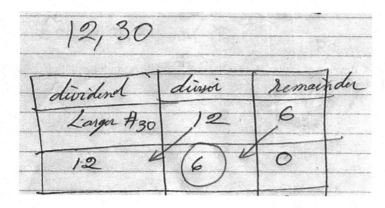

Figure 3-7. Change in the variable values during Reduction process

Test-Driven GCD

Create a test_gcd.rb test file and add a test to find the bigger number.

```
require 'minitest/autorun'

describe Gcd do
  it 'should find the bigger number' do
    gcd = Gcd.new(12, 30)
    result = gcd.bigger_number
```

```
    assert_equal 30, result
  end
end
```

The minimal implementation that will make the test pass is as follows:

```ruby
class Gcd
  def initialize(x, y)
    @x = x
    @y = y
  end

  def bigger_number
    if @x > @y
      @x
    else
      @y
    end
  end
end
```

We can now add the second test.

```ruby
it 'should return 4 for 8 and 12' do
  gcd = Gcd.new(8, 12)
  result = gcd.calculate

  assert_equal 4, result
end
```

We can now look at the algorithm we developed earlier. Here is the quick and dirty implementation based on that algorithm that passes the test:

```ruby
class Gcd
  def initialize(x, y)
    # Code same as before
  end

  def bigger_number
    # Code same as before
  end

  def reduce
    bigger_number
    remainder = 1
    dividend = bigger_number
    divisor = smaller_number
    while remainder != 0
      remainder = dividend % divisor
      dividend = divisor
      divisor = remainder
```

```
    end
    dividend
  end

  def calculate
    reduce
  end

  def smaller_number
    if @x > @y
      @y
    else
      @x
    end
  end
end
```

Let's refactor the solution to make the code readable by changing the while to until. In this case, we keep looping as long as the remainder is not 0. So,

```
while remainder != 0
```

becomes

```
until remainder == 0
```

in the reduce method. Let's add another test.

```
it 'should return 6 for 12, 30' do
  gcd = Gcd.new(12,30)
  result = gcd.calculate

  assert_equal 6, result
end
```

This test passes without requiring us to modify or add code to the existing production code. Our solution is generic so as to handle any cases. Let's now refactor the solution.

```
class Gcd
  def initialize(x, y)
    @x = x
    @y = y
    initialize_numbers
  end

  def initialize_numbers
    if @x > @y
      @bigger_number = @x
      @smaller_number = @y
```

```
    else
      @bigger_number = @y
      @smaller_number = @x
    end
  end

  def calculate
    remainder = 1
    dividend = @bigger_number
    divisor = @smaller_number
    until remainder == 0
      remainder = dividend % divisor
      dividend = divisor
      divisor = remainder
    end
    dividend
  end
end
```

We can delete the test that is coupled to the implementation of initializing the bigger and smaller numbers, leaving us with the following:

```
require 'minitest/autorun'

describe 'Gcd' do
  it 'should return 4 for 8 and 12' do
    gcd = Gcd.new(8,12)
    result = gcd.calculate

    assert_equal 4, result
  end

  it 'should return 6 for 54 and 24' do
    gcd = Gcd.new(24,54)
    result = gcd.calculate

    assert_equal 6, result
  end

  it 'should return 6 for 12,30' do
    gcd = Gcd.new(12,30)
    result = gcd.calculate

    assert_equal 6, result
  end
end
```

Transformation Priority Premise

The section will cover the Transformation Priority Premise and how to apply it to reduce impasses during a TDD programming session.

Refactorings and Transformations

Refactorings are simple operations that change the structure of code without changing its behavior. Refactorings have counterparts called *transformations*. So, what is a transformation? Transformations are simple operations that change the behavior of code. It can be used as the sole means for passing a currently failing test in the red-green-refactor cycle. Transformations have a priority, or a preferred ordering, which if maintained by the ordering of the tests will prevent long outages in the red-green-refactor cycle.

Transformation also has a direction to transform the behavior of the code from something specific to something more generic. The Transformation Priority Premise is a programming approach developed by Robert C. Martin as a refinement to make the process of Test Driven Development easier and more effective for a programmer.

The Transformation Priority Premise states that simple transformations should be preferred. We have already seen Martin's axiom, "As the tests get more specific, the code gets more generic." We will see this in action in the factorial kata.

Transformation List

So, what is this transformation list? This approach facilitates the programmer doing the simplest possible thing for the purpose of Test Driven Development, as we can specifically refer to the list of transformations and favor the simpler transformations at the top of the list. So, let's take a look at the transformation list. The transformations are ordered by their complexity. The transformations at the top of the list are simpler and less risky than the transformations lower on the list. Figure 3-8 shows the transformations list for the Transformation Priority Premise.

({}–>nil) no code at all->code that employs nil

(nil->constant)

(constant->constant+) a simple constant to a more complex constant

(constant->scalar) replacing a constant with a variable or an argument

(statement->statements) adding more unconditional statements.

(unconditional->if) splitting the execution path

(scalar->array)

(array->container)

(statement->recursion)

(if->while)

(expression->function) replacing an expression with a function or algorithm

(variable->assignment) replacing the value of a variable.

Figure 3-8. *Transformations list for the Transformation Priority Premise*

The direction of transformation priority list follows the priority as specified in the following list.

1. Initially we have no code at all, then we have code that employs nil.

2. From nil we go to constant.

3. We go from a simple constant to a more complex constant.

4. We replace the constant with a variable or an argument.

5. We add more unconditional statements.

6. We split the execution path by going from unconditional to an `if` statement.

7. We go from scalar to an array.

8. We go from an array to a container.

9. We go from statement to recursion.

10. We go from an `if` statement to a `while` statement.

11. We go from expression to a function or an algorithm.

12. We replace the value of a variable with an assignment.

When passing a test, prefer higher priority transformations. When writing a test, choose one that can be passed with higher priority transformations. When an implementation seems to require a lower priority transformation, backtrack to see if there is a simpler test to pass. If tests are chosen and implemented in the preferred order of transformations, then TDD impasses can be minimized.

Counter

The counter kata will illustrate how the Transformation Priority Premise can be applied. At the end of this kata, we will see how the code evolved from simplest to more complicated language constructs.

Problem Statement

Implement a method called `my_count` that takes a number and an array of numbers and returns a count representing the total number of elements in the array that are equal or greater than the given number.

Problem Domain Analysis

Let's say our method takes two parameters–the first parameter is n for the number used for comparison; the second is an array that contains a list of numbers to be processed. Figure 3-9 shows the number to count in the given list and the result for the given list of numbers.

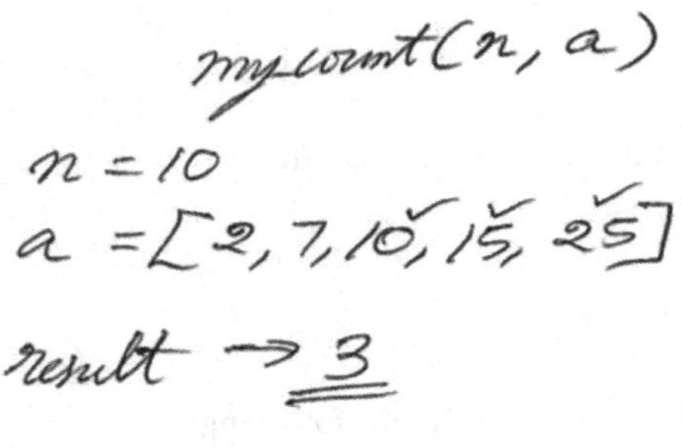

$$my\_count(n, a)$$
$$n = 10$$
$$a = [2, 7, 10, 15, 25]$$
$$result \rightarrow \underline{3}$$

Figure 3-9. Problem domain analysis for counter problem

The result in this case is 3, since there are only three numbers–10, 15, and 25–that are equal to or above 10. We can accomplish this in Ruby in just one line, in the IRB:

```
a = [2, 7, 10, 15, 25]
a.count{|x| x >= 10}
=> 3
```

We need to implement our own version of Ruby's count method called my_count. In this IRB console session we only focus on specifying what needs to be done. The details of counting, such as how many elements are in the list to be counted, when we need to terminate the loop, and so on, have been hidden inside the count method. As you already know, what needs to be done is the focus of the problem domain analysis.

Solution Domain Analysis

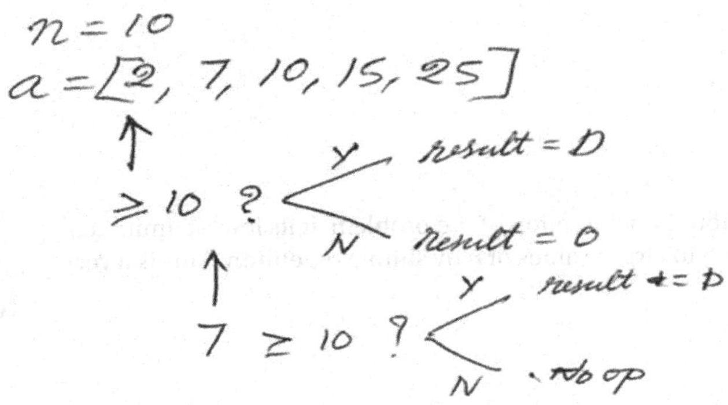

Figure 3-10. *Visual sketch of the counter problem-solving process*

Steps to Solve the Problem

```
while < n numbers have been examined do
# 1. Read the number
# 2. If current number satisfies the condition, then add one to count.
end
```

Algorithm

1. Read the number of elements to be processed.

2. Initialize the count to 0.

3. While there are still elements to be processed, repeatedly do the following:

    a. Read the number.

    b. If it satisfies the condition (>=10) then add one to count.

4. Return the total number of elements that satisfy the condition.

Logical Design

1. Read n and the array.

2. Take the first element in the array.

3. Check if element $x >= n$.

    a. If yes, then increment counter.

4. Go to the next element.

Skeleton Code

```
count = 0
i = 0

while i < n do

end
```

Terminating Condition

The condition i $==$ n is the terminating condition. Consideration of the problem at its lowest limit (i.e., $n = 0$) leads to a mechanism that can be extended to larger values of n by simple repetition. This is a very common technique in algorithm design.

Initial Condition

```
index = 0
count = 0
```

Pseudo Code

```
while index < (size of array - 1)
  extract the element from the array
  compare --> increment counter if yes
end
return count
```

Test-Driven Counter

Create a new test file, test_my_count.rb. The first test is the minimum we have to do to quickly add a new test.

```
require 'minitest/autorun'

describe MyCounter do
  it 'should return 0 for n = 0 and an empty list' do
```

```
    counter = MyCounter.new
    result = counter.count(0, [])
    assert_equal 0, result
  end
end
```

The minimal production code to make the test fail for the right reason is as follows:

```
class MyCounter
  def count(n, list)

  end
end
```

The failure message is Expected 0, Actual nil. The quick and dirty way to make this test pass is to return 0.

```
class MyCounter
  def count(n, list)
    0
  end
end
```

Add the second test, with one element in the list.

```
it 'should return 1 for 0, [0]' do
  counter = MyCounter.new
  result = counter.count(0, [0])
  assert_equal 1, result
end
```

This test fails with the failure message Expected 1, Actual 0. The quickest way to make both tests pass is to use an if-else statement.

```
class MyCounter
  def count(n, list)
    if list.include? n
      1
    else
      0
    end
  end
end
```

Add another test that is the negative test of the second test. The test is for the condition when the given number is not found in the list.

```
it 'should return 0 for 1, [0]' do
  counter = MyCounter.new
  result = counter.count(1, [0])
  assert_equal 0, result
end
```

This test passes without any modification to the production code because the `include?` method returns false, so the `else` part returns 0. Add another test for a two-element positive case.

```
it 'should return 2 for element 1 in [1,1]' do
  counter = MyCounter.new
  result = counter.count(1, [1,1])
  assert_equal 2, result
end
```

This test fails with the failure message `Expected: 2, Actual: 1`. By referring to the algorithm we developed earlier and the skeleton code, we can stop writing stupid code and implement the real solution, as follows:

```
class MyCounter
  def count(n, list)
    count = 0
    index = 0

    while index < list.size
      if list[index] == n
        count += 1
      end
      index += 1
    end
    count
  end
end
```

All four tests pass now. If you forget to increment the index or use the wrong terminating condition, your program will just hang. Add the following acceptance test.

```
it "should return 5 for element 3 in list [1,1,2,3,4,3,6,6,1]" do
  counter = MyCounter.new
  result = counter.count(3, [1,1,2,3,4,3,6,6,1])
  assert_equal 5, result
end
```

This test fails gloriously with the error message `Expected 5, Actual 2`. This test has exposed a bug in our code. By inspecting our solution, we see that the `if` condition is wrong. Change the `==` to `>=` in the `if` condition as follows:

```
if list[index] >= n
```

The code evolved from:

No code at all	➤ Returning nil
Returning nil	➤ Returning a constant
Returning a constant	➤ If-else condition
If-else condition	➤ While loop

The while programming construct is more generic than if-else. if-else is more generic than returning a constant, and so on. We see that the code became more generic as our tests became more specific. Refactoring changes the structure without changing the behavior. Transformation is change in the behavior with the least change in the structure. This forces us to write minimal code to pass the current test. Transformation and refactoring are two sides of the same coin. Red to Green is transformation. Green to Green is refactoring. The Transformation Priority Premise is not a silver bullet. It's a work in progress. Designing algorithms to solve a given problem and drawing flow charts will always help you write complex programs.

Factorial

Let's look at another example to illustrate the Transformation Priority Principle. Create a test file called test_factorial.rb with a TestFactorial class that extends from the Minitest test and we will define a method called test_zero_factorial_is_one. We invoke the calculate class method on Factorial class and pass in 0 as the argument. We expect the result to be 1. The Factorial class has a class method called calculate that takes a number as its argument.

```ruby
require 'minitest/autorun'

class Factorial
  def self.calculate(n)

  end
end

class TestFactorial < Minitest::Test
  def test_zero_factorial_is_one
    result = Factorial.calculate(0)
    assert_equal 1, result
  end
end
```

Run the test. We get the failure message Expected 1, actual nil. The simplest way to get this working is to hard code 1.

```ruby
class Factorial
  def self.calculate(n)
    1
  end
end
```

The test now will pass. Let's add the second test, test_one_factorial_is_one. In this case, the calculate method takes 1 as the argument, and we assert the result should be 1.

```ruby
  def test_one_factorial_is_one
    result = Factorial.calculate(1)
    assert_equal 1, result
  end
```

Run the test again, since the hard-coded value handles the second case also, it passes. Let's add the third test, test_two_factorial_is_two. In this case the calculate method takes 2 as the parameter, and we expect the result to be 2.

```
def test_two_factorial_is_two
  result = Factorial.calculate(2)
  assert_equal 2, result
end
```

Run the test. It fails with the failure message Expected 2, actual 1. Now this test is forcing us to add real implementation. So, if n < 2, we can just return the hard-coded value, else we will return n times calculate(n - 1), which is a recursive solution.

```
class Factorial
  def self.calculate(n)
    if n < 2
      1
    else
      n * calculate(n-1)
    end
  end
end
```

Run the test; it will pass. Let's add the fourth test, test_three_factorial_is_six. In this case, the calculate method will take 3, and we expect the result to be 6.

```
def test_three_factorial_is_six
  result = Factorial.calculate(3)
  assert_equal 6, result
end
```

Run the test; it will pass. Now we can change the recursive solution to an iterative solution. We will initialize the result to 1, and we will iterate 2 all the way up to *n*. We will multiply all the numbers with the initial value of the result equal to 1, and we will return the result.

```
class Factorial
  def self.calculate(n)
    result = 1
    2.upto(n) {|x| result *= x }
    result
  end
end
```

Run the test; it will pass. So, we were able to change the algorithm without breaking the tests. We have four tests, and that seems to be sufficient to prove that this works.

Let's look back at factorial kata and see how we used the Transformation Priority Premise. Initially, we had no code at all in the calculate method. It was just an empty method. We got the failure message Expected 1, got nil. By default, Ruby returns nil as the return value for an empty method. So, we never had to change our empty method to return nil explicitly.

```ruby
class Factorial
  def self.calculate(n)

  end
end
```

We then hard-coded the return value to 1 to get past that message and get the boundary condition working.

```ruby
class Factorial
  def self.calculate(n)
    1
  end
end
```

Then, we had an if-else statement that split the execution path and used recursion.

```ruby
class Factorial
  def self.calculate(n)
    if n < 2
      1
    else
      n * calculate(n-1)
    end
  end
end
```

These two transformations are lower on the transformation priority list. Going from no code at all to returning a hard-coded value is on the top of the transformation priority list. So, when you want to make the code generic, it's always challenging to pick things that are on the top of the list. By challenging yourself you can always figure out an easier test to write, and then you can gradually increase the complexity that will solve the problem, and you will get to a generic solution.

Next, the code evolved into a non-recursive solution that used iteration where we were using looping. That looping actually accumulated the result of multiplying all the numbers up to a given number.

```ruby
class Factorial
  def self.calculate(n)
    result = 1
    2.upto(n) {|x| result *= x }
    result
  end
end
```

We can compare the performance of the iterative and the recursive solutions of the Factorial by using the Minitest benchmark.

```ruby
require 'minitest/autorun'
require 'minitest/benchmark'

class IterativeFactorial
  def self.calculate(n)
    result = 1
    2.upto(n) {|x| result *= x }
```

151

```
    result
  end
end

class RecursiveFactorial
  def self.calculate(n)
    if n < 2
      1
    else
      n * calculate(n-1)
    end
  end
end

class TestFactorial < Minitest::Benchmark
  def bench_iterative_factorial
    assert_performance_linear 0.99 do |n|
      n.times { IterativeFactorial.calculate(20) }
    end
  end

  def bench_recursive_factorial
    assert_performance_linear 0.99 do |n|
      n.times { RecursiveFactorial.calculate(20) }
    end
  end
end
```

The output of the test shows the running times for each execution of the code under test.

```
Run options: --seed 5705
# Running:
bench_iterative_
factorial       0.000014    0.000021    0.000151    0.001323    0.011552
bench_recursive_
factorial       0.000015    0.000013    0.000102    0.001000    0.010138
Finished in 0.047717s, 41.9140 runs/s, 41.9140 assertions/s.
2 runs, 2 assertions, 0 failures, 0 errors, 0 skips
```

Summary

In this chapter, we discussed Obvious Implementation, Fake It Till You Make It, Triangulation, Reduction, and the Transformation Priority Premise. We worked through the GCD, Counter, and Factorial kata to illustrate the Transformation Priority Premise and Reduction process to solve problems.

CHAPTER 4

■ ■ ■

Importance of Test Cases

This chapter will cover the importance of designing test cases before writing tests. We will see what happens when we don't have test cases in the right sequence. We will work through reversing the digits of an integer kata to illustrate the importance of test cases. This problem uses the Reduction process. Reduction was covered in the previous chapter.

Problem Statement

Reverse the order of the digits of a given positive integer.

Problem Domain Analysis

Table 4-1 shows example input and output for transforming the given integer to its reverse.

Table 4-1. *Reverse of a Given Integer*

Input	Output
79815	51897

Solution Domain Analysis

The given number can be expressed as shown in Figure 4-1.

$$79815 = 7 \times 10^4 + 9 \times 10^3 + 8 \times 10^2 + 1 \times 10^1 + 5 \times 10^0$$

Figure 4-1. *Expressing the integer in a expanded form*

© Bala Paranj 2017
B. Paranj, *Test Driven Development in Ruby*, DOI 10.1007/978-1-4842-2638-4_4

To extract the rightmost digit, we can divide the given number by 10, as shown in Figure 4-2.

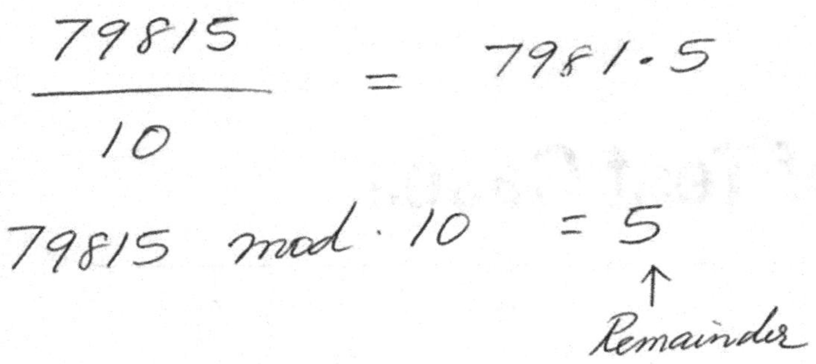

$$\frac{79815}{10} = 7981 \cdot 5$$

$$79815 \; mod \cdot 10 \; = 5$$

Remainder

Figure 4-2. Extracting the rightmost digit of the integer

Let's experiment in the IRB console.

```
$irb
> 79815 / 10
=> 7981
> 79815 / 10.0
=> 7981.5
```

We can extract the digit programmatically by using the modulo operator, like this:

```
> 79815 % 10
=> 5
```

After we extract the rightmost digit, we need to reduce the original number to a number without the rightmost digit so that we can extract the next digit. To accomplish this, we can divide the number by 10. Figure 4-3 shows the steps for reversing the given number, 79815.

Number to Reverse	Reversed Number	Step
79815	5	1
7981	51	2
798	518	3
79	5189	4
7	51897	5

Figure 4-3. *Steps in reversing a given integer*

To extract 5, we must transform 5 x 10*0 to get the reversed number 5 (5 times ten to the power of 0 is 5). To extract 51, we must transform 5 x 10 + 1 to get the reversed number 51 (five times ten plus one is 51). To extract 518, we must transform 51 x 10 + 8 to get the reversed number 518. From these examples, we can generalize the steps as follows:

```
reversed number = (previous reverse value) x 10 + (recently extracted digit)
```

Figure 4-4 shows the visual representation of the process of reversing a given integer.

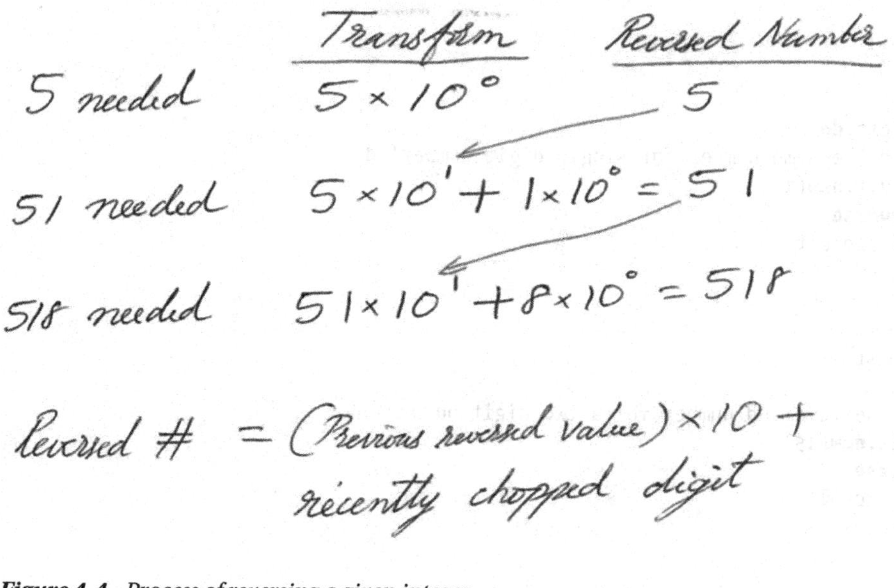

Figure 4-4. *Process of reversing a given integer*

Algorithm Description

We can now create a general outline of our algorithm.

```
while there are still digits in the number to be reversed, do
  1. Extract the rightmost digit from the number.
  2. Append this digit to right-hand end of the reversed number.
  3. Remove the rightmost digit from number.
end
```

Terminating condition is that the last number divided by 10 becomes 0.

```
while n > 0
 Do steps 1, 2 and 3.
end
```

Code

We are now going to skip the designing test cases step and jump into writing tests. We will see what happens when we skip this important step for non-trivial problems. The first test and the simple implementation are shown.

```
require 'minitest/autorun'

class ReverseDigit
  def initialize(n)
    @n = n
  end

  def reverse
    @n
  end
end

describe ReverseDigit do
  it 'should return the same number for single digit number' do
    rd = ReverseDigit.new(1)
    result = rd.reverse
    assert_equal 1, result
  end
end
```

Add the second test.

```
it 'should return the reversed number for a two-digit number' do
  rd = ReverseDigit.new(15)
  result = rd.reverse
  assert_equal 51, result
end
```

This fails. Let's experiment in the IRB console to see how we can tackle the two-digit number case.

```
>   x = 15
=> 15
> x / 10
=> 1
> x
=> 15
> x % 10
=> 5
> 1 % 10
=> 1
> 2 % 10
=> 2
> 3 % 10
=> 3
> 4 % 10
=> 4
> 5 % 10
=> 5
> 6 % 10
=> 6
> 7 % 10
=> 7
> 8 % 10
=> 8
> 9 % 10
=> 9
> 10 % 10
=> 0
> 15 % 10
=> 5
```

Change the reverse method implementation as follows:

```ruby
def reverse
  if @n % 10 == @n
    result = @n
  else
    d = @n % 10
    result = 5
    while (@n / 10) > 0
      result = (result * 10) + (@n / 10)
      @n = @n / 10
    end
  end
  result
end
```

This results in both tests passing. After referring to our algorithm and playing in the IRB console, here is the refactored solution that passes both tests:

```ruby
def reverse
  result = @n % 10
  while (@n / 10) > 0
    result = (result * 10) + (@n / 10)
    @n = @n / 10
  end
  result
end
```

Add the story test.

```ruby
it 'should return 51897 for 79815' do
  rd = ReverseDigit.new(79815)
  result = rd.reverse
  assert_equal 51897, result
end
```

It fails. What went wrong with our implementation? We took big steps. We were in red for a long time. This is because we did not have test cases that we could use as references when we wrote the tests. If we had designed the test cases that gradually increased in complexity, we would not have written the acceptance test as the third test. Let's step back and see if we can write some tests to extract the rightmost digit of any given number. Replace the existing code with the following code:

```ruby
require 'minitest/autorun'


class ReverseDigit
  def initialize(n)
    @n = n
  end

  def reverse
    return @n if @n < 10
  end

  def extract_rightmost_digit
    @n % 10
  end
end

describe ReverseDigit do
  it 'should return the same number for single digit number' do
    rd = ReverseDigit.new(1)
    result = rd.reverse
    assert_equal 1, result
  end
```

```
it 'should extract rightmost digit' do
  rd = ReverseDigit.new(1)
  result = rd.extract_rightmost_digit
  assert_equal 1, result
end

it 'should extract rightmost digit for two digit numbers' do
  rd = ReverseDigit.new(15)
  result = rd.extract_rightmost_digit
  assert_equal 5, result
end

it 'should extract rightmost digit for three digit numbers' do
  rd = ReverseDigit.new(158)
  result = rd.extract_rightmost_digit
  assert_equal 8, result
end
end
```

We can now extract the rightmost digit for any given number. Let's add the test to reverse a two-digit number.

```
it 'should return the reversed number for a two-digit number' do
  rd = ReverseDigit.new(15)
  result = rd.reverse
  assert_equal 51, result
end
```

The following implementation for reverse will make this test pass:

```
def reverse
  return @n if @n < 10
  while (@n / 10) > 0
    extracted_digit = extract_rightmost_digit
    @n = @n / 10
    reversed_digit = extracted_digit * 10 + extract_rightmost_digit
  end
  reversed_digit
end
```

Let's refactor to replace the conditional that handles the boundary case.

```
def reverse
  reversed_digit = @n
  while (@n / 10) > 0
    extracted_digit = extract_rightmost_digit
    @n = @n / 10
    reversed_digit = extracted_digit * 10 + extract_rightmost_digit
  end
  reversed_digit
end
```

Let's now handle a three-digit case.

```
it 'should return 897 for 798' do
  rd = ReverseDigit.new(798)
  result = rd.reverse
  assert_equal 897, result
end
```

The implementation that passes this test is shown here:

```
def reverse
  reversed_digit = extract_rightmost_digit * 1

  while (@n / 10) > 0
    extracted_digit = extract_rightmost_digit
    @n = @n / 10
    reversed_digit = reversed_digit * 10 + extract_rightmost_digit
  end
  reversed_digit
end
```

Let's add the story test that handles the four-digit case.

```
it 'should return 51897 for 79815' do
  rd = ReverseDigit.new(79815)
  result = rd.reverse
  assert_equal 51897, result
end
```

This test passes without any modification to the production code. We needed tests for extracting the rightmost digit of any given number before we tackled the story test. We would not have missed these tests if we had designed the test cases before coding. Sometimes developers forget or are overconfident about their ability to solve the problem, so they do not create a list of test cases before they start writing tests. It does not have to be a perfect list; it can be updated and the sequence reordered as we learn more about the problem. The test case list could be as simple as writing a few pending tests based on your initial understanding of the solution.

The following listing shows the refactored solution. The tests related to extracting the rightmost digit have been deleted.

```
require 'minitest/autorun'

class ReverseDigit
  def initialize(n)
    @n = n
  end

  def reverse
    reversed_digit = extract_rightmost_digit

    while digits_remain_to_be_reversed?
      remove_rightmost_digit
      reversed_digit = reversed_digit * 10 + extract_rightmost_digit
    end
```

```ruby
      reversed_digit
    end

    private

    def extract_rightmost_digit
      @n % 10
    end

    def remove_rightmost_digit
      @n = @n / 10
    end

    def digits_remain_to_be_reversed?
      (@n / 10) > 0
    end
end

describe ReverseDigit do
    it 'should return the same number for single digit number' do
      rd = ReverseDigit.new(1)
      result = rd.reverse
      assert_equal 1, result
    end

    it 'should return the reversed number for a two-digit number' do
      rd = ReverseDigit.new(15)
      result = rd.reverse
      assert_equal 51, result
    end

    it 'should return 897 for 798' do
      rd = ReverseDigit.new(798)
      result = rd.reverse
      assert_equal 897, result
    end

    it 'should return 51897 for 79815' do
      rd = ReverseDigit.new(79815)
      result = rd.reverse
      assert_equal 51897, result
    end
end
```

We can refactor the solution to make the loop idiomatic Ruby.

```ruby
class ReverseDigit
  def initialize(n)
    @n = n
  end
```

```ruby
def reverse
  reversed_digit = extract_rightmost_digit

  until all_digits_reversed?
    remove_rightmost_digit
    reversed_digit = reversed_digit * 10 + extract_rightmost_digit
  end
  reversed_digit
end

private

def extract_rightmost_digit
  @n % 10
end

def remove_rightmost_digit
  @n = @n / 10
end

def all_digits_reversed?
  (@n / 10) == 0
end
end
```

Summary

In this chapter, we skipped the designing test cases step and got into problematic situations. You should design a sequence of test cases that gradually increases in complexity before jumping into writing tests. This is important for non-trivial problems. Test cases do not have to be perfect in order to start writing the tests. You can update them as you learn more about the solution while working through the problem. This will minimize dead-end situations during your TDD session.

CHAPTER 5

Character-to-Number Conversion

In this chapter, we will see what happens when we don't have an algorithm to guide the implementation of the solution during the TDD session.

Problem Statement

Convert the character representation of an integer to its decimal format.

Discussion

Computers can store data in bits (zeroes and ones), which are numbers that can be converted to decimal, octal, etc. They cannot store letters or other special symbols. ASCII character encoding allows computers to store letters, text, symbols, and control characters.

Solution Domain Analysis

Let's convert the four-character sequence '1984' to the decimal number 1984. Figure 5-1 shows the characters and their ASCII-equivalent values.

© Bala Paranj 2017
B. Paranj, *Test Driven Development in Ruby*, DOI 10.1007/978-1-4842-2638-4_5

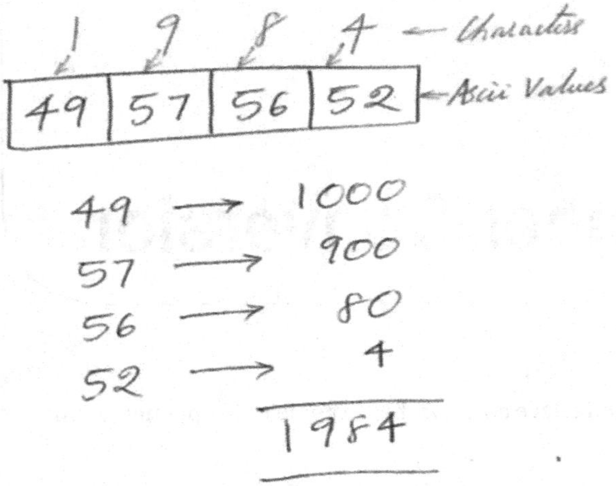

Figure 5-1. Mapping characters to ASCII values and adding them to get the final result

To do this, 49 needs to be converted to 1000, 57 to 900, 56 to 80, and 52 to 4 units. To get the decimal digit, we have to subtract 48 (ASCII value of character '0') from each of the ASCII values for the four given characters. To convert the one-character string to its decimal representation in ASCII, we can use the ord() method of the String class in Ruby. Playing in the IRB, we get the following:

```
> '0'.ord
=> 48
> '1'.ord
=> 49
> '9'.ord
=> 57
> '8'.ord
=> 56
> '4'.ord
=> 52
```

These numbers correspond to values you will find in the ASCII table. For our problem:

```
First number  = 49 - 48 = 1
Second number = 57 - 48 = 9
Third number  = 56 - 48 = 8
Fourth number = 52 - 48 = 4
```

The shifting to the left mechanism can be obtained at each step by multiplying the previous decimal value by 10 and adding it to current decimal digit. Figure 5-2 illustrates the mechanism for shifting to the left to construct the number.

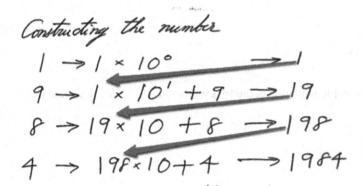

Figure 5-2. Shifting to the left to construct the result

Test Cases

We can list the test cases from the simplest to the most complicated as follows:

```
it "should convert '0' to 0"
it "should convert '1' to 1"
it "should convert '10' to 10"
it "should convert '100' to 100"
it "should convert '1000' to 1000"
```

The test cases are ordered by increasing level of difficulty. The data set is lowest to test that the solution works for any number. We are not using 1984 in the test data, but our solution should be generic enough to handle it.

```
require 'minitest/autorun'

class CharacterConverter
  def initialize(n)
    @n = n
  end

  def to_i
    @n.to_i
  end
end

describe CharacterConverter do
  it "should convert '0' to 0" do
    cc = CharacterConverter.new('0')
    result = cc.to_i
    assert_equal 0, result
  end
```

```
  it "should convert '1' to 1"
  it "should convert '10' to 10"
  it "should convert '100' to 100"
  it "should convert '1000' to 1000"
end
```

The first test passes with the simple implementation of the to_i method. Let's tackle the second test.

```
it "should convert '10' to 10" do
  cc = CharacterConverter.new('10')
  result = cc.to_i
  assert_equal 10, result
end
```

This test passes without any change to the production code. Let's add the story test.

```
it "should convert '1984' to 1984" do
  cc = CharacterConverter.new('1984')
  result = cc.to_i
  assert_equal 1984, result
end
```

This test also passes without any modification to the production code.

We don't want to use Ruby's built-in to_i method for the conversion. We want to develop our own implementation that is similar to the to_i method in Ruby. Let's not call the to_i method on the String object. Instead, we will use the ord method we discussed earlier.

```
def to_i
  '0'.ord - @n.ord
end
```

This passes only the first test. Let's add the second test from our test case list.

```
it "should convert '10' to 10" do
  cc = CharacterConverter.new('10')
  result = cc.to_i
  assert_equal 10, result
end
```

This test fails. There is gap in our problem domain analysis. We have not thought about how many digits there are in a given string, so we don't know when to terminate. If you read the Ruby documentation for the bytes method, you will see that it solves this problem for us. We can extract the ASCII code for each character using this method by playing in the IRB console.

```
> n = '1984'
> n.bytes
=> [49, 57, 56, 52]
```

We can now use this in our implementation to make the first three test cases pass.

```ruby
class CharacterConverter
  def initialize(n)
    @n = n
    @numbers = n.bytes
  end

  def to_i
    first_element = @numbers.shift
    first_number = (first_element.ord - '0'.ord)

    if @numbers.size > 0
      next_element = @numbers.shift
      next_number = (next_element.ord - '0'.ord)
      puts 'inside if'
      first_number * 10 + next_number
    else
      puts 'hi'
      first_number
    end
  end
end

describe CharacterConverter do
  it "should convert '0' to 0" do
    cc = CharacterConverter.new('0')
    result = cc.to_i
    assert_equal 0, result
  end

  it "should convert '1' to 1" do
    cc = CharacterConverter.new('1')
    result = cc.to_i
    assert_equal 1, result
  end

  it "should convert '10' to 10" do
    cc = CharacterConverter.new('10')
    result = cc.to_i
    assert_equal 10, result
  end
end
```

This implementation passes all three tests. I had to add puts statements in order to evolve the logic to get the tests passing. The puts statement is the simplest debugging tool. Why do we need a debugger when we are using TDD? The test was forcing the code to evolve quickly, so I had to see what was happening. Adding an assertion to check the code is another alternative. However, the implementation details cannot be exposed to the test, so I used the print statements. This was necessary because I did not have an algorithm as a guide for my code. I had to come up with the solution by trial and error. Now, add the story test.

```ruby
it "should convert '1984' to 1984" do
  cc = CharacterConverter.new('1984')
  result = cc.to_i
  assert_equal 1984, result
end
```

The story test fails. Let's take a step back. Make the failing test pending for now. Let's refactor to get the code ready to be generalized. The cleaned-up implementation of to_i is shown next.

```ruby
def to_i
  first_element = @numbers.shift
  first_number = (first_element.ord - '0'.ord)
  result = first_number

  if @numbers.size > 0
    next_element = @numbers.shift
    next_number = (next_element.ord - '0'.ord)
    result = first_number * 10 + next_number
  end
  result
end
```

Uncomment the story test, and it will fail. Let's change the implementation to make it pass.

```ruby
def to_i
  first_element = @numbers.shift
  first_number = (first_element.ord - '0'.ord)

  previous_number = first_number
  while @numbers.size > 0
    next_element = @numbers.shift
    next_number = (next_element.ord - '0'.ord)
    previous_number = previous_number * 10 + next_number
  end
  previous_number
end
```

The story test passes. This is a 1-2-3 punch; BOOM here is the solution example. In order to arrive at this solution, you must know how to apply the Reduction process, the terminating condition, and the initial condition that we discussed in previous chapters 2, 3 and 4. Let's now refactor this solution.

```ruby
class CharacterConverter
  def initialize(n)
    @n = n
    @numbers = n.bytes
  end

  def to_i
    first_element = @numbers.shift
    first_number = ascii_value(first_element)

    previous_number = first_number
    while not_complete?
```

```ruby
      next_element = @numbers.shift
      next_number = ascii_value(next_element)
      previous_number = previous_number * 10 + next_number
    end
    previous_number
  end

  private

  def ascii_value(n)
    n.ord - '0'.ord
  end

  def not_complete?
    @numbers.size > 0
  end
end
```

We can make the loop idiomatic, as shown in the following solution.

```ruby
class CharacterConverter
  def initialize(n)
    @n = n
    @numbers = n.bytes
  end

  def to_i
    first_element = @numbers.shift
    first_number = ascii_value(first_element)

    previous_number = first_number
    until complete?
      next_element = @numbers.shift
      next_number = ascii_value(next_element)
      previous_number = previous_number * 10 + next_number
    end
    previous_number
  end

  private

  def ascii_value(n)
    n.ord - '0'.ord
  end

  def complete?
    !(@numbers.size > 0)
  end
end
```

Summary

In this chapter, we discussed the importance of the algorithm in guiding our TDD session. We ran into problems while solving the given problem when we did not have the guidance provided by a well-designed algorithm.

CHAPTER 6

■ ■ ■

Conway's Game of Life

This chapter will discuss how we can achieve a low semantic gap in the solution, thereby resulting in domain-rich code that communicates its intent clearly. We will see that dependencies must be semantically correct and only essential dependencies must be retained. We will also review some of the solutions available online to illustrate the fact that TDD does not magically result in good design. Developers are responsible for applying good design principles to create elegant and easy to understand solutions.

Problem Statement

Conway's Game of Life (CGOL) is a cellular automaton devised by the British mathematician John Horton Conway in 1970. It is essentially a mathematical model, and is the best-known example of a cellular automaton. It is a zero-player game, meaning that its evolution is determined by its initial state, requiring no further input. One interacts with the Game of Life by creating an initial configuration and observing how it evolves.

The universe of the Game of Life is an infinite, two-dimensional, orthogonal grid of square cells, each of which is in one of two possible states, live or dead. Each cell has eight neighbors: three above, one on either side, and three below. The rules of CGOL simply govern the state of the cell in question as it relates to the state of its neighbor cells. At each step in time, the following transitions occur:

- Any live cell with fewer than two live neighbors dies, as if caused by underpopulation.

- Any live cell with more than three live neighbors dies, as if by overcrowding.

- Any live cell with two or three live neighbors lives on to the next generation.

- Any dead cell with exactly three live neighbors becomes a live cell.

The initial pattern constitutes the seed of the system. The first generation is created by applying the preceding rules simultaneously to every cell in the seed. Births and deaths happen simultaneously, and the discrete moment at which this happens is sometimes called a *tick*. In other words, each generation is a pure function of the one before. The rules continue to be applied repeatedly to create further generations. Assume cells beyond the boundary are always dead.

Problem Domain Analysis

A cell C is represented by a 1 when alive or 0 when dead, and is located in an m x m square array of cells. We calculate N–the sum of live cells in C's eight-location neighborhood. Cell C is alive or dead in the next generation based on the data in Table 6-1.

© Bala Paranj 2017
B. Paranj, *Test Driven Development in Ruby*, DOI 10.1007/978-1-4842-2638-4_6

Table 6-1. *Cell State Transition Table*

Current Cell State	Number of Live Neighbors	New Cell State	
1	0, 1	0	Lonely
1	4, 5, 6, 7, 8	0	Overcrowded
1	2, 3	1	Lives
0	3	1	Birth
0	0, 1, 2, 4, 5, 6, 7, 8	0	Barren

In this table, the first column represents the current cell state. The values in each cell represent the next cell state that depends on the number of live neighbors. Table 6-2 shows the state machine representation of the rules. State machine is a mathematical model of computation used primarily for designing algorithms and electronic circuits. Figure 6-1 shows the state machine representation of the transitions that occur between alive and dead states of a cell. There are two self-transitions and transitions for alive to dead and vice-versa.

Table 6-2. *Cell State Transition Table in a Different Format Dipicting Number of Live Neighbors vs. Cell State*

Current Cell State	Number of Live Neighbors								
C(t)	8	7	6	5	4	3	2	1	0
0	0	0	0	0	0	1	0	0	0
1	0	0	0	0	0	1	1	0	0

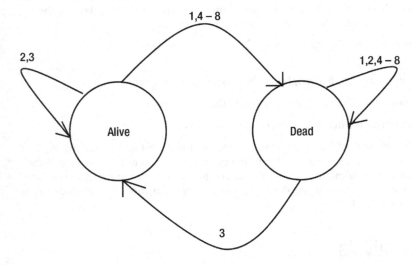

Figure 6-1. *State machine representation of the cell transitions depends on number of live neighbors*

Figure 6-2 shows that there is a hidden no-op that represents a dead cell that remains dead when the number of neighbors is not 3.

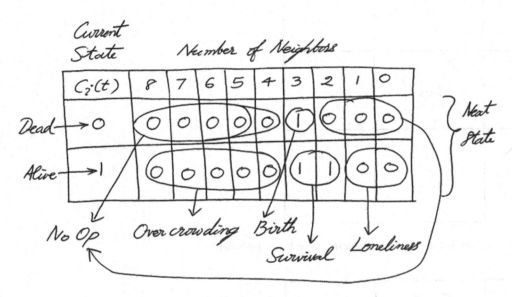

Figure 6-2. *State machine table identified with different scenarios*

Assuming the cell is alive, we can also represent the next-state values in columns, as shown in Table 6-3.

Table 6-3. *Cell State Transition for a Given Number of Live Neighbors*

0 – 1	2	3	4 – 8
Die	Stay Alive	Birth	Die

We don't need all three different representations. Their utility is in understanding the problem. They are also useful in answering the question: What happens to an alive cell in the next generation? Figures 6-3, 6-4, 6-5, and 6-6 represent the rules in a visual format using a specific number of cells. The dark cell is the focus of these diagrams. Each location in the diagram can either have a cell that is alive or dead, or it can be empty. The empty locations are not occupied by any cells, regardless of the cell state.

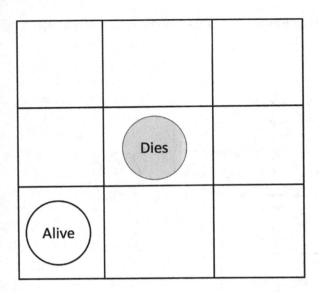

Figure 6-3. *Isolation: Any live cell with fewer than two live neighbors dies*

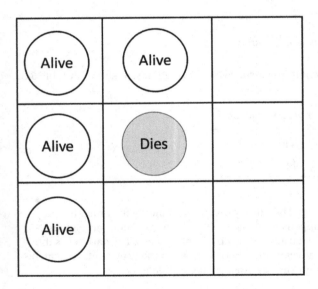

Figure 6-4. *Overcrowding: Any live cell with more than three live neighbors dies*

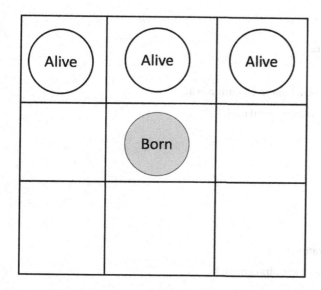

Figure 6-5. Birth: Any dead cell with exactly three live neighbors is reborn

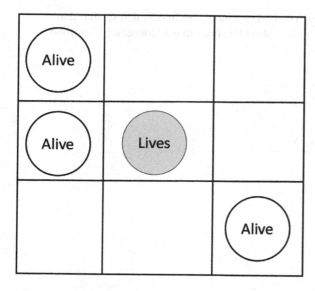

Figure 6-6. Survival: Any live cell with two or three live neighbors stays alive

Assumptions

We will make the following simplifying assumptions:

1.   The grid size is 3 by 3.

2.   Number of generations over which to observe the evolution is 3.

This means we don't have to worry about the infinite-sized grid.

Solution Domain Analysis

We need to answer questions such as:

- Where does the `tick` method belong?

- How should we represent the grid?

- How should we initialize the configuration?

- Who is responsible for applying the rules simultaneously?

Moore Neighborhood

The Moore Neighborhood is composed of nine cells: a central cell and the eight cells that surround it. Table 6-4 shows the 3 x 3 grid. Figure 6-7 shows the names of the locations in the Moore Neighborhood.

Table 6-4. *Moore Neighborhood and the Coordinates*

x - 1, y + 1	x, y + 1	x + 1, y + 1
x - 1, y	x, y	x + 1, y
x - 1, y - 1	x, y - 1	x + 1, y - 1

North West	North	North East
West	Center	East
South West	South	South East

Figure 6-7. Moore Neighborhood and the directions

We can fill the Moore Neighborhood with 0s and 1s randomly. This is called the seed. The tick method probably belongs to the game class. We will revisit and evaluate whether it is the right decision when we develop the game.

Test Cases

Let's quickly jot down the sequence of test cases that we can use as a starting point to start coding the solution. This list will change based on our understanding as we develop the game.

- A 3 x 3 grid with no alive cells will contain no alive cells in the next generation.
- A 3 x 3 grid with one alive cell will die in the next generation.
- A 3 x 3 grid with two live cells will stay alive in the next generation.

This list is directly derived from Figure 9-3, which we came up with in the section on problem domain analysis. We can add more to this list by referring back to Figure 9-3 to cover all the scenarios.

Test-Driven Game of Life

We are now ready to develop Conway's Game of Life driven by tests. Create a file called test_game_of_ life.rb with a test for the first test case and empty implementations for tick and alive_cells in the NeighborHood class.

```
require 'minitest/autorun'

class NeighborHood
  def tick
  end
```

```
    def alive_cells
    end
end

describe NeighborHood do
  it 'neighborhood with no alive cells will contain no alive cells in the next generation'
do
      neighborhood  = NeighborHood.new
      neighborhood.tick

      alive_cells = neighborhood.alive_cells

      assert_equal 0, alive_cells
  end
end
```

This test fails for the right reason. We make it pass by returning 0 in the `alive_cells` method.

The next test is written by imagining that the code we want to accomplish in the second test case already exists. We create a cell at the center location and use this to seed a new neighborhood. We then invoke `tick` as before and check that the number of alive cells in the next generation is 0. The assumption here is that when we create a cell at any given location, it will be alive by default.

```
it 'neighborhood with one alive cell will die in the next generation' do
  cell = Cell.new(0,0)
  neighborhood = NeighborHood.new
  neighborhood.seed(cell)

  neighborhood.tick

  assert_equal 0, neighborhood.alive_cells
end
```

This test fails. We have a dependency on the Cell object, which does not exist yet. We can mark this test as pending by using the `skip` method and then write a new test that documents the assumption about the cell object.

```
it 'neighborhood with one alive cell will die in the next generation' do
  skip
  cell = Cell.new(0,0)
  neighborhood = NeighborHood.new
  neighborhood.seed(cell)

  neighborhood.tick

  assert_equal 0, neighborhood.alive_cells
end
```

Create a `test_cell.rb` file with a test for the cell to document the assumption. The contents of `test_cell.rb` are as follows:

```ruby
require 'minitest/autorun'


class Cell
  def initialize(x, y)
  end
  def alive?
    true
  end
end

describe Cell do
  it 'is alive when it is created' do
    cell = Cell.new(0,0)

    assert cell.alive?
  end
end
```

The test passes. While we are at it, let's add the second test to check if the cell can transition to a dead state in `test_cell.rb`.

```ruby
it 'can transition to dead state' do
  cell = Cell.new(0, 0)
  cell.die
  refute cell.alive?
end
```

The simplest implementation that will pass both tests is shown here:

```ruby
class Cell
  def initialize(x, y)
    @alive = true
  end

  def alive?
    @alive == true
  end

  def die
    @alive = false
  end
end
```

We are not doing anything related to the coordinates yet. We do know that a cell will reside in a particular location. So, the constructor expects the values for the coordinates. Move the Cell class from `test_cell.rb` to its own file, `cell.rb`. Include `require_relative 'cell'` at the top of the `test_cell.rb` and test_game_of_life.rb files. Define an empty seed method in the NeighborHood class in the test_game_of_life.rb file that takes cell as an argument.

```
def seed(cell)
end
```

We can now run the pending test 'neighborhood with one alive cell will die in the next generation' in test_game_of_life.rb. It will pass.

Let's now tackle the third test case, which we find needs to be more precise: In a 3 x 3 grid neighborhood, a cell with two alive cells as neighbors will stay alive in the next generation. The concept of neighbors was missing in the third test case. We know which cells are neighbors by looking at the figure 6-6. We can pick any two cells who are neighboring to each other for the test by referring that diagram. The figure 6-8 shows the diagram modified for the case of two alive neighbor cells.

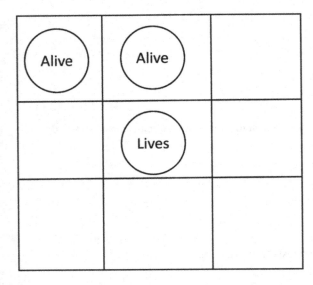

Figure 6-8. Survival: Any live cell with two live neighbors stays alive

Add the following test to test_game_of_life.rb.

```
it 'neighborhood with two alive cells as neighbors will stay alive in the next generation'
do
    c1 = Cell.new(0,0)
    c2 = Cell.new(0,1)
    c3 = Cell.new(-1,1)

    neighborhood = NeighborHood.new
    neighborhood.seed([c2,c3])

    neighborhood.tick

    assert_equal 2, neighborhood.alive_cells
end
```

180

This test fails for the right reason. Notice that we changed the signature for the seed method. We did this because we need to be able to seed the neighborhood with multiple cells. So, mark the failing test as pending and let's prepare our existing solution to be ready for real implementation. The following solution gets the code ready, and the first two tests still pass.

```
class NeighborHood
  def initialize
    @grid = []
  end

  def tick
  end

  def alive_cells
    0
  end

  def seed(cells)
    @grid = cells
  end
end
```

The second test, 'neighborhood with one alive cell will die in the next generation', is not passing in the cell in an array. Modify the seed method argument to an array that contains a cell.

```
it 'neighborhood with one alive cell will die in the next generation' do
  cell = Cell.new(0,0)
  neighborhood = NeighborHood.new
  neighborhood.seed([cell])

  neighborhood.tick

  assert_equal 0, neighborhood.alive_cells
end
```

Run the tests; the first two will still pass. We can now replace the bogus implementation for alive_cells with the real implementation.

```
def alive_cells
  @grid.size
end
```

The second test, 'neighborhood with one alive cell will die in the next generation', fails for the right reason. We don't have a real implementation for tick method yet. The tick method needs to update the neighbors count based on the rules we have already discussed. Let's play Devil's Advocate and do the minimal thing to pass the test. Provide a minimal implementation for the tick method in the NeighborHood class.

```
def tick
  @grid.clear
end
```

This implementation is obviously wrong, but it will make the first two tests pass. If we now run the third test, 'neighborhood with two alive cells as neighbors will stay alive in the next generation', it still fails. Mark this test as pending for now.

We now need to write a test for calculating the neighbors, and we need to document what we mean by neighbors in the test. In test_game_of_life.rb, add the following test:

```
it 'two cells are neighbors if they are next to each other' do
  c1 = Cell.new(0,0)
  c2 = Cell.new(0,1)
  neighborhood = NeighborHood.new
  result = neighborhood.neighbors?(c1, c2)

  assert result
end
```

We have two cells. The first one is at the center, and the second one is above the center cell. You can refer to Figure 6-9 to help you visualize the locations of these two cells.

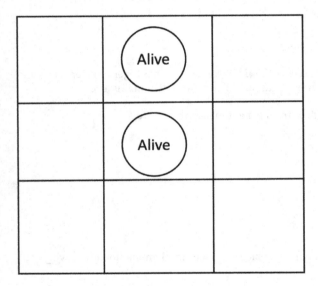

Figure 6-9. *Two live cells as neighbors*

Just by looking at this diagram, we can infer that the cell located in the center is adjacent to all the other cells surrounding it. We can use this insight and implement a simple method that works to make this test pass. Add the neighbors? method to the NeighborHood class.

```
def neighbors?(cell1, cell2)
  if cell1.center? or cell2.center?
    true
  end
end
```

We don't have the center? method implemented in cell.rb yet. So, we will add a test for the center? method in the test_cell.rb file.

```
it 'knows if it is in the center' do
  cell = Cell.new(0, 0)

  assert cell.center?
end
```

Change the constructor of the Cell class to use the co-ordinates and implement center? method as shown below:

```
class Cell
  def initialize(x, y)
    @alive = true
    @x = x
    @y = y
  end

  def center?
    (@x == 0 and @y == 0)
  end
  # alive? and die methods are same as before
end
```

All the tests in test_cell.rb will now pass. The test 'two cells are neighbors if they are next to each other' in the test_game_of_life.rb will also pass. We can now remove the skip statement in the 'neighborhood with two alive cells as neighbors will stay alive in the next generation' test. It will fail. Change the tick method in the NeighborHood class as follows:

```
def tick
  if @grid.size > 1
  else
    @grid.clear
  end
end
```

Now all four tests will pass. Moore's Neighborhood consists of eight directions, as shown in Figure 6-7. If you consider any given cell to be in a location (x,y), we can check if there is a live neighbor in any of the eight locations surrounding it. Therefore, this solution extends to an infinite grid. It is time for us to change our tests based on our understanding of the system. We can delete the 'two cells are neighbors if they are next to each other' test. We can also delete the neighbors? method in the NeighborHood class. The test

```
it 'neighborhood with two alive cells as neigbors will stay alive in the next generation'
```

needs to be updated by expressing the requirement correctly. We must count the number of neighbors for a given cell, not the number of live cells in a neighborhood. It is not intuitive to be providing the numbers as the arguments to the constructor to specify the location. It is better if we specify the location as the direction. The following is a list of neighbors for a given location in a 3 x 3 grid:

```
NorthWest : North, Center, West
NorthEast : North, Center, East
```

```
SouthWest : West, Center, South
SouthEast : East, Center, South
Center: Has everyone as its neighbors
North: NorthWest, Center, NorthEast, West, East
South: SouthWest, SouthEast, Center, East, West
East: NorthEast, SouthEast, Center, North, South
West: NorthWest, North, Center, South, SouthWest
```

We will use this as our test case list later. We can pick any of the above dataset and populate it with as many live cells as we want. Each direction has a specific coordinate, as follows:

```
NorthWest located at (-1, 1)
NorthEast  located at (1, 1)
SouthWest located at (-1, -1)
SouthEast  located at (1, -1)
Center located at (0, 0)
North located at (0, 1)
South located at (0, -1)
East located at (1, 0)
West located at (-1, 0)
```

We no longer need to map the (x,y) coordinates to a particular location in our mind. We can write a test to document this fact. Create test_location.rb with the following code:

```ruby
require 'minitest/autorun'

class Location
  NORTHWEST = [-1, 1]
end

describe Location do
  it 'NorthWest is located at (-1, 1)' do
    assert_equal [-1, 1], Location::NORTHWEST
  end
end
```

Similarly, we can document all the locations. The complete code listing is shown next. The location.rb file is as follows:

```ruby
class Location
  NORTHWEST = [-1, 1]
  NORTHEAST = [1, 1]
  SOUTHWEST = [-1, -1]
  SOUTHEAST = [1, -1]
  CENTER    = [0, 0]
  NORTH     = [0, 1]
  SOUTH     = [0, -1]
  EAST      = [1, 0]
  WEST      = [-1, 0]
end
```

The test_location.rb is as follows:

```
require 'minitest/autorun'
require_relative 'location'

describe Location do
  it 'NorthWest is located at (-1, 1)' do
    assert_equal [-1, 1], Location::NORTHWEST
  end
  it 'NorthEast is located at (1, 1)' do
    assert_equal [1, 1], Location::NORTHEAST
  end
  it 'SouthWest is located at (-1, -1)' do
    assert_equal [-1, -1], Location::SOUTHWEST
  end
  it 'SouthEast is located at (1, -1)' do
    assert_equal [1, -1], Location::SOUTHEAST
  end
  it 'Center is located at (0, 0)' do
    assert_equal [0, 0], Location::CENTER
  end
  it 'North is located at (0, 1)' do
    assert_equal [0, 1], Location::NORTH
  end
  it 'South is located at (0, -1)' do
    assert_equal [0, -1], Location::SOUTH
  end
  it 'East is located at (1, 0)' do
    assert_equal [1, 0], Location::EAST
  end
  it 'West is located at (-1, 0)' do
    assert_equal [-1, 0], Location::WEST
  end
end
```

We can now delete the 'knows if it is in the center' test from test_cell.rb. We can also delete the corresponding method center? in cell.rb, as we no longer need it.

Let's now make the constructor of the cell take the location instead of x and y values. In test_cell.rb, modify the existing tests in test_cell.rb as follows:

```
require 'minitest/autorun'
require_relative 'cell'
require_relative 'location'

describe Cell do
  it 'is alive when it is created' do
    cell = Cell.new(Location::CENTER)

    assert cell.alive?
  end
```

```
  it 'can transition to dead state' do
    cell = Cell.new(Location::CENTER)
    cell.die
    refute cell.alive?
  end
end
```

To make the updated tests pass, change the constructor of the Cell class in cell.rb as follows:

```
def initialize(location)
  @alive = true
  @x = location[0]
  @y = location[1]
end
```

Now the two updated tests in test_cell.rb will pass. We can now change the following two tests in the test_game_of_life.rb file to use the new cell constructor.

```
it 'neighborhood with one alive cell will die in the next generation' do
  cell = Cell.new(Location::CENTER)
  neighborhood = NeighborHood.new
  neighborhood.seed([cell])

  neighborhood.tick

  assert_equal 0, neighborhood.alive_cells
end
```

```
it 'a cell with two alive cells as neighbors will stay alive in the next generation' do
  c1 = Cell.new(Location::CENTER)
  c2 = Cell.new(Location::NORTH)
  c3 = Cell.new(Location::SOUTH)
  neighborhood = NeighborHood.new
  neighborhood.seed([c1,c2, c3])

  neighborhood.tick

  assert c1.alive?
end
```

Notice that the test 'a cell with two alive cells as neighbors will stay alive in the next generation' now passes all three cells in the array as the argument to the seed method. The assertion has also changed from counting the number of live cells to checking if the first cell is still alive. We are making the cell we are focusing on explicit in the assertion step. Add require_relative 'location' to the top of the test_game_of_life.rb file. All of the tests in test_game_of_life.rb will now pass.

Let's now look at the pseudo code to see what we want to accomplish.

```
if (cell is dead) AND (number-of-neighbors is 3)
    # new cell is born
    set cell alive
if (cell is alive) AND (number-of-neighbors is 2 OR 3)
```

186

```
        # Leave the cell alive
        nothing to do
if (cell is alive AND (number-of-neighbors is NOT 2 OR 3)
        # lonely or over-crowded cells die
        set cell dead
if (cell is dead) AND (number-of-neighbors is NOT 3)
        # leave cell dead
        nothing to do
```

We need to calculate the number of neighbors for a given cell before we can implement the tick method in a correct way. Let's write a test to calculate the number of neighbors for a cell that does not have any neighbors. Add the following test to test_game_of_life.rb:

```
it 'number of neighbors is 0 for a cell that is lonely' do
  c1 = Cell.new(Location::CENTER)
  neighborhood = NeighborHood.new
  neighborhood.seed([c1])

  assert_equal 0, neighborhood.number_of_neighbors_for(c1)
end
```

Add a fake implementation for the number_of_neighbors_for method in the NeighborHood class.

```
def number_of_neighbors_for(cell)
  0

end
```

The test will now pass.

Let's write the next test for the calculation of the number of neighbors. Add the following test to test_game_of_life.rb:

```
it 'number of neighbors is 1 for a cell that has a neighbor in north' do
  c1 = Cell.new(Location::CENTER)
  c2 = Cell.new(Location::NORTH)
  neighborhood = NeighborHood.new
  neighborhood.seed([c1, c2])

  assert_equal 1, neighborhood.number_of_neighbors_for(c1)
end
```

If there is a cell north of this cell, then we will return 1; otherwise, 0. In the NeighborHood class, implement the number_of_neighbors_for method as follows:

```
def number_of_neighbors_for(cell)
  north_cell = @grid.detect {|cell| cell.location == Location::NORTH}
  if north_cell
    1
  else
    0
  end
end
```

This will fail because we don't have the location method in cell.rb. Add the test for this in test_cell.rb:

```
it 'has a location' do
  cell = Cell.new(Location::NORTH)
  result = cell.location

  assert_equal Location::NORTH, result
end
```

We can delegate the call to the for class method to the Location class. Add the location method in cell.rb.

```
def location
  Location.for(@x, @y)
end
```

This will fail because we have not implemented this method in the Location class yet. Write the test first in test_location.rb.

```
it 'location for 0, 1 is north' do
  location = Location.for(0, 1)

  assert_equal Location::NORTH, location
end
```

The following implementation in the Location class will pass this test.

```
def self.for(x, y)
  if x == 0 and y == 1
    NORTH
  end
end
```

Now all the tests for cell in test_cell.rb and the Game of Life in test_game_of_life.rb will pass. We must handle all the locations for the for() class method in the Location class. We can write similar tests in test_location.rb as follows:

```
it 'location for -1, 1 is north west' do
  location = Location.for(-1, 1)

  assert_equal Location::NORTHWEST, location
end
it 'location for 1, 1 is north east' do
  location = Location.for(1, 1)

  assert_equal Location::NORTHEAST, location
end
it 'location for -1, -1 is south west' do
  location = Location.for(-1, -1)
```

```
    assert_equal Location::SOUTHWEST, location
  end
  it 'location for 1, 1 is south east' do
    location = Location.for(1, -1)

    assert_equal Location::SOUTHEAST, location
  end
  it 'location for 0, 1 is north' do
    location = Location.for(0, 1)

    assert_equal Location::NORTH, location
  end
  it 'location for 0, -1 is south' do
    location = Location.for(0, -1)

    assert_equal Location::SOUTH, location
  end
  it 'location for 1, 0 is south' do
    location = Location.for(1, 0)

    assert_equal Location::EAST, location
  end
  it 'location for -1, 0 is south' do
    location = Location.for(-1, 0)

    assert_equal Location::WEST, location
  end
  it 'location for 0, 0 is center' do
    location = Location.for(0, 0)

    assert_equal Location::CENTER, location
  end
end
```

The for class method in the Location class now implements mapping for all the locations, as shown here:

```
def self.for(x, y)
  if x == 0 and y == 1
    NORTH
  elsif x == 0 and y == -1
    SOUTH
  elsif x == 1 and y == 0
    EAST
  elsif x == -1 and y == 0
    WEST
  elsif x == 0 and y == 0
    CENTER
  elsif x == -1 and y == 1
    NORTHWEST
  elsif x == 1 and y == 1
    NORTHEAST
```

```
  elsif x == 1 and y == -1
    SOUTHEAST
  elsif x == -1 and y == -1
    SOUTHWEST
  end
end
```

Let's add the test to `test_game_of_life.rb` for a cell that has two neighbors.

```
it 'number of neighbors is 2 for a cell that has a neighbor in north and south' do
  c1 = Cell.new(Location::CENTER)
  c2 = Cell.new(Location::NORTH)
  c3 = Cell.new(Location::SOUTH)
  neighborhood = NeighborHood.new
  neighborhood.seed([c1, c2, c3])

  assert_equal 2, neighborhood.number_of_neighbors_for(c1)
end
```

We can make this test pass by modifying the `number_of_neighbors_for` method in the `NeighborHood` class, as follows:

```
def number_of_neighbors_for(cell)
  size = 0
  north_cell = @grid.detect {|c| c.location == Location::NORTH}
  south_cell = @grid.detect {|c| c.location == Location::SOUTH}

  if north_cell
    size += 1
  end
  if south_cell
    size += 1
  end
  size
end
```

Obviously, this solution will only work if the cell is at the center. Let's write a test to expose this bug.

```
it 'number of neighbors is 2 for a north west cell that has a neighbor in north and west' do
  c1 = Cell.new(Location::NORTHWEST)
  c2 = Cell.new(Location::NORTH)
  c3 = Cell.new(Location::WEST)
  neighborhood = NeighborHood.new
  neighborhood.seed([c1, c2, c3])

  assert_equal 2, neighborhood.number_of_neighbors_for(c1)
end
```

The following quick and dirty implementation for the number_of_neighbors_for method in the NeighborHood class will pass this test.

```
def number_of_neighbors_for(cell)
  size = 0
  if cell.location == Location::CENTER
    north_cell = @grid.detect {|c| c.location == Location::NORTH}
    south_cell = @grid.detect {|c| c.location == Location::SOUTH}

    if north_cell
      size += 1
    end
    if south_cell
      size += 1
    end
  elsif cell.location == Location::NORTHWEST
    north_cell = @grid.detect {|c| c.location == Location::NORTH}
    west_cell = @grid.detect {|c| c.location == Location::WEST}

    if north_cell
      size += 1
    end
    if west_cell
      size += 1
    end
  end
  size
end
```

It's time to refactor this method. The code that follows shows only the refactored methods.

```
class NeighborHood

  def number_of_neighbors_for(cell)
    size = 0
    if cell.location == Location::CENTER
      size += count_north_cell
      size += count_south_cell
    elsif cell.location == Location::NORTHWEST
      size += count_north_cell
      size += count_west_cell
    end
    size
  end

  private

  def find_cell(location)
    @grid.detect {|c| c.location == location}
  end
```

```ruby
  def count_north_cell
    count_cell(find_cell(Location::NORTH))
  end

  def count_south_cell
    count_cell(find_cell(Location::SOUTH))
  end

  def count_west_cell
    count_cell(find_cell(Location::WEST))
  end

  def count_cell(predicate)
    if predicate
      1
    else
      0
    end
  end
end
```

Let's write a test to expose the bug for the case when a cell is in the center, it has eight neighbors.

```ruby
it 'number of neighbors is 8 for a center cell that has a neighbor in all locations' do
  c1 = Cell.new(Location::CENTER)
  c2 = Cell.new(Location::NORTH)
  c3 = Cell.new(Location::SOUTH)
  c4 = Cell.new(Location::EAST)
  c5 = Cell.new(Location::WEST)
  c6 = Cell.new(Location::NORTHWEST)
  c7 = Cell.new(Location::NORTHEAST)
  c8 = Cell.new(Location::SOUTHWEST)
  c9 = Cell.new(Location::SOUTHEAST)

  neighborhood = NeighborHood.new
  neighborhood.seed([c1, c2, c3, c4, c5, c6, c7, c8, c9])

  assert_equal 8, neighborhood.number_of_neighbors_for(c1)
end
```

The following implementation of the NeighborHood class makes this test pass.

```ruby
class NeighborHood
  def initialize
    @grid = []
  end
  def tick
    if @grid.size > 1
    else
      @grid.clear
    end
```

```
  end
def alive_cells
  @grid.size
end
def seed(cells)
  @grid = cells
end
def number_of_neighbors_for(cell)
  size = 0
  if cell.location == Location::CENTER
    size += count_north_cell
    size += count_south_cell
    size += count_east_cell
    size += count_west_cell
    size += count_northwest_cell
    size += count_northeast_cell
    size += count_southwest_cell
    size += count_southeast_cell
  elsif cell.location == Location::NORTHWEST
    size += count_north_cell
    size += count_west_cell
  end
  size
end

private

def find_cell(location)
  @grid.detect {|c| c.location == location}
end
def count_north_cell
  count_cell(find_cell(Location::NORTH))
end
def count_south_cell
  count_cell(find_cell(Location::SOUTH))
end
def count_east_cell
  count_cell(find_cell(Location::EAST))
end
def count_west_cell
  count_cell(find_cell(Location::WEST))
end
def count_northwest_cell
  count_cell(find_cell(Location::NORTHWEST))
end
def count_southwest_cell
  count_cell(find_cell(Location::SOUTHWEST))
end
def count_northeast_cell
  count_cell(find_cell(Location::NORTHEAST))
end
```

```ruby
  def count_southeast_cell
    count_cell(find_cell(Location::SOUTHEAST))
  end
  def count_cell(predicate)
    if predicate
      1
    else
      0
    end
  end
end
```

Let's add the following test in `test_game_of_life.rb`:

```ruby
it 'number of neighbors is 3 for a north west cell that has a neighbor in north, west and
center' do
  c1 = Cell.new(Location::NORTHWEST)
  c2 = Cell.new(Location::NORTH)
  c3 = Cell.new(Location::WEST)
  c4 = Cell.new(Location::CENTER)
  neighborhood = NeighborHood.new
  neighborhood.seed([c1, c2, c3, c4])

  assert_equal 3, neighborhood.number_of_neighbors_for(c1)
end
```

We need to add the counting of the center cell for the northwest location conditional in the NeighborHood class.

```ruby
def number_of_neighbors_for(cell)
  size = 0
  if cell.location == Location::CENTER
    # Code same as before
  elsif cell.location == Location::NORTHWEST
    size += count_north_cell
    size += count_west_cell
    size += count_center_cell
  end
  size
end
```

We also need to add the `count_center_cell` private method to the NeighborHood class.

```ruby
def count_center_cell
  count_cell(find_cell(Location::CENTER))
end
```

The test will now pass. Add the following test to `test_game_of_life.rb`.

```ruby
it 'number of neighbors is 3 for a north east cell that has a neighbor in north, east and
center' do
  c1 = Cell.new(Location::NORTHEAST)
  c2 = Cell.new(Location::NORTH)
  c3 = Cell.new(Location::EAST)
  c4 = Cell.new(Location::CENTER)
  neighborhood = NeighborHood.new
  neighborhood.seed([c1, c2, c3, c4])

  assert_equal 3, neighborhood.number_of_neighbors_for(c1)
end
```

Change the `number_of_neighbors_for` method to handle the northeast case.

```ruby
def number_of_neighbors_for(cell)
  size = 0
  if cell.location == Location::CENTER
    # Code same as before
  elsif cell.location == Location::NORTHWEST
    # Code same as before
  elsif cell.location == Location::NORTHEAST
    size += count_north_cell
    size += count_east_cell
    size += count_center_cell
  end
  size
end
```

The test will now pass. Similarly, here is the test for southwest:

```ruby
it 'number of neighbors is 3 for a south west cell that has a neighbor in east, center and
south' do
  c1 = Cell.new(Location::SOUTHWEST)
  c2 = Cell.new(Location::SOUTH)
  c3 = Cell.new(Location::WEST)
  c4 = Cell.new(Location::CENTER)
  neighborhood = NeighborHood.new
  neighborhood.seed([c1, c2, c3, c4])

  assert_equal 3, neighborhood.number_of_neighbors_for(c1)
end
```

This will pass with the following implementation:

```ruby
def number_of_neighbors_for(cell)
  size = 0
  if cell.location == Location::CENTER
    # Code same as before
  elsif cell.location == Location::NORTHWEST
```

```ruby
  # Code same as before
  elsif cell.location == Location::NORTHEAST
  # Code same as before
  elsif cell.location == Location::SOUTHWEST
    size += count_south_cell
    size += count_west_cell
    size += count_center_cell
  end
  size
end
```

Similarly, we can implement the calculating of the number of neighbors for other cases. The refactored solution is shown here:

```ruby
class NeighborHood
  def initialize
    @grid = []
  end

  def number_of_neighbors_for(cell)
    size = 0
    if cell.location == Location::CENTER
      size = calculate_neighbors_for_center_cell
    elsif cell.location == Location::NORTHWEST
      size = calculate_neighbors_for_northwest_cell
    elsif cell.location == Location::NORTHEAST
      size = calculate_neighbors_for_northeast_cell
    elsif cell.location == Location::SOUTHWEST
      size = calculate_neighbors_for_southwest_cell
    elsif cell.location == Location::SOUTHEAST
      size = calculate_neighbors_for_southeast_cell
    elsif cell.location == Location::NORTH
      size = calculate_neighbors_for_north_cell
    elsif cell.location == Location::SOUTH
      size = calculate_neighbors_for_south_cell
    elsif cell.location == Location::EAST
      size = calculate_neighbors_for_east_cell
    elsif cell.location == Location::WEST
      size = calculate_neighbors_for_west_cell
    end
    size
  end

  private

  def find_cell(location)
    @grid.detect {|c| c.location == location}
  end
```

```ruby
def count_center_cell
  count_cell(find_cell(Location::CENTER))
end

def count_north_cell
  count_cell(find_cell(Location::NORTH))
end

def count_south_cell
  count_cell(find_cell(Location::SOUTH))
end

def count_east_cell
  count_cell(find_cell(Location::EAST))
end

def count_west_cell
  count_cell(find_cell(Location::WEST))
end

def count_northwest_cell
  count_cell(find_cell(Location::NORTHWEST))
end

def count_southwest_cell
  count_cell(find_cell(Location::SOUTHWEST))
end

def count_northeast_cell
  count_cell(find_cell(Location::NORTHEAST))
end

def count_southeast_cell
  count_cell(find_cell(Location::SOUTHEAST))
end

def count_cell(predicate)
  if predicate
    1
  else
    0
  end
end

def calculate_neighbors_for_center_cell
  size = 0
  size += count_north_cell
  size += count_south_cell
  size += count_east_cell
  size += count_west_cell
  size += count_northwest_cell
```

```
    size += count_northeast_cell
    size += count_southwest_cell
    size += count_southeast_cell
    size
  end

  def calculate_neighbors_for_northwest_cell
    size = 0
    size += count_north_cell
    size += count_west_cell
    size += count_center_cell
    size
  end

  def calculate_neighbors_for_northeast_cell
    size = 0
    size += count_north_cell
    size += count_east_cell
    size += count_center_cell
    size
  end

  def calculate_neighbors_for_southwest_cell
    size = 0
    size += count_south_cell
    size += count_west_cell
    size += count_center_cell
    size
  end

  def calculate_neighbors_for_southeast_cell
    size  = 0
    size += count_south_cell
    size += count_east_cell
    size += count_center_cell
    size
  end

  def calculate_neighbors_for_north_cell
    size = 0
    size += count_northwest_cell
    size += count_center_cell
    size += count_northeast_cell
    size += count_west_cell
    size += count_east_cell
    size
  end

  def calculate_neighbors_for_south_cell
    size = 0
    size += count_southwest_cell
```

```
      size += count_center_cell
      size += count_southeast_cell
      size += count_west_cell
      size += count_east_cell
      size
    end

    def calculate_neighbors_for_east_cell
      size = 0
      size += count_northeast_cell
      size += count_center_cell
      size += count_southeast_cell
      size += count_north_cell
      size += count_south_cell
      size
    end

    def calculate_neighbors_for_west_cell
      size = 0
      size += count_northwest_cell
      size += count_center_cell
      size += count_southwest_cell
      size += count_north_cell
      size += count_south_cell
      size
    end
end
```

The tick, alive_cells, and seed method implementations remain the same and are not shown in the preceding code. All the tests will still pass. We can write a test for overcrowding. Add the following test to test_game_of_life.rb.

```
it 'a cell with 4 alive cells will die of overcrowding' do
  c1 = Cell.new(Location::CENTER)
  c2 = Cell.new(Location::NORTH)
  c3 = Cell.new(Location::NORTHWEST)
  c4 = Cell.new(Location::WEST)
  c5 = Cell.new(Location::SOUTHWEST)
  neighborhood = NeighborHood.new
  neighborhood.seed([c1, c2, c3, c4, c5])

  neighborhood.tick

  assert c1.dead?
end
```

Now the tick method can handle the overcrowded condition, as follows:

```
def tick
  if @grid.size > 1
    @grid.each do |cell|
```

```
      neighbors_count = number_of_neighbors_for(cell)
      if neighbors_count != 2 or neighbors_count == 3
        cell.die
      end
    end
  else
    @grid.clear
  end
end
```

We also need the dead? method in the Cell class in cell.rb, which negates the alive? method to make this test pass.

```
def dead?
  !alive?
end
```

Delete the first test, 'neighborhood with no alive cells will contain no alive cells in the next generation'. It is no longer required. Delete the alive_cells method in the NeighborHood class. Modify the test 'neighborhood with one alive cell will die in the next generation' as follows:

```
it 'neighborhood with one alive cell will die in the next generation' do
  cell = Cell.new(Location::CENTER)
  c2 = Cell.new(Location::NORTH)
  neighborhood = NeighborHood.new
  neighborhood.seed([cell, c2])

  neighborhood.tick

  assert cell.dead?, 'Cell is still alive'
end
```

This test will pass with the existing implementation. Let's now write a test for the birth scenario.

```
it 'a dead cell with three alive cells as neighbors will be born in the next generation' do
  c1 = Cell.new(Location::CENTER)
  c1.die
  c2 = Cell.new(Location::NORTH)
  c3 = Cell.new(Location::NORTHWEST)
  c4 = Cell.new(Location::NORTHEAST)
  neighborhood = NeighborHood.new
  neighborhood.seed([c1, c2, c3, c4])

  neighborhood.tick

  assert c1.alive?
end
```

This test will fail. Let's implement the functionality for reproduction.

```
def tick
  if @grid.size > 1
    @grid.each do |cell|
      neighbors_count = number_of_neighbors_for(cell)
      if neighbors_count != 2 or neighbors_count == 3
        cell.die
      end
      if cell.dead? and neighbors_count == 3
        cell.born
      end
    end
  else
    @grid.clear
  end
end
```

This requires a born method in cell.rb.

```
def born
  @alive = true
end
```

Now the tests will pass. We can refactor the tick method to make it intention-revealing.

```
def tick
  if @grid.size > 1
    @grid.each do |cell|
      lonely_or_over_crowed_cells_die(cell)
      reproduction_of(cell)
    end
  else
    @grid.clear
  end
end
```

The private methods are as follows:

```
def lonely_or_over_crowed_cells_die(cell)
  neighbors_count = number_of_neighbors_for(cell)
  if neighbors_count != 2 or neighbors_count == 3
    cell.die
  end
end
```

```
def reproduction_of(cell)
  neighbors_count = number_of_neighbors_for(cell)
  if cell.dead? and neighbors_count == 3
    cell.born
  end
end
```

You can run the tests now, and they will still pass. We can write a test for the scenario where a cell has three alive cells as its neighbors, and thus it stays alive in the next generation. See the following:

```
it 'a cell with three alive cells as neighbors will stay alive in the next generation' do
  c1 = Cell.new(Location::CENTER)
  c2 = Cell.new(Location::NORTH)
  c3 = Cell.new(Location::SOUTH)
  c4 = Cell.new(Location::EAST)
  neighborhood = NeighborHood.new
  neighborhood.seed([c1, c2, c3, c4])

  neighborhood.tick

  assert c1.alive?
end
```

This test passes without any modification to the production code. The following code shows the tests for the cell, test_cell.rb. It is reproduced here to show how the born method was implemented. It is separate so as to minimize distraction during the previous discussion of the test_game_of_life.rb.

```
require 'minitest/autorun'
require_relative 'cell'
require_relative 'location'

describe Cell do
  it 'is alive when it is created' do
    cell = Cell.new(Location::CENTER)

    assert cell.alive?
  end
  it 'can transition to dead state' do
    cell = Cell.new(Location::CENTER)
    cell.die
    refute cell.alive?
  end

  it 'has a location' do
    cell = Cell.new(Location::NORTH)
    result = cell.location

    assert_equal Location::NORTH, result
  end

  it 'dead cell can be born again' do
    cell = Cell.new(Location::CENTER)
    cell.die

    cell.born

    assert cell.alive?
  end
end
```

The code listing for the cell is shown here:

```
class Cell
  def initialize(location)
    @alive = true
    @x = location[0]
    @y = location[1]
  end

  def alive?
    @alive == true
  end

  def die
    @alive = false
  end

  def location
    Location.for(@x, @y)
  end

  def dead?
    !alive?
  end

  def born
    @alive = true
  end
end
```

The complete code listing of the NeighborHood class is shown next. It uses a switch-case statement to reduce the amount of code for the number_of_neighbors_for method. The tick method has been refactored to remove the unnecessary if-else condition.

```
class NeighborHood
  def initialize
    @grid = []
  end

  def tick
    @grid.each do |cell|
      lonely_or_over_crowded_cells_die(cell)
      reproduction_of(cell)
    end
  end

  def seed(cells)
    @grid = cells
  end
```

```ruby
def number_of_neighbors_for(cell)
  size = 0
  location = cell.location
  case location
  when Location::CENTER
    size = calculate_neighbors_for_center_cell
  when Location::NORTHWEST
    size = calculate_neighbors_for_northwest_cell
  when Location::NORTHEAST
    size = calculate_neighbors_for_northeast_cell
  when Location::SOUTHWEST
    size = calculate_neighbors_for_southwest_cell
  when Location::SOUTHEAST
    size = calculate_neighbors_for_southeast_cell
  when Location::NORTH
    size = calculate_neighbors_for_north_cell
  when Location::SOUTH
    size = calculate_neighbors_for_south_cell
  when Location::EAST
    size = calculate_neighbors_for_east_cell
  when Location::WEST
    size = calculate_neighbors_for_west_cell
  end
  size
end

private

def find_cell(location)
  @grid.detect {|c| c.location == location}
end

def count_center_cell
  count_cell(find_cell(Location::CENTER))
end

def count_north_cell
  count_cell(find_cell(Location::NORTH))
end

def count_south_cell
  count_cell(find_cell(Location::SOUTH))
end

def count_east_cell
  count_cell(find_cell(Location::EAST))
end

def count_west_cell
  count_cell(find_cell(Location::WEST))
end
```

```ruby
def count_northwest_cell
  count_cell(find_cell(Location::NORTHWEST))
end

def count_southwest_cell
  count_cell(find_cell(Location::SOUTHWEST))
end

def count_northeast_cell
  count_cell(find_cell(Location::NORTHEAST))
end

def count_southeast_cell
  count_cell(find_cell(Location::SOUTHEAST))
end

def count_cell(predicate)
  if predicate
    1
  else
    0
  end
end

def calculate_neighbors_for_center_cell
  size = 0
  size += count_north_cell
  size += count_south_cell
  size += count_east_cell
  size += count_west_cell
  size += count_northwest_cell
  size += count_northeast_cell
  size += count_southwest_cell
  size += count_southeast_cell
  size
end

def calculate_neighbors_for_northwest_cell
  size = 0
  size += count_north_cell
  size += count_west_cell
  size += count_center_cell
  size
end

def calculate_neighbors_for_northeast_cell
  size = 0
  size += count_north_cell
  size += count_east_cell
  size += count_center_cell
  size
end
```

```ruby
def calculate_neighbors_for_southwest_cell
  size = 0
  size += count_south_cell
  size += count_west_cell
  size += count_center_cell
  size
end

def calculate_neighbors_for_southeast_cell
  size  = 0
  size += count_south_cell
  size += count_east_cell
  size += count_center_cell
  size
end

def calculate_neighbors_for_north_cell
  size = 0
  size += count_northwest_cell
  size += count_center_cell
  size += count_northeast_cell
  size += count_west_cell
  size += count_east_cell
  size
end

def calculate_neighbors_for_south_cell
  size = 0
  size += count_southwest_cell
  size += count_center_cell
  size += count_southeast_cell
  size += count_west_cell
  size += count_east_cell
  size
end

def calculate_neighbors_for_east_cell
  size = 0
  size += count_northeast_cell
  size += count_center_cell
  size += count_southeast_cell
  size += count_north_cell
  size += count_south_cell
  size
end

def calculate_neighbors_for_west_cell
  size = 0
  size += count_northwest_cell
  size += count_center_cell
  size += count_southwest_cell
```

```ruby
    size += count_north_cell
    size += count_south_cell
    size
  end

  def lonely_or_over_crowded_cells_die(cell)
    neighbors_count = number_of_neighbors_for(cell)
    if neighbors_count != 2 or neighbors_count == 3
      cell.die
    end
  end

  def reproduction_of(cell)
    neighbors_count = number_of_neighbors_for(cell)
    if cell.dead? and neighbors_count == 3
      cell.born
    end
  end
end
```

We have an ugly switch-case statement in the NeighborHood class. Can we get rid of it? Can we reduce the amount of code used to calculate the number of neighbors? We can use the fact that, for any given cell, the coordinates can be added to any of the surrounding coordinates to find a neighboring cell at a given location. This can simplify the logic for finding a neighbor of a given cell. The refactored solution of the NeighborHood class is shown here:

```ruby
class NeighborHood
  def initialize
    @grid = []
  end

  def tick
    @grid.each do |cell|
      lonely_or_over_crowded_cells_die(cell)
      reproduction_of(cell)
    end
  end

  def seed(cells)
    @grid = cells
  end

  def number_of_neighbors_for(cell)
    size = 0
    size = count_cell(cell, Location::NORTHWEST, size)
    size = count_cell(cell, Location::NORTHEAST, size)
    size = count_cell(cell, Location::SOUTHWEST, size)
    size = count_cell(cell, Location::SOUTHEAST, size)
    size = count_cell(cell, Location::NORTH, size)
    size = count_cell(cell, Location::SOUTH, size)
```

```
      size = count_cell(cell, Location::EAST, size)
      size = count_cell(cell, Location::WEST, size)
      size
   end

   private

   def count_cell(original, direction, size)
      result = @grid.detect{|c| c.location == (Location.add(original.location, direction))}
      if result
         size += 1
      end
      size
   end

   def lonely_or_over_crowded_cells_die(cell)
      neighbors_count = number_of_neighbors_for(cell)
      if neighbors_count != 2 or neighbors_count == 3
         cell.die
      end
   end

   def reproduction_of(cell)
      neighbors_count = number_of_neighbors_for(cell)
      if cell.dead? and neighbors_count == 3
         cell.born
      end
   end
end
```

The refactored number_of_neighbors_for method now uses a private method called count_cell. This method adds the location of the cell for which we need to find a neighbor to a specific location, which is where we search for the existence of a neighbor. This is a good example to illustrate the usefulness of a Value Object like Location. In simple terms, you can think of Value Object as something like money. We have many dollar bills; however, they don't have a unique identity. Their value is the same. We can exchange a dollar bill with another without any issue about which dollar bill we can use to purchase something. This is not possible for an object like Person, which has unique identity, and we cannot exchange our Social Security number, which identifies us in a unique way.

We have a Location class that encapsulates the coordinates and behavior related to coordinates can be assigned to the Location class, such as adding two locations to return a location as the result. You can think of adding locations as adding an offset to a cell that is always in the center to find all its surrounding neighbors. This can be extended to a cell located anywhere in our grid. Note that adding two locations is not the same as adding two arrays. Adding any two two-element arrays will result in an array with four elements that combines the elements from the addend and augend. The add method in the Location class is implemented as follows:

```
def self.add(first, second)
   [first[0]+second[0], first[1]+second[1]]
end
```

The corresponding test is as follows.

```
it 'adding two locations returns a new location' do
  result = Location.add(Location::SOUTH, Location::CENTER)

  assert_equal Location::SOUTH, result
end
```

> *Where it fits, define an operation whose return type is the same as the type of its arguments. Such an operation is closed under the set of instances of that type. A closed operation provides a high-level interface without introducing any dependency on other concepts. This pattern is most often applied to the operations of a Value Object.*

> —Eric Evans, *Domain Driven Design*

We created a Location class to wrap the primitive integers that represented coordinates. We must find domain-specific types in our application to make it expressive. We can state the relationships between the concepts in our application as follows:

- A cell resides in a particular location.

- A neighborhood consists of a grid that can hold the cells for a given grid dimension.

A cell has a dependency on the location. The direction is from the cell to the location. The Location class does not depend on any other class. It is a self-contained and standalone class. It is specific to the CGOL application we have developed. Representing domain concepts using primitive data types is called *Primitive Obsession*. We used the Location class instead of using an integer to represent the concept of location.

The neighborhood depends on both the cell and location. It is responsible for calculating the number of neighbors for a given cell. Semantically, the dependency direction and the allocation of responsibilities to the classes makes sense. Writing tests as if the code already exists will not result in a good design if the developer does not allocate responsibilities to the appropriate classes.

> *Every dependency is suspect until proven basic to the concept behind the object. The goal is not to eliminate all dependencies, but to eliminate all nonessential ones.*

> —Eric Evans, *Domain Driven Design*

The seed and tick are abstractions that we found in the problem statement, and they directly carry over to the NeighborHood class as methods. We must be able to write a paragraph about the final solution that includes the relationships between the concepts and the story that connects the concepts in simple English without using any technical terms so that anyone with no coding background can understand.

Application Statement

A neighborhood consists of a grid that can contain eight cells. Each cell occupies a particular location in the grid. A cell can be either dead or alive. A new cell will be born if the number of neighbors are exactly three. A dead cell will become alive if the number of neighbors are exactly three. A cell will die if there are more than three neighbors. A cell will also die if there are one or no neighbors. A cell that has two neighbors will survive and move on to the next generation.

Figure 6-10 shows the concepts and how they are related to other concepts. Some of the concepts become objects, and some are data structures. The concept diagram must be semantically correct to create elegant designs. In our solution, the NeighborHood class has one array to represent a grid, and the cell has one instance variable to a particular location. The grid contains eight cells.

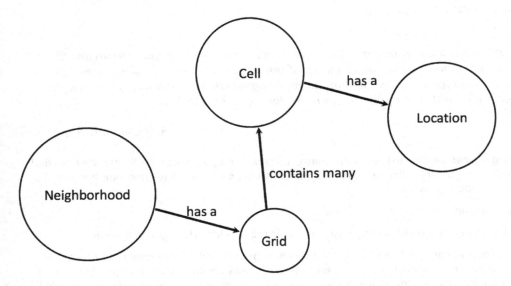

Figure 6-10. *Concepts connected by association to emphasize the dependency direction*

Refactor Solution

The refactoring step is a time to reflect on the design. Sometimes, we had to add skip to a test in the NeigborHood class and deal with dependent objects to test-drive their development. This happens when we think about the system from the outside. We discover the interfaces of the dependent classes we need just in time. In a real project, we would have to deal with a graph of objects just like we encountered in this kata. There is nothing wrong in marking a test as pending and test-driving the dependent objects.

Let's now refactor the number_of_neighbors_for method so as to use iteration.

```
def number_of_neighbors_for(cell)
  size = 0
  offsets = Location.all
  offsets.each do |offset|
    size = count_cell(cell, offset, size)
  end
  size
end
```

The all() class method in the Location class is implemented as follows:

```
def self.all
  [NORTHWEST, NORTHEAST, SOUTHWEST, SOUTHEAST, NORTH, SOUTH, EAST, WEST]
end
```

The tests will pass. Let's continue refactoring to clean up the private methods in the NeighborHood class. Update the count_cell private method and add a new find_neighbor_cell private method to the NeighborHood class.

```
def count_cell(original, offset, size)
  neighbor = find_neighbor_cell(original, offset)
  size += 1 if neighbor
  size
end

def find_neighbor_cell(original, offset)
  neighbor_location = Location.add(original.location, offset)
  @grid.detect{|cell| cell.at?(neighbor_location)}
end
```

The direction parameter has been renamed to offset. The detection of a neighbor cell has been moved from the count_cell method to the find_neighbor_cell method. Instead of asking for the location of a cell and manipulating the data to make a decision, why not ask the Cell class to perform a service that encapsulates the location data within the cell? That's what the new method at?(neighbor_location) of the Cell class does. It returns a boolean value to indicate the presence or absence of a cell in a given location. This method is implemented as shown next. It requires storing the location in an instance variable.

```
class Cell
  def initialize(location)
    @alive = true
    @location = location
  end
  def at?(location)
    @location == location
  end
end
```

The corresponding tests in test_cell.rb for the at? method are shown here:

```
it 'returns true if a cell is located in the specified location' do
  cell = Cell.new(Location::CENTER)
  result = cell.at?(Location::CENTER)

  assert result
end

it 'returns false if a cell is not located in the specified location' do
  cell = Cell.new(Location::CENTER)
  result = cell.at?(Location::NORTH)

  refute result
end
```

Delete the 'has a location' test in test_cell.rb and the location method in cell.rb. The tests for test_cell.rb will now pass. Add attr_reader :location to cell.rb. The tests in test_game_of_life.rb will now pass. Conceptually, there is a disconnect between the Location.all method and its implementation. This method does not return all the locations; it excludes the center location. Since this method does not have behavior, we can remove it and define an OFFSETS constant in the Location class. This makes it clear that we are storing the offsets. It can be used to find a neighbor of a cell located anywhere in the grid.

```ruby
class Location
  OFFSETS = [NORTHWEST, NORTHEAST, SOUTHWEST, SOUTHEAST, NORTH, SOUTH, EAST, WEST]
  # Rest of the code is same as before and is not shown here
end
```

The number_of_neighbors_for method in the NeighborHood class can now use this constant.

```ruby
def number_of_neighbors_for(cell)
  size = 0
  offsets = Location::OFFSETS
  offsets.each do |offset|
    size = count_cell(cell, offset, size)
  end
  size
end
```

The tests in test_game_of_life.rb will pass. We no longer need the for() class method that converted given coordinates to a location. The final Location class looks as shown here:

```ruby
class Location
  NORTHWEST = [-1, 1]
  NORTHEAST = [1, 1]
  SOUTHWEST = [-1, -1]
  SOUTHEAST = [1, -1]
  CENTER    = [0, 0]
  NORTH     = [0, 1]
  SOUTH     = [0, -1]
  EAST      = [1, 0]
  WEST      = [-1, 0]

  OFFSETS = [NORTHWEST, NORTHEAST, SOUTHWEST, SOUTHEAST, NORTH, SOUTH, EAST, WEST]

  def self.add(first, second)
    [first[0]+second[0], first[1]+second[1]]
  end
end
```

The corresponding tests in test_location.rb are shown here:

```ruby
require 'minitest/autorun'
require_relative 'location'

describe Location do
  it 'NorthWest is located at (-1, 1)' do
    assert_equal [-1, 1], Location::NORTHWEST
  end
```

```ruby
    # Similar tests is same as before and is not shown here

    it 'adding two locations returns a new location' do
      result = Location.add(Location::SOUTH, Location::CENTER)

      assert_equal Location::SOUTH, result
    end
    it 'returns a list of offsets for any cell' do
      offsets = Location::OFFSETS
      expected = [Location::NORTHWEST, Location::NORTHEAST,
        Location::SOUTHWEST, Location::SOUTHEAST, Location::NORTH,
        Location::SOUTH, Location::EAST, Location::WEST]

      assert_equal expected, offsets
    end
  end
end
```

We no longer have the tests for the for() method, since we no longer need that method. The final Cell class is shown here:

```ruby
class Cell
  attr_reader :location

  def initialize(location)
    @alive = true
    @location = location
  end

  def alive?
    @alive == true
  end

  def die
    @alive = false
  end

  def dead?
    !alive?
  end

  def born
    @alive = true
  end

  def at?(location)
    @location == location
  end
end
```

Take a look at the NeighborHood class and ask yourself the following questions:

- Is most of the methods operating on the same data?

- Are there too many private methods that are not operating on the instance variables of the object?

- Is there any hidden abstraction that can be made explicit by moving the private methods to a new class?

These are some of the questions that we ask ourselves to evaluate whether the NeighborHood class captures only one abstraction. By constantly revising our design decisions as the software grows, we don't let private methods grow in number and thus hide abstractions that can be extracted to a new class that can be tested separately. Collaborators can be difficult to find if we don't reflect on the resulting design during the refactoring step and at the end of the TDD session.

Code Review

This section will review three solutions to CGOL. It will be a quick tour, pointing out some of the things that can be improved upon.

> TDD does not drive towards good design, it drives away from a bad design. If you know what good design is, the result is a better design.

> —Nat Pryce, *Growing Object Oriented System Guided by Tests*

Let's first review the solution by Derek Barber found at https://github.com/derekbarber/game_of_life.

```
class Game
  attr_accessor :world, :seeds
  def initialize(world=World.new, seeds=[])
    @world = world
    seeds.each do |seed|
      @world.cell_grid[seed[0]][seed[1]].alive = true
    end
  end

  def tick!
    next_round_live_cells = []
    next_round_dead_cells = []

    @world.cells.each do |cell|
      neighbour_count = self.world.live_neighbours_around_cell(cell).count
      # Rule 1:
      # Any live cell with fewer than two live neighbors dies        if cell.alive? and
neighbour_count < 2
        next_round_dead_cells << cell
      end
      # Rule 2
      # Any live cell with two or three live neighbors lives on to the next generation
```

```ruby
      if cell.alive? and ([2, 3].include? neighbour_count)
        next_round_live_cells << cell
      end
      # Rule 3
      # Any live cell with more than three live neighbors dies        if cell.alive? and
neighbour_count > 3
        next_round_dead_cells << cell
      end
      # Rule 4
      # Any dead cell with exactly three live neighbors becomes a live cell
      if cell.dead? and neighbour_count == 3
        next_round_live_cells << cell
      end
    end

    next_round_live_cells.each do |cell|
      cell.revive!
    end
    next_round_dead_cells.each do |cell|
      cell.die!
    end
  end
end
```

The rules are documented as comments. It is better to extract the rules into small methods with names that describe the rules. Since our code becomes self-describing, we can delete the comments.

```ruby
class World
  attr_accessor :rows, :cols, :cell_grid, :cells

  def initialize(rows=3, cols=3)
    @rows = rows
    @cols = cols
    @cells = []

    @cell_grid = Array.new(rows) do |row|
      Array.new(cols) do |col|
        cell = Cell.new(col, row)
        cells << cell
        cell
      end
    end
  end

  def live_neighbours_around_cell(cell)
    live_neighbours = []
    # It detects a neighbour to the North
    if cell.y > 0
      candidate = self.cell_grid[cell.y - 1][cell.x]
      live_neighbours << candidate if candidate.alive?
    end
```

```ruby
    # It detects a neighbour to the North-East
    if cell.y > 0 && cell.x < (cols - 1)
      candidate = self.cell_grid[cell.y - 1][cell.x + 1]
      live_neighbours << candidate if candidate.alive?
    end
    # It detects a neighbour to the East
    if cell.x < (cols - 1)
      candidate = self.cell_grid[cell.y][cell.x + 1]
      live_neighbours << candidate if candidate.alive?
    end
    # It detects a neighbour to the South-East
    if cell.x < (cols - 1) && cell.y < (rows - 1)
      candidate = self.cell_grid[cell.y + 1][cell.x + 1]
      live_neighbours << candidate if candidate.alive?
    end
    # It detects a neighbour to the South
    if cell.y < (rows - 1)
      candidate = self.cell_grid[cell.y + 1][cell.x]
      live_neighbours << candidate if candidate.alive?
    end
    # It detects a neighbour to the South-West
    if cell.y < (rows - 1) && cell.x > 0
      candidate = self.cell_grid[cell.y + 1][cell.x - 1]
      live_neighbours << candidate if candidate.alive?
    end
    # It detects a neighbour to the West
    if cell.x > 0
      candidate = self.cell_grid[cell.y][cell.x - 1]
      live_neighbours << candidate if candidate.alive?
    end
    # It detects a neighbour to the North-West
    if cell.x > 0 && cell.y > 0
      candidate = self.cell_grid[cell.y - 1][cell.x - 1]
      live_neighbours << candidate if candidate.alive?
    end

    live_neighbours
  end

  def live_cells
    cells.select { |cell| cell.alive }
  end

  def randomly_populate
    cells.each do |cell|
      cell.alive = [true, false].sample
    end
  end
end
```

The same thing can be said about the live_neighbours_around_cell method in the World class. The neighbor-detection conditionals can be moved to small private methods with expressive names. This will make the comments redundant. The live_neighbours_around_cell method suffers from Primitive Obsession, since the coordinate integer values of 0 and 1 are spread throughout this method. The domain concept location is hidden in this method. The duplication of 0 and 1 provides an implicit clue to the hidden abstraction that needs to be extracted during the refactoring step. We named the World class as NeighborHood to represent the Moore's Neighborhood concept found in the domain. We want to achieve traceability from the initial requirements to our code by keeping the semantic gap between the domain and the code as low as possible. The Cell class is very similar to our solution, and there is not much to be done to improve upon it. To save some trees, the code for Cell will not be provided here.

TDD doesn't drive good design. TDD gives you immediate feedback about what is likely to be bad design.

—Kent Beck

Let's now review the solution by Anderson Dias found at https://github.com/andersondias/conway-game-of-life-ruby.

```ruby
class Cell
  attr_reader :world, :x, :y
  def initialize(world, x, y)
    @world, @x, @y = world, x, y
    @live = false
  end

  def dead?
    !@live
  end

  def dead!
    @live = false
  end

  def live?
    @live
  end

  def live!
    @live = true
  end

  def toggle!
    @live = !@live
  end

  def neighbours
    neighbours = []
    neighbours.push(@world.cell_at(self.x - 1, self.y - 1))
    neighbours.push(@world.cell_at(self.x - 1, self.y))
    neighbours.push(@world.cell_at(self.x - 1, self.y + 1))
```

```
      neighbours.push(@world.cell_at(self.x, self.y - 1))
      neighbours.push(@world.cell_at(self.x, self.y + 1))

      neighbours.push(@world.cell_at(self.x + 1, self.y - 1))
      neighbours.push(@world.cell_at(self.x + 1, self.y))
      neighbours.push(@world.cell_at(self.x + 1, self.y + 1))

      neighbours
    end

    def live_neighbours
      self.neighbours.select do |n|
         n && n.live?
      end
    end
  end
end
```

The dependency of the Cell class on the World class is in the wrong direction. Conceptually, the cell is not aware of the world. The world (or neighborhood, in our solution) is aware of the cells that it contains in its grid. The wrong dependency direction has lead to the wrong allocation of responsibility to calculate the number of neighbors. This solution also suffers from Primitive Obsession, since the location is accessed using integer values. The domain-specific concept, Location, is missing. There is not much to be done to improve on the World class, and it will not be shown here.

■ **Note**   It is easy to see code duplication and eliminate it during the refactoring step. However, it is difficult to see the data duplication in code that could be a sign of hidden abstraction. We must reflect about data duplication and consider expressing the hidden domain concept in a class during the refactoring step. You might also accomplish this by aiming for a low semantic gap in the solution. If you read the problem domain analysis section, you will find the word *location* used in the analysis. The language we use to describe a problem affects the code quality.

Let's now review the code from the book *The Four Rules of Simple Design* by Corey Haines. The author does not discuss the explicit relationship of the test name to the actual test code. Here is the test:

```
def test_after_adding_a_cell_the_world_is_not_empty
  world = World.new
  world.set_living_at(1, 1)
  assert_false world.empty?
end
```

The problem here is that the concept of *cell* is mentioned in the test name, but it is not found in the test code. There is a bit of confusion when the code states you are setting living_at to a world. What is living_ at at that coordinate in the World class? The test can be rewritten in the following way to make the concept of *cell* explicit and to ensure the test code is consistent with the test name.

```
def test_after_adding_a_cell_the_world_is_not_empty
  world = World.new
  world.add(Cell.new(1, 1))
  assert_false world.empty?
end
```

It also expresses what is being conveyed in the name of the test in the form of test code. This results in a design that uses composition. This test is also tied to the implementation. We can make it focus on intent and express the concepts found in the domain by rewriting it as follows:

```
def test_after_adding_a_cell_the_world_is_populated
  world = World.new
  world.add(Cell.new(1, 1))
  assert world.populated?
end
```

Terms such as *overcrowded, lonely, birth,* and so forth are found in the domain. The test must look for opportunities to express them instead of thinking in terms of data structure, such as *array*.

A solution that has small and focused classes can be combined in different ways to implement features and will result in an elegant design. We also used the concept of *seed*, found in the problem domain, directly in code. This raised the level of abstraction of the seeding API. We used the seed method to populate as many cells as we desired in the grid. We were able to express our intent to seed the game rather than using an implementation-level API such as the living_at() method, which is capable of populating only one cell. The Four Rules of Simple Design stated by the author of that book are:

1. Tests Pass

2. Express Intent

3. No Duplication

4. Small

This is not sufficient to come up with elegant solutions. Ironically, the API shown in the book violates the Express Intent guideline. We can choose a better name for a method that expresses intent by asking the following question: Which method has the name that provides the answer to the questions *Why?* and *What is the purpose of this method?* We have discussed several design principles and illustrated how to apply them to create elegant solutions throughout this book.

EXERCISES

The Dead Cell Scenario

The solution does not check if a cell is dead when the number of neighbors is counted. Write a failing test to expose the bug and fix it to make the test pass.

Draw a concept diagram for the code in the "Code Review" section. Is it semantically correct?

Summary

In this chapter, we discussed how missing abstractions can manifest themselves as data duplication in the code. The effort we put into finding the key abstractions is worth it because it will result in less code and more elegant solutions. We worked through the Game of Life kata and reviewed some of the solutions found online to illustrate that TDD does not magically create good designs. As developers, we are responsible for applying good design principles during the refactoring step. Recognizing that data duplication might be hiding an essential domain concept is crucial to coming up with better designs.

CHAPTER 7

■ ■ ■

Gilded Rose

In this chapter, we will work on the Gilded Rose kata to focus on refactoring a legacy code base to add a new feature. We will follow Kent Beck's guideline for making a desired change.

> *For each desired change, make the change easy (warning: this may be hard), then make the easy change.*

> —Kent Beck

Kent Beck's guideline is at a strategic level. How do we go about making the code easy to change? To answer that question, we need a plan at the tactical level that fits into the higher level strategy. We need a list of concrete things to look for in the code, and we need to apply the refactorings in the right sequence to transform the code to the desired form and structure. So, in order to discover the concrete things to work on, we need to discuss form and structure.

Form vs. Structure

Form is the visible shape of something. It relates to the external shape, best thought of as a silhouette. *Structure* is the arrangement of and relations between the elements of something complex. It goes beyond the visible. It is the internal development and relationship between parts. You can think of the structure as an X-Ray or CT scan. Figure 7-1 shows the concept diagram for form.

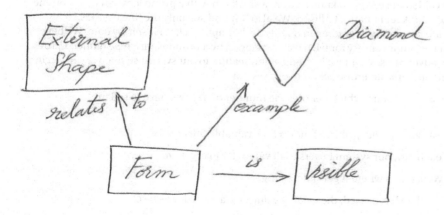

Figure 7-1. Concept diagram of form

© Bala Paranj 2017
B. Paranj, *Test Driven Development in Ruby*, DOI 10.1007/978-1-4842-2638-4_7

Figure 7-2 shows the concept diagram of structure.

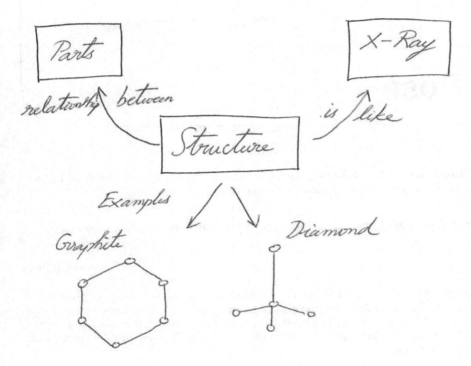

Figure 7-2. *Concept diagram of structure*

We will see what the form and structure look like for the code in this kata after the introduction of the refactoring kata and the code we need to work on.

Problem Statement

Hi, and welcome to Team Gilded Rose. As you know, we are a small inn with a prime location in a prominent city. We are run by a friendly innkeeper named Allison. We also buy and sell only the finest goods. Unfortunately, our goods are constantly degrading in quality as they approach their sell-by date. We have a system in place that updates our inventory for us. It was developed by a no-nonsense type named Leroy, who has moved on to new adventures. Your task is to add a new feature to our system so that we can begin selling a new category of items. First, an introduction to our system.

- All items have a SellIn value, which denotes the number of days we have to sell the item.

- All items have a Quality value, which denotes how valuable the item is.

- At the end of each day, our system lowers both values for every item.

Pretty simple, right? Well, this is where it gets interesting.

- Once the sell-by date has passed, the Quality value degrades twice as fast.

- The Quality value of an item is never negative.

- "Aged Brie" actually increases in Quality value the older it gets.

- The Quality value of an item is never more than 50.

- "Sulfuras," being a legendary item, never has to be sold and never decreases its Quality value.

- "Backstage passes," like aged brie, increase in Quality value as SellIn value approaches; Quality value increases by 2 when there are 10 days or less and by 3 when there are 5 days or less, but Quality value drops to 0 after the concert.

We have recently signed a supplier of "conjured" items. This requires an update to our system.

- "Conjured" items degrade in quality twice as fast as normal items do.

Just for clarification, an item can never have its Quality value increase above 50; however, "Sulfuras" is a legendary item and as such its Quality value is 80, and it never alters. (Source: http://iamnotmyself. com/2011/02/13/refactor-this-the-gilded-rose-kata/.)

Feel free to make any changes to the UpdateQuality method and add any new code you feel is needed, as long as everything still works correctly. However, do not alter the Item class or Items property, as those belong to the goblin in the corner who will insta-rage and one-shot you, as he doesn't believe in shared code ownership. (You can make the UpdateQuality method and Items property static if you'd like; we'll cover for you).

Initial Setup

The original Gilded Rose kata does not have any tests. We cannot refactor without any tests. Michael Feather's book *Working Effectively with Legacy Code* discusses how to write characterization tests for a legacy code base with no tests. The discussion on characterization tests is out of scope of this book. If you are interested in learning how to write characterization tests, watch the RailsConf presentation by Randy Coulman, "Getting a Handle on Legacy Code," found at http://confreaks.tv/videos/railsconf2015-getting-a-handle-on-legacy-code. We will use Randy Coulman's initial setup code that has the characterization tests as the starting point for our kata. You can find his github repo at https://github.com/randycoulman/GildedRose. My repository at https://github.com/bparanj/gildie contains the files required in order to start working on this kata. You can either clone my repository or create the files from scratch, as shown in this chapter. Create a gilded_rose.rb file with the following code:

```ruby
require_relative 'item.rb'

class GildedRose
  @items = []

  def initialize
    @items = []
    @items << Item.new("+5 Dexterity Vest", 10, 20)
    @items << Item.new("Aged Brie", 2, 0)
    @items << Item.new("Elixir of the Mongoose", 5, 7)
    @items << Item.new("Sulfuras, Hand of Ragnaros", 0, 80)
    @items << Item.new("Backstage passes to a TAFKAL80ETC concert", 15, 20)
    @items << Item.new("Conjured Mana Cake", 3, 6)
  end
```

```ruby
def update_quality
  for i in 0..(@items.size-1)
    if (@items[i].name != "Aged Brie" && @items[i].name != "Backstage passes to a
    TAFKAL80ETC concert")
      if (@items[i].quality > 0)
        if (@items[i].name != "Sulfuras, Hand of Ragnaros")
          @items[i].quality = @items[i].quality - 1
        end
      end
    else
      if (@items[i].quality < 50)
        @items[i].quality = @items[i].quality + 1
        if (@items[i].name == "Backstage passes to a TAFKAL80ETC concert")
          if (@items[i].sell_in < 11)
            if (@items[i].quality < 50)
              @items[i].quality = @items[i].quality + 1
            end
          end
          if (@items[i].sell_in < 6)
            if (@items[i].quality < 50)
              @items[i].quality = @items[i].quality + 1
            end
          end
        end
      end
    end
    if (@items[i].name != "Sulfuras, Hand of Ragnaros")
      @items[i].sell_in = @items[i].sell_in - 1;
    end
    if (@items[i].sell_in < 0)
      if (@items[i].name != "Aged Brie")
        if (@items[i].name != "Backstage passes to a TAFKAL80ETC concert")
          if (@items[i].quality > 0)
            if (@items[i].name != "Sulfuras, Hand of Ragnaros")
              @items[i].quality = @items[i].quality - 1
            end
          end
        else
          @items[i].quality = @items[i].quality - @items[i].quality
        end
      else
        if (@items[i].quality < 50)
          @items[i].quality = @items[i].quality + 1
        end
      end
    end
  end
end
```

Form

How can we make the change easy for this class? First, we need to evaluate where we are now. Then, we must set a target to aim for in the resulting code that will make it easy to add the new feature. So, we need to ask ourselves the following questions:

- What does the easy-to-change code look like for the guilded_rose.rb file?

- What is the sequence of transformations that will lead to our desired target?

At this point, we don't know enough about the code to answer the second question. But, we do know that we need to start with very small changes and gradually work toward big refactorings. We need to zoom out to get a big-picture view of the update_quality method in gilded_rose.rb. So, ignore the details of the update_quality method for now and look at the big-picture view, as shown here:

```
def update_quality
  for loop
    if
      if
        if

        end
      end
    else
      if
        if
          if
            if

            end
          end
          if
            if

            end
          end
        end
      end
    end
    if

    end
    if
      if
        if
          if

          end
        end
      else
```

```
            end
          else
            if

            end
          end
        end
      end
end
```

We see a lot of nested if-else and if conditionals. There are too many levels of indentations. This procedural code makes it difficult to locate where we need to make changes to add the new feature. If we zoom in a bit by looking only at the if statements, we see a lot of negative conditionals, hard-coded strings, and integers that make understanding the code difficult. For instance, we don't know what the integers in the if statements represent. If the code is difficult to read, we cannot understand it; therefore, making changes will be difficult. What we would like to see is a form that has flat if-else clauses limited to the number of items in the database. We have six items, so we can aim for a form that looks like the following:

```
def update_quality
  if

  elsif

  elsif

  elsif

  elsif

  else

  end
end
```

This also makes it easy to locate the code related to a given item and make changes to either modify existing functionality or add a new feature.

Structure

The structure is invisible in the code. How can we pass this code through a CT scanner to view its structure? How can we develop the X-ray vision to see the structure of the code? In this case, the execution paths at runtime provide us the structure of the code. We need to trace the execution path for a given item. Figure 7-3 shows the execution path for the item Sulfuras, Hand of Ragnaros.

```
def update_quality
  for i in 0..(@items.size-1)
    if (@items[i].name != "Aged Brie" && @items[i].name != "Backstage passes to a TAFKAL80ETC concert")
      if (@items[i].quality > 0)
        if (@items[i].name != "Sulfuras, Hand of Ragnaros")
          @items[i].quality = @items[i].quality - 1
        end
      end
    else
      if (@items[i].quality < 50)
        @items[i].quality = @items[i].quality + 1
        if (@items[i].name == "Backstage passes to a TAFKAL80ETC concert")
          if (@items[i].sell_in < 11)
            if (@items[i].quality < 50)
              @items[i].quality = @items[i].quality + 1
            end
          end
          if (@items[i].sell_in < 6)
            if (@items[i].quality < 50)
              @items[i].quality = @items[i].quality + 1
            end
          end
        end
      end
    end
    if (@items[i].name != "Sulfuras, Hand of Ragnaros")
      @items[i].sell_in = @items[i].sell_in - 1;
    end
    if (@items[i].sell_in < 0)
      if (@items[i].name != "Aged Brie")
        if (@items[i].name != "Backstage passes to a TAFKAL80ETC concert")
          if (@items[i].quality > 0)
            if (@items[i].name != "Sulfuras, Hand of Ragnaros")
              @items[i].quality = @items[i].quality - 1
            end
          end
        else
          @items[i].quality = @items[i].quality - @items[i].quality
        end
      else
        if (@items[i].quality < 50)
          @items[i].quality = @items[i].quality + 1
        end
      end
    end
  end
end
```

Figure 7-3. *Execution path for Sulfuras, Hand of Ragnaros*

All the conditionals return false, and no code gets executed for Sulfuras, Hand of Ragnaros. Figure 7-4 shows the execution path for the item +5 Dexterity Vest.

227

```ruby
def update_quality
  for i in 0..(@items.size-1)
    if (@items[i].name != "Aged Brie" && @items[i].name != "Backstage passes to a TAFKAL80ETC concert")
      if (@items[i].quality > 0)
        if (@items[i].name != "Sulfuras, Hand of Ragnaros")
          @items[i].quality = @items[i].quality - 1
        end
      end
    else
      if (@items[i].quality < 50)
        @items[i].quality = @items[i].quality + 1
        if (@items[i].name == "Backstage passes to a TAFKAL80ETC concert")
          if (@items[i].sell_in < 11)
            if (@items[i].quality < 50)
              @items[i].quality = @items[i].quality + 1
            end
          end
          if (@items[i].sell_in < 6)
            if (@items[i].quality < 50)
              @items[i].quality = @items[i].quality + 1
            end
          end
        end
      end
    end
    if (@items[i].name != "Sulfuras, Hand of Ragnaros")
      @items[i].sell_in = @items[i].sell_in - 1;
    end
    if (@items[i].sell_in < 0)
      if (@items[i].name != "Aged Brie")
        if (@items[i].name != "Backstage passes to a TAFKAL80ETC concert")
          if (@items[i].quality > 0)
            if (@items[i].name != "Sulfuras, Hand of Ragnaros")
              @items[i].quality = @items[i].quality - 1
            end
          end
        else
          @items[i].quality = @items[i].quality - @items[i].quality
        end
      else
        if (@items[i].quality < 50)
          @items[i].quality = @items[i].quality + 1
        end
      end
    end
  end
end
```

Figure 7-4. *Execution path for +5 Dexterity Vest*

Figure 7-5 shows the execution path for Elixir of the Mongoose.

```ruby
def update_quality
  for i in 0..(@items.size-1)
    if (@items[i].name != "Aged Brie" && @items[i].name != "Backstage passes to a TAFKAL80ETC concert")
      if (@items[i].quality > 0)
        if (@items[i].name != "Sulfuras, Hand of Ragnaros")
          @items[i].quality = @items[i].quality - 1
        end
      end
    else
      if (@items[i].quality < 50)
        @items[i].quality = @items[i].quality + 1
        if (@items[i].name == "Backstage passes to a TAFKAL80ETC concert")
          if (@items[i].sell_in < 11)
            if (@items[i].quality < 50)
              @items[i].quality = @items[i].quality + 1
            end
          end
          if (@items[i].sell_in < 6)
            if (@items[i].quality < 50)
              @items[i].quality = @items[i].quality + 1
            end
          end
        end
      end
    end
    if (@items[i].name != "Sulfuras, Hand of Ragnaros")
      @items[i].sell_in = @items[i].sell_in - 1;
    end
    if (@items[i].sell_in < 0)
      if (@items[i].name != "Aged Brie")
        if (@items[i].name != "Backstage passes to a TAFKAL80ETC concert")
          if (@items[i].quality > 0)
            if (@items[i].name != "Sulfuras, Hand of Ragnaros")
              @items[i].quality = @items[i].quality - 1
            end
          end
        else
          @items[i].quality = @items[i].quality - @items[i].quality
        end
      else
        if (@items[i].quality < 50)
          @items[i].quality = @items[i].quality + 1
        end
      end
    end
  end
end
```

Figure 7-5. *Execution path for Elixir of the Mongoose*

By comparing the execution paths of the +5 Dexterity Vest and the Elixir of the Mongoose, we see that they have the same code paths. Figure 7-6 shows the execution path for Aged Brie.

```ruby
def update_quality
  for i in 0..(@items.size-1)
    if (@items[i].name != "Aged Brie" && @items[i].name != "Backstage passes to a TAFKAL80ETC concert")
      if (@items[i].quality > 0)
        if (@items[i].name != "Sulfuras, Hand of Ragnaros")
          @items[i].quality = @items[i].quality - 1
        end
      end
    else
      if (@items[i].quality < 50)
        @items[i].quality = @items[i].quality + 1
        if (@items[i].name == "Backstage passes to a TAFKAL80ETC concert")
          if (@items[i].sell_in < 11)
            if (@items[i].quality < 50)
              @items[i].quality = @items[i].quality + 1
            end
          end
          if (@items[i].sell_in < 6)
            if (@items[i].quality < 50)
              @items[i].quality = @items[i].quality + 1
            end
          end
        end
      end
    end
    if (@items[i].name != "Sulfuras, Hand of Ragnaros")
      @items[i].sell_in = @items[i].sell_in - 1;
    end
    if (@items[i].sell_in < 0)
      if (@items[i].name != "Aged Brie")
        if (@items[i].name != "Backstage passes to a TAFKAL80ETC concert")
          if (@items[i].quality > 0)
            if (@items[i].name != "Sulfuras, Hand of Ragnaros")
              @items[i].quality = @items[i].quality - 1
            end
          end
        else
          @items[i].quality = @items[i].quality - @items[i].quality
        end
      else
        if (@items[i].quality < 50)
          @items[i].quality = @items[i].quality + 1
        end
      end
    end
  end
end
```

Figure 7-6. *Execution path for Aged Brie*

Figure 7-7 shows the execution path for Backstage Passes to a TAFKAL80ETC concert.

```
def update_quality
  for i in 0..(@items.size-1)
    if (@items[i].name != "Aged Brie" && @items[i].name != "Backstage passes to a TAFKAL80ETC concert")
      if (@items[i].quality > 0)
        if (@items[i].name != "Sulfuras, Hand of Ragnaros")
          @items[i].quality = @items[i].quality - 1
        end
      end
    else
      if (@items[i].quality < 50)
        @items[i].quality = @items[i].quality + 1
        if (@items[i].name == "Backstage passes to a TAFKAL80ETC concert")
          if (@items[i].sell_in < 11)
            if (@items[i].quality < 50)
              @items[i].quality = @items[i].quality + 1
            end
          end
          if (@items[i].sell_in < 6)
            if (@items[i].quality < 50)
              @items[i].quality = @items[i].quality + 1
            end
          end
        end
      end
    end
    if (@items[i].name != "Sulfuras, Hand of Ragnaros")
      @items[i].sell_in = @items[i].sell_in - 1;
    end
    if (@items[i].sell_in < 0)
      if (@items[i].name != "Aged Brie")
        if (@items[i].name != "Backstage passes to a TAFKAL80ETC concert")
          if (@items[i].quality > 0)
            if (@items[i].name != "Sulfuras, Hand of Ragnaros")
              @items[i].quality = @items[i].quality - 1
            end
          end
        else
          @items[i].quality = @items[i].quality - @items[i].quality
        end
      else
        if (@items[i].quality < 50)
          @items[i].quality = @items[i].quality + 1
        end
      end
    end
  end
end
```

Figure 7-7. *Execution paths of Backstage Passes to a TAFKAL80ETC concert*

Let's compare Aged Brie with Backstage Passes. The first half of the method has similar code paths. The lower part of the method needs to execute code at one more level in nested if-else for Backstage Passes. To make this clear, here is the code that highlights the execution path for Aged Brie:

```ruby
def update_quality
  for i in 0..(@items.size-1)
    if (@items[i].name != "Aged Brie" && @items[i].name != "Backstage")
      # Not executed
    else
      # executed
    end
    if (@items[i].name != "Sulfuras")
      @items[i].sell_in = @items[i].sell_in - 1;
    end
    if (@items[i].sell_in < 0)
      if (@items[i].name != "Aged Brie")
        # Not executed
      else
        # executed
      end
    end
  end
end
```

The code that highlights the execution path for Backstage Passes is shown here:

```ruby
def update_quality
  for i in 0..(@items.size-1)
    if (@items[i].name != "Aged Brie" && @items[i].name != "Backstage")
      # Not executed
    else
      # Executed
    end
    if (@items[i].name != "Sulfuras")
      # Executed
    end
    if (@items[i].sell_in < 0)
      if (@items[i].name != "Aged Brie")
        if (@items[i].name != "Backstage")
          # Not executed
        else
          # Executed
        end
      else
        # Not executed
      end
    end
  end
end
```

By tracing the execution paths for different items, we find that they're similar, but entangled, as shown in Figure 7-8.

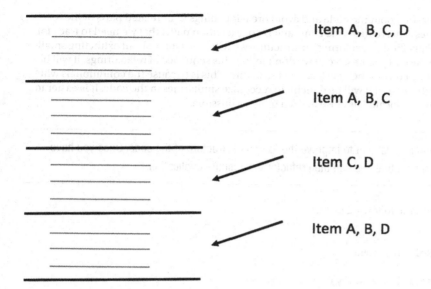

Figure 7-8. *Entangled structure of update_quality method with nested if-else statements*

How can we make the execution paths simple? The if condition must handle only one type of item, and the logic for handling that item should be within each if-elsif clause, as shown in Figure 7-9.

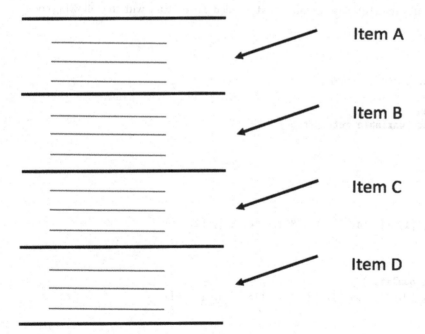

Figure 7-9. *Desired target structure of update_quality method with localized logic for each item*

We will then be able to reason about the code and avoid breaking things in unrelated parts of the method when we make changes. This reduces the combination of execution paths that we need to trace for a given item. After we hit our specified target form and structure, we will then worry about extracting small methods and classes to make the code expressive. If we don't follow this sequence of refactorings, it will be very difficult to mold the existing code to the new form and structure. This is because the conditionals will be spread across different methods, and it will be difficult to recognize similarities in the code. It is easier to recognize similarities if the code is located as close to each other as possible.

> ■ **Note**   Early-stage refactorings must aim to improve the form and structure of the code. Once you have attained the preferred form and structure, we can then refactor to eliminate duplication.

Create an `item.rb` file with the following code:

```ruby
class Item
  attr_accessor :name, :sell_in, :quality

  def initialize (name, sell_in, quality)
    @name = name
    @sell_in = sell_in
    @quality = quality
  end
end
```

We are not allowed to modify the `item` class. Create a `test_gilded_rose.rb` file with the following code:

```ruby
require 'minitest/autorun'
require_relative "gilded_rose"

class CharacterizationTest < Minitest::Test
  def setup
    @rose = GildedRose.new
    @items = @rose.instance_variable_get(:@items)
  end

  attr_reader :rose, :items

  def test_after_1_day
    rose.update_quality
    assert_items([9, 19], [1, 1], [4, 6], [0, 80], [14, 21], [2, 5])
  end

  def test_after_2_days
    2.times { rose.update_quality }
    assert_items([8, 18], [0, 2], [3, 5], [0, 80], [13, 22], [1, 4])
  end

  def test_after_3_days
    3.times { rose.update_quality }
    assert_items([7, 17], [-1, 4], [2, 4], [0, 80], [12, 23], [0, 3])
  end
```

```ruby
def test_after_4_days
  4.times { rose.update_quality }
  assert_items([6, 16], [-2, 6], [1, 3], [0, 80], [11, 24], [-1, 1])
end

def test_after_5_days
  5.times { rose.update_quality }
  assert_items([5, 15], [-3, 8], [0, 2], [0, 80], [10, 25], [-2, 0])
end

def test_after_6_days
  6.times { rose.update_quality }
  assert_items([4, 14], [-4, 10], [-1, 0], [0, 80], [9, 27], [-3, 0])
end

def test_after_7_days
  7.times { rose.update_quality }
  assert_items([3, 13], [-5, 12], [-2, 0], [0, 80], [8, 29], [-4, 0])
end

def test_after_8_days
  8.times { rose.update_quality }
  assert_items([2, 12], [-6, 14], [-3, 0], [0, 80], [7, 31], [-5, 0])
end

def test_after_9_days
  9.times { rose.update_quality }
  assert_items([1, 11], [-7, 16], [-4, 0], [0, 80], [6, 33], [-6, 0])
end

def test_after_10_days
  10.times { rose.update_quality }
  assert_items([0, 10], [-8, 18], [-5, 0], [0, 80], [5, 35], [-7, 0])
end

def test_after_11_days
  11.times { rose.update_quality }
  assert_items([-1, 8], [-9, 20], [-6, 0], [0, 80], [4, 38], [-8, 0])
end

def test_after_12_days
  12.times { rose.update_quality }
  assert_items([-2, 6], [-10, 22], [-7, 0], [0, 80], [3, 41], [-9, 0])
end

def test_after_13_days
  13.times { rose.update_quality }
  assert_items([-3, 4], [-11, 24], [-8, 0], [0, 80], [2, 44], [-10, 0])
end
```

```ruby
def test_after_14_days
  14.times { rose.update_quality }
  assert_items([-4, 2], [-12, 26], [-9, 0], [0, 80], [1, 47], [-11, 0])
end

def test_after_15_days
  15.times { rose.update_quality }
  assert_items([-5, 0], [-13, 28], [-10, 0], [0, 80], [0, 50], [-12, 0])
end

def test_after_16_days
  16.times { rose.update_quality }
  assert_items([-6, 0], [-14, 30], [-11, 0], [0, 80], [-1, 0], [-13, 0])
end

def test_after_17_days
  17.times { rose.update_quality }
  assert_items([-7, 0], [-15, 32], [-12, 0], [0, 80], [-2, 0], [-14, 0])
end

def test_after_25_days
  25.times { rose.update_quality }
  assert_items([-15, 0], [-23, 48], [-20, 0], [0, 80], [-10, 0], [-22, 0])
end

def test_after_26_days
  26.times { rose.update_quality }
  assert_items([-16, 0], [-24, 50], [-21, 0], [0, 80], [-11, 0], [-23, 0])
end

def test_after_27_days
  27.times { rose.update_quality }
  assert_items([-17, 0], [-25, 50], [-22, 0], [0, 80], [-12, 0], [-24, 0])
end

private

def assert_items(*expected_items)
  expected_items.zip(items) do |(sell_in, quality), item|
    assert_equal(sell_in, item.sell_in, "#{item.name} sell_in")
    assert_equal(quality, item.quality, "#{item.name} quality")
  end
end
end
```

You don't need to know anything about these tests. We will run the characterization tests after every refactoring. You can run these tests by executing ruby test_gilded_rose.rb in a terminal. All the tests will pass. Let's begin refactoring by making very small changes. Delete the semicolon in line 42 of gilded_rose.rb. We can also delete the unnecessary braces in the if conditional of the update_quality method in gilded_rose.rb. The method will now look as shown next. This minor cleanup did not affect the structure of the program. It reduced the noise so that the code is easier to read.

```ruby
def update_quality
  for i in 0..(@items.size-1)
    if (@items[i].name != "Aged Brie" && @items[i].name != "Backstage passes to a
TAFKAL80ETC concert")
      if @items[i].quality > 0
        if @items[i].name != "Sulfuras, Hand of Ragnaros"
          @items[i].quality = @items[i].quality - 1
        end
      end
    else
      if @items[i].quality < 50
        @items[i].quality = @items[i].quality + 1
        if @items[i].name == "Backstage passes to a TAFKAL80ETC concert"
          if @items[i].sell_in < 11
            if @items[i].quality < 50
              @items[i].quality = @items[i].quality + 1
            end
          end
          if @items[i].sell_in < 6
            if @items[i].quality < 50
              @items[i].quality = @items[i].quality + 1
            end
          end
        end
      end
    end
    if @items[i].name != "Sulfuras, Hand of Ragnaros"
      @items[i].sell_in = @items[i].sell_in - 1
    end
    if @items[i].sell_in < 0
      if @items[i].name != "Aged Brie"
        if @items[i].name != "Backstage passes to a TAFKAL80ETC concert"
          if @items[i].quality > 0
            if @items[i].name != "Sulfuras, Hand of Ragnaros"
              @items[i].quality = @items[i].quality - 1
            end
          end
        else
          @items[i].quality = @items[i].quality - @items[i].quality
        end
      else
        if @items[i].quality < 50
          @items[i].quality = @items[i].quality + 1
        end
      end
    end
  end
end
```

All the tests will still pass. We can now tackle the duplication in indexing in the items collection. Replace the outer for loop in the update_quality method, shown below.

```ruby
for i in 0..(@items.size-1)
  # Code same as before
end
```

with each method that loops through items, as follows:

```ruby
def update_quality
  @items.each do |item|
    if (item.name != "Aged Brie" && item.name != "Backstage passes to a TAFKAL80ETC
concert")
      if item.quality > 0
        if item.name != "Sulfuras, Hand of Ragnaros"
          item.quality = item.quality - 1
        end
      end
    else
      if item.quality < 50
        item.quality = item.quality + 1
        if item.name == "Backstage passes to a TAFKAL80ETC concert"
          if item.sell_in < 11
            if item.quality < 50
              item.quality = item.quality + 1
            end
          end
          if item.sell_in < 6
            if item.quality < 50
              item.quality = item.quality + 1
            end
          end
        end
      end
    end
    if item.name != "Sulfuras, Hand of Ragnaros"
      item.sell_in = item.sell_in - 1
    end
    if item.sell_in < 0
      if item.name != "Aged Brie"
        if item.name != "Backstage passes to a TAFKAL80ETC concert"
          if item.quality > 0
            if item.name != "Sulfuras, Hand of Ragnaros"
              item.quality = item.quality - 1
            end
          end
        else
          item.quality = item.quality - item.quality
        end
      else
        if item.quality < 50
          item.quality = item.quality + 1
        end
      end
```

```
      end
    end
end
```

The tests will still pass. Let's now tackle the following specification: "Sulfuras," being a legendary item, never has to be sold or have a decrease in its Quality value. This means we don't need to process the item if it is Sulfuras. We can skip it by checking for this item in the beginning of the loop. Delete all three conditionals for an item that is not Sulfuras:

```
if item.name != "Sulfuras, Hand of Ragnaros"
  # Some code here must not be deleted
end
```

The refactored update_quality method now looks as shown here:

```
def update_quality
  @items.each do |item|
    next if item.name == "Sulfuras, Hand of Ragnaros"
    if (item.name != "Aged Brie" && item.name != "Backstage passes to a TAFKAL80ETC
concert")
      if item.quality > 0
        item.quality = item.quality - 1
      end
    else
      if item.quality < 50
        item.quality = item.quality + 1
        if item.name == "Backstage passes to a TAFKAL80ETC concert"
          if item.sell_in < 11
            if item.quality < 50
              item.quality = item.quality + 1
            end
          end
          if item.sell_in < 6
            if item.quality < 50
              item.quality = item.quality + 1
            end
          end
        end
      end
    end
    item.sell_in = item.sell_in - 1
    if item.sell_in < 0
      if item.name != "Aged Brie"
        if item.name != "Backstage passes to a TAFKAL80ETC concert"
          if item.quality > 0
            item.quality = item.quality - 1
          end
        else
          item.quality = item.quality - item.quality
        end
      else
```

```
      if item.quality < 50
        item.quality = item.quality + 1
      end
    end
  end
 end
end
```

The tests will still pass. We can use the += and -= to increment and decrement values. The refactored method now looks as shown here:

```
def update_quality
  @items.each do |item|
    next if item.name == "Sulfuras, Hand of Ragnaros"
    if (item.name != "Aged Brie" && item.name != "Backstage passes to a TAFKAL80ETC
concert")
      if item.quality > 0
        item.quality -= 1
      end
    else
      if item.quality < 50
        item.quality += 1
        if item.name == "Backstage passes to a TAFKAL80ETC concert"
          if item.sell_in < 11
            if item.quality < 50
              item.quality += 1
            end
          end
          if item.sell_in < 6
            if item.quality < 50
              item.quality += 1
            end
          end
        end
      end
    end
    item.sell_in -= 1
    if item.sell_in < 0
      if item.name != "Aged Brie"
        if item.name != "Backstage passes to a TAFKAL80ETC concert"
          if item.quality > 0
            item.quality -= 1
          end
        else
          item.quality -= item.quality
        end
      else
        if item.quality < 50
          item.quality += 1
        end
      end
```

```
      end
    end
end
```

The readability of the code is improving. The tests will still pass. We see duplication in the conditional `item.quality < 50`.

This is required in order to enforce the business rule stated in the requirements: The Quality of an item is never more than 50. We can move this check into a method that will increase the quality only if it passes the check.

```
def increase_quality_for(item)
  if item.quality < 50
    item.quality += 1
  end
end
```

The update_quality method can now be simplified as follows:

```
def update_quality
  @items.each do |item|
    next if item.name == "Sulfuras, Hand of Ragnaros"
    if (item.name != "Aged Brie" && item.name != "Backstage passes to a TAFKAL80ETC
concert")
      if item.quality > 0
        item.quality -= 1
      end
    else
      increase_quality_for(item)
      if item.name == "Backstage passes to a TAFKAL80ETC concert"
        if item.sell_in < 11
          increase_quality_for(item)
        end
        if item.sell_in < 6
          increase_quality_for(item)
        end
      end
    end
    item.sell_in -= 1
    if item.sell_in < 0
      if item.name != "Aged Brie"
        if item.name != "Backstage passes to a TAFKAL80ETC concert"
          if item.quality > 0
            item.quality -= 1
          end
        else
          item.quality -= item.quality
        end
      else
        increase_quality_for(item)
      end
    end
  end
end
```

We were able to eliminate four conditionals that checked that the Quality value was less than 50 before increasing the value by one. Similarly, we can extract a method to decrease the Quality value and enforce the following business rule: The Quality of an item is never negative.

```
def decrease_quality_for(item)
  if item.quality > 0
    item.quality -= 1
  end
end
```

The update_quality method can now be simplified as shown here:

```
def update_quality
  @items.each do |item|
    next if item.name == "Sulfuras, Hand of Ragnaros"
    if (item.name != "Aged Brie" && item.name != "Backstage passes to a TAFKAL80ETC
concert")
      decrease_quality_for(item)
    else
      increase_quality_for(item)
      if item.name == "Backstage passes to a TAFKAL80ETC concert"
        if item.sell_in < 11
          increase_quality_for(item)
        end
        if item.sell_in < 6
          increase_quality_for(item)
        end
      end
    end
    item.sell_in -= 1
    if item.sell_in < 0
      if item.name != "Aged Brie"
        if item.name != "Backstage passes to a TAFKAL80ETC concert"
          decrease_quality_for(item)
        else
          item.quality -= item.quality
        end
      else
        increase_quality_for(item)
      end
    end
  end
end
```

The tests will still pass. Let's now convert negation into a positive conditional for the following conditional:

```
if item.name != "Backstage passes to a TAFKAL80ETC concert"
  decrease_quality_for(item)
else
  item.quality -= item.quality
end
```

This can be rewritten by flipping the `if` and `else` parts by checking for the positive condition.

```
if item.name == "Backstage passes to a TAFKAL80ETC concert"
  item.quality -= item.quality
else
  decrease_quality_for(item)
end
```

The tests will still pass. We can do the same for the outer if-else condition.

```
if item.name != "Aged Brie"
  if item.name == "Backstage passes to a TAFKAL80ETC concert"
    item.quality -= item.quality
  else
    decrease_quality_for(item)
  end
else
  increase_quality_for(item)
end
becomes:
if item.name == "Aged Brie"
  increase_quality_for(item)
else
  if item.name == "Backstage passes to a TAFKAL80ETC concert"
    item.quality -= item.quality
  else
    decrease_quality_for(item)
  end
end
```

The tests will still pass. We can use `elsif` to eliminate the nested `if` and `else` in the preceding code. So, the code can be refactored as shown here:

```
if item.name == "Aged Brie"
  increase_quality_for(item)
elsif item.name == "Backstage passes to a TAFKAL80ETC concert"
  item.quality -= item.quality
else
  decrease_quality_for(item)
end
```

The tests will still pass. Let's replace the hard-coded strings with constants. The refactored method is as shown here:

```
class GildedRose
  SULFURAS = "Sulfuras, Hand of Ragnaros"
  BACKSTAGE_PASSES = "Backstage passes to a TAFKAL80ETC concert"
  AGED_BRIE = "Aged Brie"

  def update_quality
    @items.each do |item|
      next if item.name == SULFURAS
```

```ruby
      if (item.name != AGED_BRIE && item.name != BACKSTAGE_PASSES)
        decrease_quality_for(item)
      else
        increase_quality_for(item)
        if item.name == BACKSTAGE_PASSES
          if item.sell_in < 11
            increase_quality_for(item)
          end
          if item.sell_in < 6
            increase_quality_for(item)
          end
        end
      end
      item.sell_in -= 1
      if item.sell_in < 0
        if item.name == AGED_BRIE
          increase_quality_for(item)
        elsif item.name == BACKSTAGE_PASSES
          item.quality -= item.quality
        else
          decrease_quality_for(item)
        end
      end
    end
  end
  # Rest of the code same as before
end
```

The tests will still pass.

DeMorgan's Laws

Let's now tackle negation in the conditionals.

```ruby
if (item.name != AGED_BRIE && item.name != BACKSTAGE_PASSES)
```

This appears at the top of the `update_quality` method. The next refactoring is based on Randy Coulman's presentation "Gilding the Rose: Refactoring Legacy Code" at the GoGaRuCo 2014 Ruby Conference. We can apply DeMorgan's Laws to make this conditional positive and flip the code within if-else. DeMorgan's Laws states the following:

not (A and B) ➤ (not A) or (not B)
not (A or B) ➤(not A) and (not B)

```ruby
item.name != AGED_BRIE && item.name != BACKSTAGE_PASSES
```

can be negated as follows:

```ruby
!(item.name != AGED_BRIE && item.name != BACKSTAGE_PASSES)
```

This can be converted to the *OR* form by applying DeMorgan's Law as follows:

```
!(item.name != AGED_BRIE) || !(item.name != BACKSTAGE_PASSES)
```

This can be simplified as follows:

```
item.name == AGED_BRIE || item.name == BACKSTAGE_PASSES
```

We can now refactor the code as follows:

```
def update_quality
  @items.each do |item|
    next if item.name == SULFURAS
    if (item.name == AGED_BRIE || item.name == BACKSTAGE_PASSES)
      increase_quality_for(item)
      if item.name == BACKSTAGE_PASSES
        if item.sell_in < 11
          increase_quality_for(item)
        end
        if item.sell_in < 6
          increase_quality_for(item)
        end
      end
    else
      decrease_quality_for(item)
    end
    item.sell_in -= 1
    if item.sell_in < 0
      if item.name == AGED_BRIE
        increase_quality_for(item)
      elsif item.name == BACKSTAGE_PASSES
        item.quality -= item.quality
      else
        decrease_quality_for(item)
      end
    end
  end
end
```

Making Temporal Dependency Explicit

You can see the line item.sell_in -= 1 that is between two if-else clauses. What is the purpose of this line of code? The specification says: All items have a SellIn value that denotes the number of days we have to sell the item. This method updates the number of days left to sell the item. Let's extract that line into the intention-revealing method update_number_of_days_left_to_sell(item).

```
def update_number_of_days_left_to_sell(item)
  item.sell_in -= 1
end
```

We need to group things that are related. It will make the code easy to read. Can we move the updating of days left to sell up to the top to separate it from the code related to the update of quality? Let's move the update_number_of_days_left_to_sell(item) method to the top, as shown here:

```ruby
def update_quality
  @items.each do |item|
    next if item.name == SULFURAS
    update_number_of_days_left_to_sell(item)
    if (item.name == AGED_BRIE || item.name == BACKSTAGE_PASSES)
      increase_quality_for(item)
      if item.name == BACKSTAGE_PASSES
        if item.sell_in < 11
          increase_quality_for(item)
        end
        if item.sell_in < 6
          increase_quality_for(item)
        end
      end
    else
      decrease_quality_for(item)
    end
    if item.sell_in < 0
      if item.name == AGED_BRIE
        increase_quality_for(item)
      elsif item.name == BACKSTAGE_PASSES
        item.quality -= item.quality
      else
        decrease_quality_for(item)
      end
    end
  end
end
```

The test will fail. This means we have an implicit temporal dependency. This line of code must be in that particular location to pass all the tests. This is because there are two conditionals that check that the sell_in value is less than 11 and 6 to update the quality. Since we have decremented the sell_in value by one, if we change those numbers to 10 and 5, the tests will pass. This also expresses the requirement clearly, because the requirement states the following:

"Backstage passes," like aged brie, increase in Quality as their SellIn value approaches; Quality increases by 2 when there are 10 days or less and by 3 when there are 5 days or less, but Quality drops to 0 after the concert.

You can see 10 days and 5 days in the problem statement instead of 11 and 6 in the solution before refactoring. We can now refactor the following part of the update_quality method:

```ruby
if (item.name == AGED_BRIE || item.name == BACKSTAGE_PASSES)
  increase_quality_for(item)
  if item.name == BACKSTAGE_PASSES
    if item.sell_in < 11
      increase_quality_for(item)
    end
```

```
  if item.sell_in < 6
    increase_quality_for(item)
  end
 end
else
 decrease_quality_for(item)
end
```

We can simplify it as follows:

```
if item.name == AGED_BRIE
  increase_quality_for(item)
elsif item.name == BACKSTAGE_PASSES
  increase_quality_for(item)
  if item.sell_in < 10
    increase_quality_for(item)
  end
  if item.sell_in < 5
    increase_quality_for(item)
  end
else
  decrease_quality_for(item)
end
```

The tests will pass. We were able to accomplish this because of the requirement we just looked at. Let's now refactor the code:

```
item.sell_in < 0
```

The purpose of this line of code is to check if the item has expired. We can extract a method to reveal the intent of this line of code.

```
def expired?(item)
  item.sell_in < 0
end
```

The update_quality method can use this method.

```
if expired?(item)
  if item.name == AGED_BRIE
    increase_quality_for(item)
  elsif item.name == BACKSTAGE_PASSES
    item.quality -= item.quality
  else
    decrease_quality_for(item)
  end
end
```

The entire method is shown here:

```ruby
def update_quality
  @items.each do |item|
    next if item.name == SULFURAS
    update_number_of_days_left_to_sell(item)
    if item.name == AGED_BRIE
      increase_quality_for(item)
    elsif item.name == BACKSTAGE_PASSES
      increase_quality_for(item)
      if item.sell_in < 10
        increase_quality_for(item)
      end
      if item.sell_in < 5
        increase_quality_for(item)
      end
    else
      decrease_quality_for(item)
    end
    if expired?(item)
      if item.name == AGED_BRIE
        increase_quality_for(item)
      elsif item.name == BACKSTAGE_PASSES
        item.quality -= item.quality
      else
        decrease_quality_for(item)
      end
    end
  end
end
```

The tests will pass. We have made the implicit temporal dependency explicit by moving the update_number_of_days_left_to_sell method to the top.

Improving the Structure

Let's now work on improving the structure by refactoring the update_quality method to localize the handling of aged brie and backstage passes. We will do this by moving the expired? check at the bottom to be inside the conditionals, as follows:

```ruby
def update_quality
  @items.each do |item|
    next if item.name == SULFURAS
    update_number_of_days_left_to_sell(item)
    if item.name == AGED_BRIE
      increase_quality_for(item)
      increase_quality_for(item) if expired?(item)
    elsif item.name == BACKSTAGE_PASSES
      increase_quality_for(item)
      if item.sell_in < 10
        increase_quality_for(item)
      end
```

```
      if item.sell_in < 5
        increase_quality_for(item)
      end
      if expired?(item)
        item.quality -= item.quality
      end
    else
      decrease_quality_for(item)
      decrease_quality_for(item) if expired?(item)
    end
  end
end
```

This method now has the desired structure we had in mind at the beginning of this chapter. The tests will pass.

Express Intent

The else condition handles the following requirement: Once the sell-by date has passed, Quality degrades twice as fast.

Instead of commenting in the code to communicate how it is related to the requirement, we can make it explicit in our code.

```
def decrease_quality_twice(item)
  decrease_quality_for(item)
  decrease_quality_for(item)
end
```

We have to call the decrease_quality_for method twice because it has the guard condition to make sure the quality does not become negative, as per the requirements. We still need to decrease the quality by a factor of 1 for other items. The code for update_quality now looks as shown here:

```
def update_quality
  @items.each do |item|
    next if item.name == SULFURAS
    update_number_of_days_left_to_sell(item)
    if item.name == AGED_BRIE
      increase_quality_for(item)
      increase_quality_for(item) if expired?(item)
    elsif item.name == BACKSTAGE_PASSES
      increase_quality_for(item)
      if item.sell_in < 10
        increase_quality_for(item)
      end
      if item.sell_in < 5
        increase_quality_for(item)
      end
      if expired?(item)
        item.quality -= item.quality
      end
    else
```

```ruby
    if expired?(item)
      decrease_quality_twice(item)
    else
      decrease_quality_for(item)
    end
  end
  end
end
```

We can extract a method to handle the quality update.

```ruby
def update_quality_for(item)
  if item.name == AGED_BRIE
    increase_quality_for(item)
    increase_quality_for(item) if expired?(item)
  elsif item.name == BACKSTAGE_PASSES
    increase_quality_for(item)
    if item.sell_in < 10
      increase_quality_for(item)
    end
    if item.sell_in < 5
      increase_quality_for(item)
    end
    if expired?(item)
      item.quality -= item.quality
    end
  else
    if expired?(item)
      decrease_quality_twice(item)
    else
      decrease_quality_for(item)
    end
  end
end
```

The update_quality method becomes simpler.

```ruby
def update_quality
  @items.each do |item|
    next if item.name == SULFURAS
    update_number_of_days_left_to_sell(item)
    update_quality_for(item)
  end
end
```

We can extract the logic for aged brie and backstage pass as separate methods.

```ruby
def update_aged_brie_quality(item)
  increase_quality_for(item)
  increase_quality_for(item) if expired?(item)
end
```

```ruby
def update_backstage_pass_quality(item)
  increase_quality_for(item)
  if item.sell_in < 10
    increase_quality_for(item)
  end
  if item.sell_in < 5
    increase_quality_for(item)
  end
  if expired?(item)
    item.quality -= item.quality
  end
end
```

The update_quality_for method becomes simpler.

```ruby
def update_quality_for(item)
  if item.name == AGED_BRIE
    update_aged_brie_quality(item)
  elsif item.name == BACKSTAGE_PASSES
    update_backstage_pass_quality(item)
  else
    if expired?(item)
      decrease_quality_twice(item)
    else
      decrease_quality_for(item)
    end
  end
end
```

What do the numbers 0, 5, and 10 represent? Is it days, weeks, months, years? It's not clear, so we define constants to represent them.

```ruby
ZERO_DAYS = 0
FIVE_DAYS = 5
TEN_DAYS = 10
```

Now the expired? and update_backstage_pass_quality methods can use these constants to reveal the units clearly.

```ruby
def update_backstage_pass_quality(item)
  increase_quality_for(item)
  if item.sell_in < TEN_DAYS
    increase_quality_for(item)
  end
  if item.sell_in < FIVE_DAYS
    increase_quality_for(item)
  end
  if expired?(item)
    item.quality -= item.quality
  end
end
```

```ruby
def expired?(item)
  item.sell_in < ZERO_DAYS
end
```

Tell-Don't-Ask Principle

We should not ask for data; we should tell an object to do some work with its internal data. Change the update_quality_for method as follows:

```ruby
def update_quality_for(item)
  if item.name == AGED_BRIE
    aged_brie = AgedBrie.new(item)
    aged_brie.update
  elsif item.name == BACKSTAGE_PASSES
    update_backstage_pass_quality(item)
  else
    if expired?(item)
      decrease_quality_twice(item)
    else
      decrease_quality_for(item)
    end
  end
end
```

Create an aged_brie.rb file with the code shown here:

```ruby
require_relative 'item'


class AgedBrie
  def initialize(item)
    @item = item
  end
  def update
    increase_quality
    increase_quality if expired?
  end
  def increase_quality
    if @item.quality < 50
      @item.quality += 1
    end
  end
  def expired?
    @item.sell_in < 0
  end
end
```

Add require_relative 'aged_brie' to the top of gilded_rose.rb. Delete the update_aged_brie_quality method in gilded_rose.rb. The tests will now pass.

Let's now tackle the backstage pass. Create a `backstage_pass.rb` file.

```ruby
require_relative 'item'

class BackstagePass
  def initialize(item)
    @item = item
  end
  def update
    increase_quality
    if @item.sell_in < 10
      increase_quality
    end
    if @item.sell_in < 5
      increase_quality
    end
    if expired?
      @item.quality -= @item.quality
    end
  end
  def increase_quality
    if @item.quality < 50
      @item.quality += 1
    end
  end
  def expired?
    @item.sell_in < 0
  end
end
```

Delete the update_backstage_pass_quality method in gilded_rose.rb. Add require_relative 'backstage_pass' to the top of gilded_rose.rb. Change the update_quality_for method in gilded_rose.rb as follows:

```ruby
def update_quality_for(item)
  if item.name == AGED_BRIE
    aged_brie = AgedBrie.new(item)
    aged_brie.update
  elsif item.name == BACKSTAGE_PASSES
    backstage = BackstagePass.new(item)
    backstage.update
  else
    if expired?(item)
      decrease_quality_twice(item)
    else
      decrease_quality_for(item)
    end
  end
end
```

The tests will now pass. Create a new file, regular_item.rb, with the following code:

```ruby
require_relative 'item'

class RegularItem
  def initialize(item)
    @item = item
  end
  def update
    if expired?
      decrease_quality_twice
    else
      decrease_quality
    end
  end
  def expired?
    @item.sell_in < 0
  end
  def decrease_quality
    if @item.quality > 0
      @item.quality -= 1
    end
  end

  private
  def decrease_quality_twice
    decrease_quality
    decrease_quality
  end
end
```

Add require_relative 'regular_item' to the top of gilded_rose.rb. Modify the update_quality_for method as follows:

```ruby
def update_quality_for(item)
  if item.name == AGED_BRIE
    aged_brie = AgedBrie.new(item)
    aged_brie.update
  elsif item.name == BACKSTAGE_PASSES
    backstage = BackstagePass.new(item)
    backstage.update
  else
    regular_item = RegularItem.new(item)
    regular_item.update
  end
end
```

Delete the decrease_quality_for and decrease_quality_twice methods in gilded_rose.rb. The tests will now pass. We can now extend the BackstagePass class from the RegularItem class. Change require_relative 'item' to require_relative 'regular_item'. Delete the constructor and the expired? method in the BackstagePass class.

```ruby
require_relative 'regular_item'

class BackstagePasses < RegularItem
  def update
    increase_quality
    if @item.sell_in < 10
      increase_quality
    end
    if @item.sell_in < 5
      increase_quality
    end
    if expired?
      @item.quality -= @item.quality
    end
  end
  def increase_quality
    if @item.quality < 50
      @item.quality += 1
    end
  end
end
```

Inheritance

We can inherit the behavior of expired? from the Super class. The tests will pass. We can make a similar change to the AgedBrie class.

```ruby
require_relative 'regular_item'

class AgedBrie < RegularItem
  def update
    increase_quality
    increase_quality if expired?
  end
  def increase_quality
    if @item.quality < 50
      @item.quality += 1
    end
  end
end
```

The tests will pass. We can now move the duplicated method increase_quality found in AgedBrie and BackstagePass to the superclass RegularItem as a protected method. We can now simplify the AgedBrie and BackstagePass classes.

```ruby
require_relative 'regular_item'

class BackstagePass < RegularItem
  def update
    increase_quality
```

```ruby
      if @item.sell_in < 10
        increase_quality
      end
      if @item.sell_in < 5
        increase_quality
      end
      if expired?
        @item.quality -= @item.quality
      end
    end
end

require_relative 'regular_item'

class AgedBrie < RegularItem
  def update
    increase_quality
    increase_quality if expired?
  end
end
```

The unnecessary methods in gilded_rose.rb are removed in the following code:

```ruby
require_relative 'aged_brie'
require_relative 'backstage_pass'
require_relative 'regular_item'

class GildedRose
  @items = []

  SULFURAS = "Sulfuras, Hand of Ragnaros"
  BACKSTAGE_PASSES = "Backstage passes to a TAFKAL80ETC concert"
  AGED_BRIE = "Aged Brie"

  def initialize
    @items = []
    @items << Item.new("+5 Dexterity Vest", 10, 20)
    @items << Item.new("Aged Brie", 2, 0)
    @items << Item.new("Elixir of the Mongoose", 5, 7)
    @items << Item.new("Sulfuras, Hand of Ragnaros", 0, 80)
    @items << Item.new("Backstage passes to a TAFKAL80ETC concert", 15, 20)
    @items << Item.new("Conjured Mana Cake", 3, 6)
  end

  def update_quality
    @items.each do |item|
      next if item.name == SULFURAS
      update_number_of_days_left_to_sell(item)
      update_quality_for(item)
    end
  end
```

```ruby
  def update_quality_for(item)
    if item.name == AGED_BRIE
      aged_brie = AgedBrie.new(item)
      aged_brie.update
    elsif item.name == BACKSTAGE_PASSES
      backstage = BackstagePass.new(item)
      backstage.update
    else
      regular_item = RegularItem.new(item)
      regular_item.update
    end
  end
  def update_number_of_days_left_to_sell(item)
    item.sell_in -= 1
  end
end
```

The tests still pass. This code is now easy to change. We are ready to make the easy change. Let's implement the new feature to handle the conjured item.

Implementing the New Feature

The new requirement states the following: Conjured items degrade in Quality twice as fast as normal items.

Change the visibility of the decrease_quality_twice method in regular_item.rb from *private* to *protected* because the subclass for ConjuredItem needs it. Create conjured_item.rb with the following code:

```ruby
require_relative 'regular_item'

class ConjuredItem < RegularItem
  def update
    decrease_quality
    if expired?
      decrease_quality
    end
  end
end
```

Modify the update_quality_for method in gilded_rose.rb to handle the conjured items.

```ruby
def update_quality_for(item)
  if item.name == AGED_BRIE
    aged_brie = AgedBrie.new(item)
    aged_brie.update
  elsif item.name == BACKSTAGE_PASSES
    backstage = BackstagePass.new(item)
    backstage.update
  elsif item.name == CONJURED
    conjured = ConjuredItem.new(item)
    conjured.update
  else
```

```
    regular_item = RegularItem.new(item)
    regular_item.update
  end
end
```

Add require_relative 'conjured_item' to the top of the gilded_rose.rb file. Define the constant for a conjured item at the top, CONJURED = "Conjured". The tests will pass. We spent a lot of time and effort to make the change easy to do, and we finally made the easy change that in the end took much less effort. The RegularItem class does not extend from the Item class. While inheritance is indeed a way to reuse code, there is no behavior in the Item class that we can reuse via inheritance. We are asking the item for the name and making a decision based on the name. Why not ask the Item class to provide a service for us that uses its own internal data? It's a good idea, but we will not tackle that issue because of the constraint specified in the requirements document.

Express Domain Concepts

Let's parameterize the decrease_quality method so that we can control the amount of decrease. For this refactoring, we will retain the old interface to prevent the tests from breaking. Define a new method, decrease_quality_by, in the RegularItem class.

```
def decrease_quality_by(factor)
  @item.quality -= factor
  if @item.quality < 0
    @item.quality = 0
  end
end
```

We can call this method with any number, so the quality might become negative. We need a guard condition that checks for negative quality and resets it to 0. This enforces the business rule: The quality of an item is never negative.

Change the update method in the RegularItem class to use this new method.

```
def update
  if expired?
    decrease_quality_by(2)
  else
    decrease_quality_by(1)
  end
end
```

The expired? check enforces the following business rule: Once the sell-by date has passed, quality degrades twice as fast.

The tests will still pass. The update method in the ConjuredItem class is the same as in its superclass RegularItem. This is a problem because in legacy code we do not know if the requirements are out of date or if the code has a bug. The developers who can answer our question have moved on to new adventures. So, we will leave the duplication in the solution.

Delete the decrease_quality and decrease_quality_twice methods in the RegularItem class. The tests will pass. Now, define an increase_quality_by method in the RegularItem class.

```
def increase_quality_by(factor)
  @item.quality += factor
  if @item.quality > 50
    @item.quality = 50
  end
end
```

This method has a guard condition to check for the limit of quality and set it to 50 if it exceeds 50. This enforces the following business rule: The quality of an item is never more than 50.

Change the update method in the AgedBrie class.

```
class AgedBrie < RegularItem
  def update
    if expired?
      increase_quality_by(2)
    else
      increase_quality_by(1)
    end
  end
end
```

The tests will still pass. Change the update method in the BackstagePass class to use the new increase_quality_by method.

```
class BackstagePass < RegularItem
  def update
    increase_quality_by(1)
    if @item.sell_in < 10
      increase_quality_by(1)
    end
    if @item.sell_in < 5
      increase_quality_by(1)
    end
    if expired?
      @item.quality -= @item.quality
    end
  end
end
```

The tests will pass. Delete the increase_quality method in the RegularItem class. The tests will pass.

Let's make this business rule, The quality of an item is never more than 50, explicit in the code. Change the following methods in the RegularItem class:

```
def increase_quality_by(factor)
  @item.quality += factor
  enforce_quality_of_an_item_is_not_more_than(50)
end
```

```
private

def enforce_quality_of_an_item_is_not_more_than(limit)
  if @item.quality > limit
    @item.quality = limit
  end
end
```

The tests will still pass. Let's now make this business rule, The quality of an item is never negative, explicit in the code. In the RegularItem class, change the decrease_quality_by method.

```
def decrease_quality_by(factor)
  @item.quality -= factor
  enforce_quality_of_an_item_is_never_negative
end
```

Define a private method to express the business intent.

```
def enforce_quality_of_an_item_is_never_negative
  if @item.quality < 0
    @item.quality = 0
  end
end
```

The complete code listing for RegularItem is as shown here:

```
require_relative 'item'


class RegularItem
  def initialize(item)
    @item = item
  end

  def update
    if expired?
      decrease_quality_by(2)
    else
      decrease_quality_by(1)
    end
  end

  protected

  def expired?
    @item.sell_in < 0
  end

  def increase_quality_by(factor)
    @item.quality += factor
    enforce_quality_of_an_item_is_not_more_than(50)
```

```
end

def decrease_quality_by(factor)
  @item.quality -= factor
  enforce_quality_of_an_item_is_never_negative
end

private

def enforce_quality_of_an_item_is_not_more_than(limit)
  if @item.quality > limit
    @item.quality = limit
  end
end

def enforce_quality_of_an_item_is_never_negative
  if @item.quality < 0
    @item.quality = 0
  end
end
end
```

The refactorings were focused on making the code express the business rules clearly by defining intent-revealing private methods. It is now easier to understand and locate the relevant code when you want to change any of the values for a given business rule. This makes maintenance easier.

Retrospective

Bad form and structure result in brittle code, thus making it difficult to make changes to the code. Table 7-1 shows the sequence of refactorings for this kata. This sequence is not strictly rigid. However, it is important that the refactoring of the form and structure comes before any refactoring related to design changes, such as extracting new classes.

Table 7-1. *The Sequence of Refactorings*

Sequence	Refactoring	Purpose
1	Syntax Noise	Readability
2	Negative Conditionals	Form
3	Hardcoded Strings and Integers	Readability
4	Localizing Logic	Structure
5	Design Changes	Design
6	Express Intent	Readability

The key takeaway of this kata is that we need to first focus on improving the form and structure before looking at doing object-oriented design. Form and structure provide the big picture. The refactorings that are related to lower-level details will fit the outline provided by the earlier refactorings that improved the form and structure of the code. The initial micro-refactorings, such as removing semi-colons and unnecessary braces, using decrement/increment syntax, and so on, did not alter the existing bad form and structure. It simply improved the readability of the code. Only after we achieved the desired form and structure in the code, we focused on refactoring that extracted classes and made code express intent.

We gradually reduced the complexity of the code. We ran the tests very frequently. We began refactoring in the green state and ended our refactoring in the green state. We focused on creating similarities in the code while working on transforming the code to a better form and structure. We resisted the temptation to prematurely eliminate duplication because our priority was to improve the form and structure.

EXERCISE

Rename the RegularItem Class to NormalItem

The requirements document has no reference to a regular item. To make the code reflect the domain, rename the `RegularItem` class to `NormalItem` and make sure all the tests pass.

Replace Magic Numbers with Constants

Replace the hard-coded integers 0, 5, and 10 with constants that express the units clearly, and make sure all the tests pass. Define a constant `MAX_QUALITY` for the hard-coded integer 50.

Summary

In this chapter, we worked on a refactoring kata to illustrate why we need to make the code easy to change before we can add a new feature to legacy code. We used characterization tests as the safety net during our refactoring process. We learned about DeMorgan's Laws and how they can be applied to simplify conditionals in code. The sequence of refactorings affects how quickly we can make the code easy to change. We learned that recognizing bad form and structure in code is important so that we can target our refactorings to attain the preferred form and structure of the code.

CHAPTER 8

Dealing with Third-Party APIs

This chapter will cover integration testing and using fixtures to speed up tests that go over the network to interact with third-party servers. Stripe is an online payment platform that processes credit card transactions. We will be using the stripe gem that is published by Stripe to develop a monthly subscription feature. We can subscribe a customer to an existing subscription plan, update a subscription, and cancel an existing subscription to a plan. The update feature will enable customers to upgrade or downgrade their subscription.

Subscription Plan

You can sign up for a Stripe account at https://dashboard.stripe.com/register. You can view your API credentials here: https://dashboard.stripe.com/account. There are two keys that you need in order to run the code examples: test secret key, which looks like sk_test_abcde12345, and test publishable key, which looks like pk_test_xyz_123. We will install the gem and start playing with it in the IRB console to get familiar with the Stripe API request and response. You can install the gem by running the following command in a terminal:

```
gem install stripe
```

Create a Plan

The Stripe API documentation says that we can create a subscription plan by creating a Stripe::Plan instance that takes the amount, subscription interval, subscription plan name, currency, and subscription plan ID.

```
require "stripe"
Stripe.api_key = "sk_test_BQokikJOvB2"

Stripe::Plan.create(
  :amount => 2000,
  :interval => 'month',
  :name => 'Amazing Gold Plan',
  :currency => 'usd',
  :id => 'gold')
```

© Bala Paranj 2017
B. Paranj, *Test Driven Development in Ruby*, DOI 10.1007/978-1-4842-2638-4_8

In this case, we are using gold as the value for the plan ID that will charge subscribed customers 20 USD every month. The amount value is in cents. The interval specifies frequency of billing for subscription. In this case, it is a monthly subscription. The ID is a unique string that identifies the plan to subscribe a customer. It could be a string or a primary key from your own database. For more details on the fields, read the Stripe API docs at https://stripe.com/docs/api#plans.

Delete a Plan

```
plan = Stripe::Plan.retrieve('gold')
plan.delete
```

The plan ID in this case is gold. It can be from your database or stored as a constant in your server-side code. Usually, you create plans just once and you can delete them from your account dashboard. In a real project, deleting a plan occurs rarely, and you may not need the programmatic way of deleting it.

Stripe Customer

Next, we need a customer object in order to subscribe a given customer to a subscription plan.

We need a token before we can create a customer. The token represents the credit card number that the customer provides. Let's create a token using the Stripe API:

```
card = { :number => "4242424242424242", :exp_month => 8, :exp_year => 2020, :cvc => "314" }
response = Stripe::Token.create(:card => card)
puts response['id']
```

```
> tok_14Tj2w2eRoTz
```

Real web applications will use Stripe.js JavaScript to create tokens because the credit card number is never sent to our servers. This makes PCI compliance easy. The credit card number in our case is a test credit card, and the expiration date must be in the future. We pass in the hash containing the credit card details to create the Stripe token. We can extract the value of the Stripe token by using the ID key in the response hash. We can now create a customer using the token generated in the preceding call as follows:

```
response = Stripe::Customer.create(:description => "desc goes here",
                                   :card => "tok_14Tj2w2e3RoTz")
puts response
```

The JSON response we get from the server is as follows:

```
{
  "id": "cus_4cz7I6SnCZIrYF",
  "object": "customer",
  "created": 1408579761,
  "livemode": false,
  "description": "desc goes here",
  "email": null,
  "delinquent": false,
  "metadata": {},
  "subscriptions": {"object":"list","total_count" ...}
```

```
  "discount": null,
  "account_balance": 0,
  "currency": null,
  "cards": {"object":"list","total_count" ...}
  "default_card": "card_14Tj2w2eZvKYlCh"
}
```

In this example, the Stripe::Customer ID is cus_4cz7I6SnCZIrYF.

Subscribe a Customer to a Plan

We first retrieve an existing customer object and create a subscription by calling create on the subscriptions method on the customer.

```
customer = Stripe::Customer.retrieve('cus_4cz7rYF')
subscription = customer.subscriptions.create({:plan => 'gold'})

puts subscription.class
puts subscription.id
puts subscription
```

The output of this code is shown here:

```
Stripe::Subscription
sub_4dFhAPa595XZsN
{
  "id": "sub_4dFhAPa595XZsN",
  "plan": {"id":"gold","interval":"month","name":"Basic","created"}
  "object": "subscription",
  "start": 1408641490,
  "status": "active",
  "customer": "cus_4cz7IYF",
  "cancel_at_period_end": false,
  "current_period_start": 1408641490,
  "current_period_end": 1411319890,
  "ended_at": null,
  "trial_start": null,
  "trial_end": null,
  "canceled_at": null,
  "quantity": 1,
  "application_fee_percent": null,
  "discount": null,
  "metadata": {}
}
```

For writing tests, we will check that subscription.id has some value. Since we cannot predict the value, we will just check for its existence.

Test-Driven Stripe Library

In this section, we will write integration tests to implement the subscription to a plan, updating and cancelling an existing subscription. We will also write unit tests that run faster than integration tests. We need both the slow-running integration tests as well as the unit tests. In our case, integration tests prove that our software can integrate with the third-party software. The fast-running unit tests are run more frequently by developers. The unit tests need updates of the fixture files if the JSON structure changes in a future Stripe API version.

Integration Tests

We need to set the credentials as environment variables. In a terminal, you can run

```
export STRIPE_SECRET_KEY = 'sk_test_oAU7tWq2QgwED55FT2TGgBVf'
```

and

```
export STRIPE_PUBLISHABLE_KEY='pk_test_OiqVwPdGjusTz82m6IzsQKN6'
```

You can verify they are set correctly by running the following command in a terminal:

```
echo $STRIPE_SECRET_KEY
```

Install the stripe gem by running the following command:

```
gem install stripe
```

We will be using stripe gem version 1.57.1 in this book. Create a subscription_integration_test.rb file with the test to subscribe a customer to a gold plan.

```
require 'minitest/autorun'
require 'stripe'
require_relative 'subscription'

describe Subscription do
  before do
    Stripe.api_key = ENV['STRIPE_SECRET_KEY']
  end

  it 'subscribe a customer to gold plan' do
    email = 'bugs_bunny@rubyplus.com'
    stripe_token = Stripe::Token.create(card: {
                                          number: "4242424242424242",
                                          exp_month:  7,
                                          exp_year:  2020,
                                          cvc: "314"
                                          })
    # This plan must already exist in your Stripe Test account
    plan_id = 'gold'

    customer = Subscription.create(email, stripe_token.id, plan_id)
```

```
# If there is no exception and the response JSON has the new customer ID then the test
passes
assert customer.id.size > 5
  end
end
```

The require statement at the top includes the stripe gem. We also include the subscription.rb file that we are developing. The before method sets up the Stripe api_key that is required to make the remote calls to the Stripe server. The test creates a token for a credit card. The token, the customer email, and the plan_id are passed to the create class method in Subscription. In the assert step, we check that the customer ID size is greater than 5. The reason is that we cannot predict the exact value of the customer ID. If there is no exception and the JSON response has a customer ID, we assume the subscription call to the Stripe server succeeded. We can make this test pass by implementing the create method as follows:

```
class Subscription
  def self.create(email, stripe_token, plan_id, description='none')
    Stripe::Customer.create(email:        email,
                            description: description,
                            card:        stripe_token,
                            plan:        plan_id)
  end
end
```

In test mode, you can view the new subscription in the Stripe dashboard of your account. Copy the customer ID for the new subscriber from the Stripe dashboard. The second test will update the subscription of this customer to a new plan.

```
it 'update subscription to a new plan' do
  # This must be an existing customer id who already has a subscription for gold plan
  customer_id = 'cus_9hIOOYk3q1dnBe'
  new_plan_id = 'silver'

  subscription = Subscription.update(customer_id, new_plan_id)

  assert_equal new_plan_id, subscription.plan.id
end
```

Make sure that you have created a silver plan by using either the Stripe dashboard or the IRB console as shown in the section "Create a Plan." We can make this test pass with the following implementation of the update class method in subscription.rb.

```
def self.update(customer_id, plan_id)
  customer = Stripe::Customer.retrieve(customer_id)
  customer.update_subscription(plan: plan_id)
end
```

Ideally, we should make only one remote call. In reality, the Stripe API requires us to make two remote calls. We need to first retrieve the customer with a given ID, then we must update the subscription to the new plan. You can also check the Stripe dashboard to verify that the customer's plan has been changed to Silver. Let's add the third test, one to cancel a subscription for an existing subscribed customer.

```
it 'can cancel subscription for a subscriber' do
  email = 'daffy@rubyplus.com'
  stripe_token = Stripe::Token.create(card: {
                                        number: "4242424242424242",
                                        exp_month: 7,
                                        exp_year: 2020,
                                        cvc: "314"})
  plan_id = 'gold'
  customer = Subscription.create(email, stripe_token.id, plan_id)

  subscription = Subscription.cancel(customer.id)

  assert_equal 'canceled', subscription.status
end
```

We create a token and create a new subscription. This is the Arrange part of the test. We then cancel the subscription for this customer and assert that the subscription status is canceled. The implementation that makes this test pass is as follows:

```
def self.cancel(customer_id)
  customer = Stripe::Customer.retrieve(customer_id)
  customer.cancel_subscription
end
```

This is similar to updating the subscription. We have to make two remote calls to the Stripe servers. The output of running all the tests is shown here:

```
Run options: --seed 22515
# Running:
...
Finished in 2.578222s, 1.1636 runs/s, 1.1636 assertions/s.
3 runs, 3 assertions, 0 failures, 0 errors, 0 skips
```

You can see that it took over 2.5 seconds to run three tests. The reason for the slow tests is that we are going over the network. Integration tests are required in order to make sure that our software can integrate with third-party software. If we upgrade the Stripe gem, these integration tests will catch any backward-incompatible changes to the API. They act as a safety net. We can run the integration tests on a continuous integration server whenever a developer checks in the code.

Unit Tests

How can we write faster tests? If tests can be run faster, developers are more likely to run them frequently. Fortunately, Stripe provides us with helper methods that allow us to create Stripe objects from a hash. When we played in the IRB, we saw the JSON structure of the response from the Stripe server. This JSON response is the contract between our software and the third-party Stripe library. We can create a file that contains the JSON to create the hash required to construct Stripe objects. Ideally, the unit tests will not touch the file system. In reality, this may not be possible, especially when dealing with a third-party API. Create a `fixtures` folder, then create a `customer.json` file with the contents shown here:

```json
{
    "id": "cus_6XToBT4GczhYXA",
    "object": "customer",
    "created": 1435909465,
    "livemode": false,
    "description": "none",
    "email": "bugs.bunny@rubyplus.com",
    "delinquent": false,
    "metadata": {},
    "subscriptions": {
        "object": "list",
        "total_count": 1,
        "has_more": false,
        "url": "/v1/customers/cus_6XToBT4GczhYXA/subscriptions",
        "data": [
            {
                "id": "sub_6XTocuXPlSg8iS",
                "plan": {
                    "id": "gold",
                    "interval": "month",
                    "name": "Amazing Gold Plan",
                    "created": 1415160352,
                    "amount": 2000,
                    "currency": "usd",
                    "object": "plan",
                    "livemode": false,
                    "interval_count": 1,
                    "trial_period_days": null,
                    "metadata": {},
                    "statement_descriptor": null
                },
                "object": "subscription",
                "start": 1435909465,
                "status": "active",
                "customer": "cus_6XToBT4GczhYXA",
                "cancel_at_period_end": false,
                "current_period_start": 1435909465,
                "current_period_end": 1438587865,
                "ended_at": null,
                "trial_start": null,
                "trial_end": null,
                "canceled_at": null,
                "quantity": 1,
                "application_fee_percent": null,
                "discount": null,
                "tax_percent": null,
                "metadata": {}
            }
```

```
            ]
        },
        "discount": null,
        "account_balance": 0,
        "currency": "usd",
        "sources": {
            "object": "list",
            "total_count": 1,
            "has_more": false,
            "url": "/v1/customers/cus_6XToBT4GczhYXA/sources",
            "data": [
                {
                    "id": "card_16KOqTKmUHg13gkFBwOQHqf7",
                    "object": "card",
                    "last4": "4242",
                    "brand": "Visa",
                    "funding": "credit",
                    "exp_month": 9,
                    "exp_year": 2020,
                    "fingerprint": "JbFvkc6RO9g2yFua",
                    "country": "US",
                    "name": null,
                    "address_line1": null,
                    "address_line2": null,
                    "address_city": null,
                    "address_state": null,
                    "address_zip": null,
                    "address_country": null,
                    "cvc_check": "pass",
                    "address_line1_check": null,
                    "address_zip_check": null,
                    "tokenization_method": null,
                    "dynamic_last4": null,
                    "metadata": {},
                    "customer": "cus_6XToBT4GczhYXA"
                }
            ]
        },
        "default_source": "card_16KOqTKmUHg13gkFBwOQHqf7"
}
```

Create a subscription_unit_test.rb file.

```ruby
require 'minitest/autorun'
require 'stripe'
require_relative 'subscription'

describe Subscription do

  it 'subscribe customer to a plan' do
    email = 'bugs.bunny@rubyplus.com'
```

```
    plan_id = 'gold'
    stripe_token = 'value does not matter'

    hash = JSON.parse(File.read("fixtures/customer.json"))
    customer = Stripe::Customer.construct_from(hash)

    Stripe::Customer.stub :create, customer do
      customer = Subscription.create(email, stripe_token, plan_id)

      assert_equal 'cus_6XToBT4GczhYXA', customer.id
      assert_equal 'gold', customer.subscriptions.data[0].plan.id
    end
  end
end
```

One of the common mistakes developers make is mocking a third-party API. Mocking is a design technique. You cannot drive the design of a third-party API. However, we can stub them.

Stubs provide canned answers to calls made during the test.

—Martin Fowler

In this unit test for subscribing a customer to a plan, we read the JSON from the fixtures file and parse it to a hash. We then create a Stripe customer object from this hash. We stub the create method of the Stripe::Customer class of the stripe gem and return the customer object we created from the fixtures file. We call the create class method in our Subscription class and pass in the required fields, such as email, stripe_token, and plan_id. We then assert on the value of the customer ID and the plan name of the subscribed customer's plan. Unfortunately, the Stripe API does not provide us with a method that encapsulates the knowledge about the structure of the object graph. The test is tied to the structure of the graph of objects because we have to navigate through the complicated object structure to find the plan ID in the assert step. One of the design options we have is to create a StripeMapper class that will encapsulate accessing the object graph. The constructor will take the Stripe::Customer object, and the method would return either primitives or an application-specific domain object. This design is a good choice for a real project. This test passes without making any changes to the implementation. This unit test now runs fast. You don't need an Internet connection to run this test.

```
ruby subscription_unit_test.rb
Run options: --seed 31092
# Running:
.
Finished in 0.002541s, 393.6168 runs/s, 787.2336 assertions/s.
1 runs, 2 assertions, 0 failures, 0 errors, 0 skips
```

As you can see from the preceding output, this test ran in a fraction of a second. It runs much faster than the integration test. Add the second test for updating the subscription as follows:

```
it 'update subscription will update an existing subscribed plan' do
  existing_customer_id = 'cus_6XToBT4GczhYXA'
  new_plan_id = 'silver'

  hash = JSON.parse(File.read("fixtures/customer.json"))
  customer = Stripe::Customer.construct_from(hash)
```

```ruby
  subscription_hash = JSON.parse(File.read("fixtures/subscription.json"))
  subscription = Stripe::Subscription.construct_from(subscription_hash)

  Stripe::Customer.stub :retrieve, customer do
    customer.stub :update_subscription, subscription do
      result_subscription = Subscription.update(existing_customer_id, new_plan_id)

      assert_equal 'silver', result_subscription.plan.id
      assert_equal 'active', result_subscription.status
    end
  end
end
```

This test is similar to the first test. We are stubbing the retrieve method of Stripe::Customer as well as the update_subscription of Stripe::Customer. In the fixtures folder, create a subscription.json file with the following contents:

```json
{
    "id": "sub_6XTRPLoPvFkZAd",
    "plan": {
        "id": "silver",
        "interval": "month",
        "name": "Silver",
        "created": 1415672471,
        "amount": 1500,
        "currency": "usd",
        "object": "plan",
        "livemode": false,
        "interval_count": 1,
        "trial_period_days": null,
        "metadata": {},
        "statement_descriptor": null
    },
    "object": "subscription",
    "start": 1435908724,
    "status": "active",
    "customer": "cus_6XTROqQpg2yLCv",
    "cancel_at_period_end": false,
    "current_period_start": 1435908120,
    "current_period_end": 1438586520,
    "ended_at": null,
    "trial_start": null,
    "trial_end": null,
    "canceled_at": null,
    "quantity": 1,
    "application_fee_percent": null,
    "discount": null,
    "tax_percent": null,
    "metadata": {}
}
```

This test will pass without making any changes to the implementation. Add the third test for cancelling an existing subscription.

```ruby
it 'cancel subscription returns subscription with canceled status' do
  existing_customer_id = 'cus_6XToBT4GczhYXA'

  customer_hash = JSON.parse(File.read("fixtures/customer.json"))
  customer = Stripe::Customer.construct_from(customer_hash)

  canceled_subscription_hash = JSON.parse(File.read("fixtures/canceled_subscription.json"))
  subscription = Stripe::Subscription.construct_from(canceled_subscription_hash)

  Stripe::Customer.stub :retrieve, customer do
    customer.stub :cancel_subscription, subscription do
      result = Subscription.cancel(existing_customer_id)

      assert_equal 'canceled', result.status
    end
  end
end
```

Create `canceled_subscription.json` in the fixtures folder.

```json
{
    "id": "sub_6XTRPLoPvFkZAd",
    "plan": {
        "id": "silver",
        "interval": "month",
        "name": "Silver",
        "created": 1415672471,
        "amount": 1500,
        "currency": "usd",
        "object": "plan",
        "livemode": false,
        "interval_count": 1,
        "trial_period_days": null,
        "metadata": {},
        "statement_descriptor": null
    },
    "object": "subscription",
    "start": 1435908724,
    "status": "canceled",
    "customer": "cus_6XTROqQpg2yLCv",
    "cancel_at_period_end": false,
    "current_period_start": 1435908120,
    "current_period_end": 1438586520,
    "ended_at": 1435910365,
    "trial_start": null,
    "trial_end": null,
    "canceled_at": 1435910365,
    "quantity": 1,
```

```
    "application_fee_percent": null,
    "discount": null,
    "tax_percent": null,
    "metadata": {}
}
```

The new test and all the existing tests will pass. You can see the Stripe API version in your Stripe dashboard. In this case, the version is 2016-07-06 (latest). This version is compatible with stripe gem version 1.57.1.

Make Your Code Robust

Disconnect your machine from the network by turning off the wireless or Ethernet connection. Run the integration tests. They will fail with the following error message:

```
Stripe::APIConnectionError: Unexpected error communicating when trying to connect to Stripe.
You may be seeing this message because your DNS is not working. To check, try running 'host
stripe.com' from the command line.
```

This error message is not very helpful to developers who will use our library. This problem is the result of the lack of Internet connectivity and not DNS servers. This can also happen when you work in a coffee shop or library and forget to click on the "I agree" option to connect to the Internet. According to the Stripe API documentation, the api_connection_error happens because of a failure to connect to Stripe's API server. Here is the output of host stripe.com when there is an Internet connection:

```
$ host stripe.com
stripe.com has address 54.208.102.207
stripe.com mail is handled by 10 aspmx.l.google.com.
stripe.com mail is handled by 20 alt1.aspmx.l.google.com.
stripe.com mail is handled by 20 alt2.aspmx.l.google.com.
stripe.com mail is handled by 30 aspmx2.googlemail.com.
stripe.com mail is handled by 30 aspmx3.googlemail.com.
```

Here is the output of host stripe.com when there is no Internet connection:

```
$ host stripe.com
;; connection timed out; no servers could be reached
```

The error message must include the likely cause of the problem and also provide the possible solution. We need to check for Internet connectivity and communicate clearly to a developer who can take action to fix this problem. The simplest way to check for Internet connectivity is to use Net::HTTP.

```
> require 'net/http'
=> true
> Net::HTTP.get('example.com', '/index.html')
=> "<!doctype html><html>more html will be here for good Internet connectivity</html>"
> Net::HTTP.get('example.com', '/index.html')
SocketError: getaddrinfo: nodename nor servname provided, or not known
```

Even though the error message is cryptic, the SocketError in this case is due to no connection to the Internet. Let's write the test for checking Internet connectivity.

```
it 'raises SocketError when there is no Internet connectivity' do
  assert_raises SocketError do
    Subscription.cancel('bogus customer id')
  end
end
```

This fails, with the following error message:

```
Subscription#test_0004_raises exception SocketError when there is no Internet connectivity
[subscription_unit_test.rb:62]:
[SocketError] exception expected, not
Class: <Stripe::AuthenticationError>
Message: <"No API key provided. Set your API key using \"Stripe.api_key = <API-KEY>\". You
can generate API keys from the Stripe web interface. See https://stripe.com/api for details,
or email support@stripe.com if you have any questions.">
```

To make this test pass, we have to disconnect our machine from the Internet. How can we make the test pass without disconnecting our machine from the network? It is not possible to disconnect from the network when we run our tests in a continuous integration environment. How can we simulate network connectivity failure when we have working network connection? We can use a stub to simulate network connectivity failure. Change the test as follows:

```
it 'raises SocketError when there is no Internet connectivity' do
  raises_exception = ->(a, b){ raise SocketError.new }
  Net::HTTP.stub :get, raises_exception do
    assert_raises SocketError do
      Subscription.cancel('bogus customer id')
    end
  end
end
```

This test stubs the get method in Ruby's Net::HTTP library and raises the SocketError. The code within the stubbed block runs with the simulated network failure. The Subscription class now has the network connectivity check. To run this code, make sure you have set the values for your stripe credentials.

```
class Subscription
  def self.cancel(customer_id)
    check_internet_connectivity
    customer = Stripe::Customer.retrieve(customer_id)
    customer.cancel_subscription
  end

  def self.check_internet_connectivity
    require 'net/http'
    begin
      Net::HTTP.get('example.com', '/index.html')
    rescue SocketError => se
```

```
        message = "Problem with Internet connection. Check your Internet and try again"
        raise se, message
      end
    end
end
```

We catch the exception due to network connection failure and reraise the exception with a meaningful error message. The test will now pass. Network connectivity is not 100 percent reliable. We can write code to recover from transient network connectivity issues by retrying the request a few times before throwing an exception.

Besides network connectivity issues, our library can raise exceptions for many other reasons, such as a failed credit card transaction, invalid expiration date, authentication errors, and so on. Our library must deal with such exceptions gracefully. Some of the questions we need to answer are the following:

1. Can the user do something to correct the error?

2. Can the system retry the request?

3. Who can fix the problem?

A customer can provide a valid credit card to recover from a credit card decline. The credit card number 4000000000000069 can be used to simulate a decline due to expired card. In this case, the Stripe API will throw a Stripe::CardError exception. We must notify the user about the reason for the decline so that they can use a different card to complete the transaction. The integration and unit tests will be similar to the tests we have already written.

Authentication errors can occur if the API keys were changed by someone. In this case, the request cannot be retried by the system or the customer; it can only be fixed by someone who can provide us the correct API keys. Customers can only retry for problems that they can rectify, such as over credit limit problems, wrong card number, incorrect expiration date, and so on.

Summary

In this chapter, we discussed how to write integration and unit tests for code that deals with third-party APIs. We also saw how to speed up the tests by using fixtures to avoid going over the network in unit tests. We discussed the power of stubs to gain control of operating system services, such as communicating over a network.

CHAPTER 9

Pair Ranking

Pair ranking is a voting system developed in 1987 by Nicolaus Tideman. It selects a single winner using votes that express preferences. It can also be used to create a sorted list of winners.

Problem Domain Analysis

Let's say we need to rank four choices: A, B, C, and D. To pair-rank these choices, we list them in a column, one beneath the other:

```
Choice A
Choice B
Choice C
Choice D
```

We then ask: Which is better, A or B? We mark the choice we decide is better–say, B.

```
Choice A
Choice B |
Choice C
Choice D
```

We then ask why B is better and record our reasoning separately. The voting yields only our preference if we don't ask why we favor B over A. The question identifies the rationale, which is the most important part of the process. Now, which is better, A or C? We mark C and record our reasoning.

```
Choice A
Choice B |
Choice C |
Choice D
```

Which is better, A or D? We mark D and record our reasoning.

```
Choice A
Choice B |
Choice C |
Choice D |
```

© Bala Paranj 2017
B. Paranj, *Test Driven Development in Ruby*, DOI 10.1007/978-1-4842-2638-4_9

Which is better, B or C? We mark B and record our reasoning.

```
Choice A
Choice B ||
Choice C |
Choice D |
```

Which is better, B or D? We mark B and record our reasoning.

```
Choice A
Choice B |||
Choice C |
Choice D |
```

Which is better, C or D? We mark C and record our reasoning.

```
Choice A
Choice B |||
Choice C ||
Choice D |
```

We systematically compare each item with every other item. Choice B has three votes, C has two votes, D has one, and A has none. The item with the most votes is ranked first. In this case, that's choice B. Table 9-1 summarizes the result.

Table 9-1. *Pair-Ranking Result*

Choices	Votes	Ranking
A	0	4
B	3	1
C	2	2
D	1	3

If two items end up with the same number of votes, we rank the two items head to head to break the tie. The solution domain analysis, designing test cases, and developing the solution driven by tests are left as an exercise for the reader.

Solution

The following is one way to solve the problem. Create a `pair_rank.rb` file with the following code:

```ruby
module PairRank
  # Value Object
  # - Pair - Consists of two options
  # - Choice - Selected option from a given pair
  # - Criteria - Rationale for the preference. Why was the choice was made?
  class RationalChoice
    attr_reader :choice, :criteria, :pair
```

```ruby
  def initialize(pair, choice, criteria)
    @choice = choice
    @criteria = criteria
    @pair = pair
  end

  def to_s
    "You selected #{@choice} because of #{@criteria} for #{@pair}"
  end
end

class Combination
  def initialize(options)
    @list = options.combination(2).to_a
    @index = -1
  end

  def pair
    @index += 1
    @list[@index]
  end
end

class PairRank
  attr_reader :decisions

  def initialize(options)
    @options = options
    @decisions = []
    @votes = Hash.new(0)
    @combination = Combination.new(@options)
  end

  def combinations
    @options.combination(2).to_a
  end

  def combination
    @combination.pair
  end

  def score_for(choice)
    @votes[choice]
  end

  def tied_pair
    return [] if zeros?

    find_tie
  end
```

```ruby
  def break_tie(pair, choice, criteria)
    make_rational_choice(pair, choice, criteria)
  end

  def make_rational_choice(pair, choice, criteria)
    rc = RationalChoice.new(pair, choice, criteria)
    make(rc)
  end

  private

  # All choices with 0 scores mean the pair-ranking process has not begun
  def zeros?
    list = @options.collect{|choice| score_for(choice)}
    list.uniq == [0]
  end

  def tie(combination)
    first = score_for(combination[0])
    second = score_for(combination[1])
    first == second
  end

  def make(rational_choice)
    store(rational_choice)
    vote_for(rational_choice)
  end

  def has_tie?
    !tied_pair.empty?
  end

  def vote_for(rational_choice)
    @votes[rational_choice.choice] += 1
  end

  # For display at the end of the pair-ranking process
  def store(rational_choice)
    @decisions << rational_choice
  end

  def find_tie
    result = []
    combinations.each do |combination|
      if tie(combination)
        result = combination
        break
      end
    end
    result
  end
  end
end
```

Create combination_test.rb as shown here:

```ruby
require 'minitest/autorun'
require_relative 'pair_rank'

class CombinationTest < Minitest::Test
  include PairRank

  def test_get_first_pair_given_options
    options = ['A', 'B', 'C']
    c = Combination.new(options)
    result = c.pair
    assert_equal ['A', 'B'], result
  end

  def test_get_second_pair_given_options
    options = ['A', 'B', 'C']
    c = Combination.new(options)
    c.pair
    result = c.pair
    assert_equal ['A', 'C'], result
  end

  def test_get_third_pair_given_options
    options = ['A', 'B', 'C']
    c = Combination.new(options)
    c.pair
    c.pair
    result = c.pair
    assert_equal ['B', 'C'], result
  end

  def test_get_pair_when_there_is_no_pair
    options = ['A', 'B', 'C']
    c = Combination.new(options)
    c.pair
    c.pair
    c.pair
    result = c.pair
    assert_equal nil, result
  end
end
```

Create pair_rank_test.rb as shown here:

```ruby
require 'minitest/autorun'
require_relative 'pair_rank'

class PairRankTest < Minitest::Test
  include PairRank

  def test_score_is_zero_for_the_element_that_did_not_get_vote
    options = []
    pr = PairRank.new(options)
    result = pr.score_for('A')
    assert_equal 0, result
  end

  def test_first_combination
    options = ['A', 'B', 'C']
    pr = PairRank.new(options)
    result = pr.combination
    assert_equal ['A', 'B'], result
  end

  def test_second_combination
    options = ['A', 'B', 'C']
    pr = PairRank.new(options)
    pr.combination
    result = pr.combination
    assert_equal ['A', 'C'], result
  end

  def test_in_the_beginning_all_scores_are_zero_so_its_not_a_tie
    options = ['A', 'B', 'C', 'D']
    pr = PairRank.new(options)
    result = pr.tied_pair
    assert_equal [], result
  end

  def test_complete_session_when_there_is_no_tie
    criteria = 'test'
    options = ['A', 'B', 'C']
    pr = PairRank.new(options)
    pair = pr.combination
    choice = 'A'
    pr.make_rational_choice(pair, choice, criteria)
    pair = pr.combination
    choice = 'A'
    pr.make_rational_choice(pair, choice, criteria)
    pair = pr.combination
    choice = 'B'
    pr.make_rational_choice(pair, choice, criteria)
```

```ruby
  assert_equal 2, pr.score_for('A')
  assert_equal 1, pr.score_for('B')
  assert_equal 0, pr.score_for('C')
end

def test_score_complete_session_where_there_are_ties
  criteria = 'test'
  options = ['A', 'B', 'C']
  pr = PairRank.new(options)
  pair = pr.combination
  choice = 'A'
  pr.make_rational_choice(pair, choice, criteria)
  pair = pr.combination
  choice = 'C'
  pr.make_rational_choice(pair, choice, criteria)
  pair = pr.combination
  choice = 'B'
  pr.make_rational_choice(pair, choice, criteria)

  assert_equal 1, pr.score_for('A')
  assert_equal 1, pr.score_for('B')
  assert_equal 1, pr.score_for('C')
end

def test_get_tie_for_a_complete_session_when_there_are_ties
  criteria = 'test'
  options = ['A', 'B', 'C']
  pr = PairRank.new(options)
  pair = pr.combination
  choice = 'A'
  pr.make_rational_choice(pair, choice, criteria)
  pair = pr.combination
  choice = 'C'
  pr.make_rational_choice(pair, choice, criteria)
  pair = pr.combination
  choice = 'B'
  pr.make_rational_choice(pair, choice, criteria)

  assert_equal ['A', 'B'], pr.tied_pair
end

def test_process_ties_for_a_complete_session_when_there_are_ties
  criteria = 'test'
  options = ['A', 'B', 'C']
  pr = PairRank.new(options)
  pair = pr.combination
  choice = 'A'
  pr.make_rational_choice(pair, choice, criteria)
  pair = pr.combination
  choice = 'C'
  pr.make_rational_choice(pair, choice, criteria)
```

```
      pair = pr.combination
      choice = 'B'
      pr.make_rational_choice(pair, choice, criteria)

      pr.break_tie(pr.tied_pair, 'A', criteria)
      assert_equal ['B', 'C'], pr.tied_pair

      pr.break_tie(pr.tied_pair, 'B', criteria)
      assert_equal ['A', 'B'], pr.tied_pair

      pr.break_tie(pr.tied_pair, 'A', criteria)
      assert_equal [], pr.tied_pair
  end

  def test_rational_choice_custom_string
      rc = RationalChoice.new('pair', 'choice', 'criteria')
      expected = "You selected choice because of criteria for pair"
      result = rc.to_s
      assert_equal expected, result
  end
end
```

Summary

In this chapter, we discussed pair ranking and saw one way to code the solution. The concepts found in the domain, such as choice, rationale, and so on, are carried over to the code. We did this deliberately to reduce the semantic gap between the requirements and the code.

Index

A

Abstraction, 77, 94
  symbolic, 25
  visual, 25
Acceptance criterion, 70
Additive changes, 102
Application programming interface (API)
  design, 13
ASCII, 163–164
Assertions, 28
  custom, 48
  multiple, 37, 47–48
  single, 47

B

Bad inputs, 27
Black box, 11, 17, 16
boolean return value, 54
Boundary case, 134
Boundary conditions, 27, 50
Boundary object, 92, 94
Bowling game scoring program, 9–10

C

Canonical test structure, 30
Cellular automaton, 171
Characterization tests, 223
Character-to-Number Conversion
  ASCII table, 164
  solution domain analysis, 163–164
  test cases, 165–169
Constraints. *See* Fizz Buzz
Conway's Game of Life (CGOL)
  application statement, 209
  code review, 214–219
  driven by tests, 177–179, 181–209
  problem domain analysis, 171, 173–174, 176
  problem statement, 171
  refactor solution, 210–214
  solution domain analysis, 176
Customer, subscribe to plan, 265

D

Data duplication, 218, 220
Debugging tool, 167
Decimal-to-octal conversion problem, 39
Defect localization, 48, 104
Degenerate case, 26
DeMorgan's Laws, 244–245, 262
Devil's Advocate, 14–15, 181
Difference reduction, 102–103
Divide and conquer strategy, 26
Documentation
  comments, 11
  executable, 11
  wiki, 11
Domain, 2
  concepts, 258–261
  expert, 2
  knowledge, 3
  objects, 92, 94
  problem, 2
  solution, 2
Domain-rich code, 171

E

Euclidean Algorithm, 139
Executable documentation, 11
Express intent, 249–250, 261

F

Factorial, 149–152
Failing test, 14
Fake It Till You Make It, 127–129

© Bala Paranj 2017
B. Paranj, *Test Driven Development in Ruby*, DOI 10.1007/978-1-4842-2638-4

Get the eBook for only $4.99!

Why limit yourself?

Now you can take the weightless companion with you wherever you go and access your content on your PC, phone, tablet, or reader.

Since you've purchased this print book, we are happy to offer you the eBook for just $4.99.

Convenient and fully searchable, the PDF version enables you to easily find and copy code—or perform examples by quickly toggling between instructions and applications.

To learn more, go to http://www.apress.com/us/shop/companion or contact support@apress.com.

Printed in the United States
By Bookmasters